A GREEN ROSE

THE MEMOIR OF LORNA PATERSON

J Krivine

Copyright © 2013 J Krivine
All rights reserved.
ISBN: 1480014419
ISBN 13: 9781480014411

I'm only a witness, and there are other witnesses whose evidence will have to be weighed with mine, and other people will sit in judgment. I think the final outcome will be a just verdict. I don't ask for any part in Orde's glory, I only ask that my evidence should be taken into account and not swept aside or denigrated as it has been up to now, or that my motives should have aspersions cast upon them. Because truly I have tried to serve the truth.

> *"And fair Margaret and rare Margaret*
> *And Margaret of veritie*
> *Gin ere ye love anither man*
> *Ne'er love him as ye did me"*

LORNA, HEREFORDSHIRE, 1987

Part I

Chapter I

When I was fifteen years old in 1931, I went by sea from England to Western Australia. My grandmother had died unexpectedly and mother made up her mind to go out there to see her father - I understood she didn't like him - and papa reluctantly agreed to accompany her; I was brought along with the trunks. We occupied three first class cabins because my parents always slept apart, but it was a rule mother made that we should eat breakfast together in the dining room. This was not a cruise ship in the modern sense, it was a vessel for people who had to get from England to Australia, often on pressing business, there was no other way in those days. Mother was the most attractive woman on the boat and I was the second most attractive. I wore sunglasses which were a new thing, no one else on board had them, and when on deck I wore an unfashionably long coat, so it wasn't possible to know how old I was, I was completely mysterious, I might have been Myrna Loy. To allay the boredom, my mother played bridge, sipping champagne and nibbling dried biscuits, her patent antidote to sea sickness from which she suffered all her life. Mother played bridge, papa drank, and I tormented the young officers of the crew. My parents didn't introduce me to anybody, I read books from morn to dusk, and was perfectly content to do so.

When we disembarked at Perth grandfather was not there to greet us, in fact he had disappeared and no-one knew where he was. He was apprised of our visit, papa had send telegrams to his office, and his office manager confirmed that he had read them, but he had gone. Mother didn't take it personally, she checked us into a hotel and went straight to a lawyer to set about liquidating his businesses. This was made possible by the fact that grandpa had, over time, put most of his assets in his wife's name for purposes of good housekeeping, confident of pre-deceasing her, and mother was confident that grandmamma had left her everything, so it was just a matter of reading the will. Mother's lawyer could find no such will, which set in motion a most extraordinary treasure hunt in which the three of us turned the house upside down looking for the thing, expecting and perhaps fearing that grandfather would walk through the door at any minute, after all it was still his house; and he did. Grandfather, whose name was Herbert John Wigmore, was a tough, self-reliant type who had built up a large business in agricultural feeds and implements, and he was a very rich man. When he clapped eyes first on his daughter and then on his grand-daughter whom he was seeing for the first time, he appeared a little stunned and didn't seem to know or care that his home was in the process of being burgled. You would think that mother would have been shame-faced in this situation, but far from it; she tore into the poor fellow – there had evidently been another woman – and he completely broke down in front of us, it was most unmanly, and not what I had been led to expect from my Australian forebear. What passed between father and daughter, and to what backdrop, is of no consequence; we re-embarked for England with the loot, or at least some of it, and I never saw grandfather again.

On the return journey, having just turned sixteen, I think something had changed in me because I had grown out of merchant seamen, I was now intent in finding a suitable English husband, and after docking at Singapore there was an intake of a few presentable young men on board, mainly military. The Cathay was newer and smaller than the outbound vessel, about 10,000 tons, and had above-average kitchens and bars on account of the Italian crew. I took lunch and dinner in my cabin, and if I ventured out at all, it was to spend time with an old man I had met on the first week out. He was in fact an old soldier called Reginald Buckland, and because the history of warfare was a passion of mine, I latched onto him to hear him speak of his profession. You would think it would please an old soldier to recount his adventures to an eager girl, but not at all, and finally it was I who did the talking and he the listening; it occurred to me that he may once have had a daughter of my age and lost her, because he treated me with such remarkable warmth and kindness, and I told him everything there was to tell, it's something one does at sea, I believe.

The long boring passages across half the world were punctuated by stopovers at harbours over each of which casually fluttered the Union Jack. Britain owned, Britain ruled, Britain administered, there was an army of British men going about the business of empire unhindered (thus it had been and thus it always would be, was it not the perfection of civilization?), I just needed to find one for myself. On the fifth week at sea I was leaning over the rails at Port Said, watching the embarkation of passengers, when

I spotted him. He was a wild creature with the nose of an eagle, he didn't ascend the gangplank, he prowled up it, he was unkempt, his uniform was dusty and disheveled, one could be in no doubt that he had come directly from great danger. He had under his arm a small cage, and without being discourteous he showed no courtesy to people around him, that is to say he betrayed no awareness of their existence, he appeared terribly sure of himself without being in any way superior in manner, in other words, he was exactly like me; all this I deduced in the space of the few seconds I had him in view at a distance of about one hundred feet. I ran to my cabin to change into a suitable outfit and then I went looking for the man with the cage. I was in a state of happiness and terror such as has only happened to me three times in my life, I wanted this man in a most acquisitive manner. Carnally? Good gracious, he looked as if he needed a good bath. No, I felt as if he were a missing part of me that I had not known existed, and I was certain that with this part I would be complete. The corollary being that having discovered that such a part existed, I should not be able to continue living without it. So I was in a perfectly desperate state because I knew nothing of the customs of courtship, my life was at stake. Should I rugby tackle him on the foredeck, or throw a net over him while he was eating in the dining room? But the man had disappeared from view, I could find him nowhere, I traveled every deck and every companionway, I wondered if he had fallen overboard.

Over breakfast the following morning, I was so unhappy that mother asked me if I was ill. I told her cryptically that I had seen the man I should like to marry, and in saying these words I shocked myself because marriage had not been in my mind, I simply had to belong to this man, and he to me. She paid no attention to my little declaration because it did not seem to be a proper reply to her question, and it made absolutely no sense. After two days of scanning and loitering I went to the purser's office to ask to see the passenger list. The chief purser knew me by now so he took it out, laid it on the desk and discretely left the office. I scribbled down the twenty or so names of the most recent arrivals, and returned to my cabin. I had narrowed it down to four possibles according to rank, I reconnoitered their lairs, when suddenly my quarry broke cover directly in my path, I bolted in blind panic, and lost him again. I had now not eaten properly for 48 hours, I had cried myself to sleep every night since that first sighting, I was in a state of utter despair, because with every passing moment the ship was edging closer to Marseilles and soon he would disembark and I would never see him again in my life. I had no-one to turn to…but that was not true! I left my cabin and found dear Reginald in our usual place in the top lounge, and told him everything in a hoarse whisper. 'But my dear', said he, 'I believe that the man you are talking about is sitting on the other side of the room, and if I am not mistaken he is watching you closely.'

I was, at that time in my life, starting to develop myopia, and myopia is a terrible thing for a young woman, worse than smallpox, spectacles being a paramount obstacle to sexual attraction. I positively refused to wear the eyeglasses that mother had had made for me in Perth, except in a cinema, or if I could do so without being observed. 'That is quite impossible' I said, 'it must be someone else! Describe him.' Reginald proceeded to describe the man who was watching me, without taking his eyes off his newspaper. I was of course in a state of pure terror.

'What kind of nose does he have?'
'Roman', said Reginald.
'Why is it that I can never find him?'
'Have you tried in the library?'
'Of course not! I haven't gone near the library since he came on board.'

'I think that is where I saw the young man yesterday,' said Reginald, calmly.

'Oh God.'

'Well, he's pretending not to look at you now.' He managed this conversation barely moving his lips. I rested my hand on his arm for reassurance, cleared my throat, and stood up slowly. I straightened my skirt and walked stiffly to the door. I passed through it into the companionway until I was out of sight, broke into a run to my cabin, and threw myself on my bed and howled.

The following morning, I ate a hearty breakfast in silence, returned to my cabin to check myself in the mirror, and headed for the library. He was seated at a desk buried in a book, he didn't look up as I entered. I walked directly to the desk adjacent to his desk and sat down. I realized that I didn't have a book. We were now sitting side by side, I believe I was shaking quite badly. I took a deep breath, turned my head half- way in his direction, while looking directly ahead, and uttered the words I had been rehearsing, annunciating carefully. 'Do you come from Egypt or Arabia?' I saw him slowly close his book. I moved my head slightly to look at his hands which were delicate for a man, the book was Wordsworth's Intimations of Immortality, and he turned to me and he said, 'I come from the Sudan', and now out of the corner of my eye I saw he was smiling at me, I couldn't breathe. He had the most beautiful voice I'd heard in my life.

I have no recollection whatever of what was said beyond this point, but he talked to me without pause for the rest of the day and the following day. We ate sandwiches together and walked the deck together, I believe that we were oblivious to the world. I was less oblivious than he, because I saw some of the looks we were getting on account of the fact that everyone knew my age. My appetite had returned, I was sleeping well, on the third day the Cathay docked in

Marseilles where we all had to get off. Oh dear. I knew he was called Orde – was there ever a more beautiful name? – and I knew a great deal about what he thought and read, and how he felt about God, but I didn't know very much about what he actually did, who his people were or where he came from, and I had no idea if he was married or spoken for, because our connection was of the mind, ethereal and above such considerations. But now that the voyage was coming to an end I was starting to wonder whether or not I should be anxious. What comes next? He said to me, a propos nothing,

'I shall see you on the train.'

'Yes, of course' said I, and went off to pack my trunk like a good and happy girl.

France may indeed be a beautiful country but I didn't notice it. There was a knock on the door of our compartment and he stepped in and introduced himself to papa, so papa, being possessed of impeccable manners, invited him to join us for dinner. My parents had not addressed a single question to me about the considerably older man with whom I had spent every waking moment for the last two and a half days. We all ate grilled plaice and broccoli and boiled potatoes, followed by crepes suzettes, the food on those old wagons-lits was as good as in any stationary restaurant. He was not exactly reserved with my parents, and not exactly deferential to papa, but he spoke little, leaving the floor to mother who couldn't seem to stem the flow. It was through papa's casual but pointed questions - when he could get a word in - that I learnt that he was 31 years old, the son of a retired colonel living in Godalming, had innumerable siblings, and that he regularly wrote letters to his mother. The unfortunate thing about this meal was the fact that he didn't speak to me and rarely looked at me, and when I could bare being ignored by him no longer, I calmly asked, and pointedly,

'And when do you return to the Sudan?' to which he replied,

'It hasn't been settled.' He didn't say it coldly or with indifference, it was spoken plainly and without emphasis or any bodily or facial gesture that might betray a deeper feeling, but it was spoken to me and for my benefit alone, and he looked directly at me for the first time in our short acquaintance.

When the train stopped in Paris, I saw him running down the platform. Was it something I had said? I was certain he was leaving me for good, I fainted in my seat. When I came to, the train was racing through northern France and I heard traces of his voice in the corridor speaking to mama, I closed my eyes and fell into a deep sleep. We arrived at Calais on a Friday. On parting he asked papa if he might call on us on Tuesday at our hotel – we were staying at the Browns Hotel in Dover Street – and papa politely consented. This was of course the longest weekend of my life, the longest in history. I told my parents nothing and they were sensible enough not to ask, they were biding their time. I couldn't read a book or a newspaper, I couldn't think, I couldn't take myself for a walk. I persuaded mother to go with me to a matinee on Saturday, I have no recollection of the film, and again on Sunday and again on Monday, in this way I accounted for ten hours in the interminable void between Calais and the Browns Hotel.

He arrived at the hotel dressed in a suit, shaved, his hair cut and combed, I was shocked by his appearance, he looked so much older, like a bank manager really, all the wildness gone, subdued, and he looked like he hadn't slept. He didn't address my parents who were sitting with me in the lounge, he spoke directly to me, gently asking – entreating – me to come and sit with him by the fireplace which was some distance away from my parents, it was clear that he had something very important to say. It was common practice in those days, when a young man had an important announcement to make with regards his intentions towards a woman or a girl, which is what I rather hoped to be the case, he would ask to speak to her father. He led me away and papa just stared. He was a different man to the man I had known on the boat, and nothing he had told me on the boat prepared me for what he now had to say. He had his back to my parents and I was facing them across the room. If they were watching me they would have seen my face white as marble and expressionless. He spoke quietly and unhesitatingly, and without any preamble. I remember every word of it, it is seared into my memory. I have not made up anything, I don't think I could have made up anything half as grim as the facts, so what I tell you now you must accept as coming from him.

When he was about 24 he came to know a very pretty and very nice girl called Peggy Jelley. She was one of three sisters of whom one was married, her father was a retired colonel, and they lived under rather straightened circumstances in a modest house at a place called Farham. He liked her very much, he told me that actually he wanted to make a pass at her younger sister Mary, who had the most beautiful legs he'd ever seen and he'd tried her first, but she was a lesbian and was having an affair with a naval commander's wife called Marlene Morse. I mention her name only to demonstrate that I haven't forgotten anything, indeed I can't, it is bitten deep into my mind. He went to a dance with Peggy and kissed her passionately, whereupon Peggy announced to him and to their circle that they were engaged, it wasn't a challenge or a gambit; that is how she understood the world at the age of 23, and for all he knew at the age of 24 she was correct. He was about to go off to the Sudan for six years, he'd been seconded to the Camel Corps of the Sudan Defense Force, and Peggy allowed herself to be seduced by him on the eve of his departure. Every year he returned to England on three months leave, and Peggy would be there at the quayside waiting for him. She wrote him letters and sent him parcels to keep his spirits up. Their summers together in England were like a constantly renewable honeymoon, he was a welcome guest in Colonel Jelley's home, they drove through the countryside in the Colonel's car, his parents had met Peggy's parents, he was considered part of the Jelley family, she adored him and he was very fond of her, but he did not feel that their lives were intertwined. He was deeply troubled, saw no purpose for himself in the world, felt abandoned by God, adrift without compass, in danger of wasting his life, he told her of his doubts, warned her off him, said that he would only make her unhappy, that she could do better, but still he accepted her love and her favours. Peggy understood Orde, she knew he wasn't in love with her, so she set out the terms for the grounds on which she would release him; she promised that if he should ever fall in love with somebody else, she would not hold him to his commitment. They were together for six years, Peggy was no longer 23, Orde was now 30, and as such he was now entitled to a marriage allowance and married quarters, his stint in the Sudan was coming to an end, he could prevaricate no longer. So they named the day. Banns were posted, engagement photographs taken, invitations sent out, wedding lists prepared, Peggy was fitted for the wedding dress, all was hustle and bustle at the Colonel's home in Farham.

Meanwhile, as a finale to his Sudan days, Orde planned and executed a remarkable but quixotic expedition into the Libyan desert in search of a 'lost oasis'. It was a feat of navigation and endurance, and his report found its way into the Journal of the Royal Geographical Society. Before he set out he went to the P&O offices in Cairo to book his return passage, and he asked them to put him on their newest ship which was called the Strathneva

- it was about 25,000 tons - because he hoped that he might meet a girl with whom he could fall in love. The Strathneva was the largest ship in the P&O fleet, there was more room for girls on board (these were his exact words to me). Then he went into the desert and when he came out again he sat under a palm tree and communed with God. He said, 'give me a sign that I don't have to marry Peggy, or that I do. I want a sign'. He went to Cairo and visited the shipping office and asked if they had his ticket. They said yes but they were sorry, they couldn't put him on the Strathneva, they had put him instead on a smaller vessel named Cathay. Orde took this as the sign that he must marry Peggy and that everything was going forward on this particular path in his life.

Peggy was to meet him at the quayside on his return. He telegraphed her from Paris to tell her to wait for him in London. The instant she saw his face she understood what had happened and why the telegram. He told her he could not marry her. They went back to the apartment she had borrowed from a friend, and the night was spent in floods of tears. The family was all assembled in Farham awaiting the happy couple. They arrived after a miserable journey and the news was broken, and one by one they attacked him and tried to get him to honour his obligation. At the very end of the weekend, just before he was due to leave, the brother-in-law said, "come out for a walk with me", and they went off to some course, I can't remember if it was a golf course or a race course, and for a long time they walked and the brother-in-law said, "now my dear fellow, I know just how you feel, before I married Suzie I felt exactly the same, horror-stricken, I thought I couldn't go through with it, I even considered running away, and then I said to myself, 'be a man, you can't let her down at the last moment' and do you know my dear fellow, it's not nearly as bad as you think".

A Green Rose

As I sat by the fireplace, I studied this man closely, he was torn between pity and compassion which was perfectly genuine, and horror at what he'd done, and his narrow escape. At this point in the story, he allowed himself a kind of brutal laughter, black laughter. Peggy's family was livid and utterly humiliated, the old colonel was ready to ruin him which he was perfectly entitled to do, it would have been the end of Orde's military career. Breaking an engagement was actionable in those days, but Peggy would have no part of it. Even in her great distress and bitterness she respected Orde, and remembered her own terms.

I listened to this infamous account in silence, it went on for about an hour according to papa, there is much that I have omitted for Orde didn't spare himself. The words brutal and unfeeling come to mind, I don't recall if he used them or if I thought them. Orde had delicately omitted my unwitting part in the affair. I was a sixteen year old girl he'd known for three days, into whose hand he had dropped this poisoned chalice, what did he imagine I would do? I remember we sat there in silence for I don't know how long, he didn't take his eyes off me, there was no appeal in his expression, rather a challenge. I then told him the following story, which had been much in my thoughts in recent days. When I was five years old I was living in Ceylon, I received a summons from my mother, to join her downstairs in the drawing room. When I arrived I found her sitting on the sofa, and cross-legged on the floor in front of her was an exotic looking man dressed in military khaki, his name was Karum Bux. He had a reputation throughout the sub-continent as a see-er of the future, he may have been a Sikh, I don't recall. He'd been telling my mother's fortune and she wanted him to tell mine. I sat down beside her, extended my sweaty little hand, the lines in my palm were outlined in black, I hadn't washed my hands for some time and I wished I could have sat upon them instead of displaying them. But Karum Bux took my small hand into his own and looked at it. And then he turned to my mother and he said, 'ah, now I understand! I told you that you had one son, and you told me that you had no sons and I would not believe you. Now I see the hand of this small girl, she has the head of a man and the heart of a man too. If she had been a man she would have been a judge'. And then he went on, 'she will marry a famous soldier'. In this manner did I accept Orde's proposal of marriage, and as we had begun, so surely would we go on.

Chapter 2

I was born in Ceylon. I was a nannied child and had to pass my whole time in the company of a hard, unkind woman, I only parted from her when I was seven years old, and she made my first years unhappy. I hardly saw my mother and father, in those days one visited one's parents after tea for perhaps an hour, and otherwise one saw them not at all. But I was happy when we were in Ceylon because I was surrounded by such a variety of sensual experience. We lived in a very nice house – there used to be a photograph of it hanging on the wall of Jonathan's bedroom – it had a lovely garden, my father was fond of ferns, so am I, and he had built up a marvelous collection. It was tended by his head gardener who I think was a Burmese called Thungurum, a dear little yellow man, great expert on orchids and ferns, and my father's collection was quite famous. Not only did he grow ferns out of the ground, but he grew tree ferns as well. Of course everything in Ceylon grew to an extraordinary size, the climate there was not a climate of hot and cold, but a climate of wet or dry, it was always hot, but when the Monsoon came twice a year the downpour resulted not only in moulds sprouting out of your ear, but in the most wonderful growth in the garden. Amazing how a certain fern, for instance, which in this country produces its tiny leaves about the size of a pin head, in Ceylon it grows to the size of a two shilling piece.

The Singhalese themselves are handsome, intelligent, and honest, or they were in those days. They were finely cut, fine broad features, slender bodies, they looked rather like coffee coloured Greeks of antiquity. To see a beautiful Singhalese girl combing out her blue-black hair, and sleeking it down with coconut oil outside her palm leaf hut in the early morning was something to remember. We had an extremely good-looking butler called John, dressed like all our servants in a white sarong and a white mess jacket, and like all of them barefoot. We hardly ever came home in the evening without seeing John come down the great staircase, it was a beautiful double staircase that joined like rivulets into a stream, and came down the center of the hall, and John would be walking down, beautiful as a Greek god of course, expression of suffering on his face. 'So, John', my mother would say, 'not another needle in your foot?' 'Yes, lady, another needle' John would say. I think he put them there himself so that my mother could take them out again for him. One of the pictures that flash upon my inward eye is of John and my father coming out of the dressing room one evening, where John had been putting my father into his evening clothes. My father was wearing black trousers with braid down the side and a pleated Cambric shirt. It was too hot in Ceylon to wear stiff shirts, so men wore ruffled shirts, or pleated ones and a black bow tie and patent leather pumps on his feet, and they came out into the ballroom – believe it or not we had a ballroom although I never remember seeing a ball take place in it – a lovely room with polished floor and chandeliers. John was carrying a sash, a long sash of dark red silk, and he handed one end to my father who tucked it into his waistband, and then John stood off from him, and my father lifted his hands like a dancer, and he twirled the whole length of the sash until John tucked the other end into his waist, and then he put on his white jacket. I shall never forget the sight of that handsome man under the glittering light, and the hot dark night outside.

It was from the great round balcony that ran the width of the house that I saw the Indian Rope trick. I believe I'm one of the few people left in the world who has actually seen the Indian Rope Trick, instead of just knowing somebody else who's seen it, so I shall record it for posterity. Now this balcony was a very large one, very wide, and it was bounded by a great white marble balustrade. And it was on the second floor, I think the house only had two floors, and down below it was a lawn, and of course the rustling palm trees, coconut palm, flowers disposed about. My parents had given strict instructions that no wandering entertainers such as flute players or snake charmers should be allowed within the garden, which was a sad privation for the servants and for me. So one day when my parents were out, one afternoon about teatime, the head houseboy who was my greatest friend, his name was Azuvathum, whispered in my nanny's ear that there was a snake charmer below, and would the little missy like to see him. Well now my nanny, although she was quite inhumane, she was also bored, and she wanted to see the snake charmer too, so she gave permission, and took me out onto the balcony, sat me on the balustrade and held me there while all the servants lined up beside us and we looked over, and the entertainment began.

A Green Rose

We had, as you can imagine the most perfect view, it was like sitting in the dress circle of a well-constructed theater. Down below us on the grass stood a little man, he was not a Singhalese, I think, he was very thin, he wore nothing except a turban and a loin cloth made of a bright red material with yellow flowers on it, like cheap curtaining. He had with him two flat circular baskets such as snake charmers use to carry their snakes about in, and a tall flagilay, a native instrument like a penny whistle with a big bulge in the middle. This was a very common form of musical instrument in Ceylon and one often heard the delightful twiddling of it in the early morning, or in the middle of the night, in fact people seemed to play it all day long. To us of course the music could not have been easily learned, it seemed to be without a tune, but it always fitted in with its surroundings, and it was invariably played by the snake charmers, the snakes danced to these little instruments. The snakes were cobras without exception, a deadly creature, of course the story ran that their poison fangs were extracted before they were trained but I don't know, I've seen some very strange things in Ceylon and I wouldn't be surprised if some of the snake charmers had entires, as you might call them. Now this little man removed the lid of one of his baskets, he sat down at a short distance, crossed his legs and began to play his flagilay, just like any other snake charmer. And slowly, up from the basket came two flat grey heads, and presently the entire length of these massive cobras which then in the most elegant manner swayed and insinuated themselves to and fro in a sort of rhythm with the music, and after a while his music changed and grew slower, and they sank back again. And he put the lid on the basket.

Now I was enchanted of course, and clapped like mad, and waved to him and smiled, and he looked up at me with a great flash of white teeth and he went over to the other basket and, removing the lid, he lifted out a length of rope, neatly coiled, a sort of browny yellow colour, hardly substantial but about the thickness of two fingers. He held the coil, one end of it in his left hand, and with his right hand he threw the coil upwards in a swift, neat movement so that it straightened itself out to its full length and there it stiffened and stood. He took his left hand away and it hung in mid-air. He looked back at me, and seeing on my face the delight, he took a little running jump, leapt onto the rope and swarmed up to the top where he was on a level with me on the balcony. He then turned and gave me another delightful smile, slid down, put the basket underneath the rope, snapped his fingers, and the whole thing fell, neatly coiled, into place. I saw it, nanny saw it, the servants saw it, no one guffawed, no one winked, it happened as I have described it. I was a little girl of six, I was a sensible and intelligent little girl, and I perfectly understood the astonishing nature of what I had seen, but being a child I accepted it as being part of the natural order.

Ceylon was a little India without the stresses of India, without its vast spaces and without its vast problems. It's supposed to be the Garden of Eden; Adam's Peak is the great snow mountain in the middle and it's a flowery place, its climate around the edges is very hot and wet, but in the center in the highlands it's a wonderful climate, like a perpetual fresh summer's day in England. There are leopards in the trees, and you have log fires at night. They kept a good deal of state in those days, as they did in India. The governor was a great man, people curtseyed to him, scarlet outriders in his carriage, the races were very smart affairs, people played a lot of polo, many young men of good family went out there to make some money - how sensible - and altogether the light shone on fair women and brave men. And my father, who was known to his friends as Walter, immediately became a part of this scene, he was very good-looking in that black almost Spanish way, he had a splendid physique and he was marvelous at games, the only game he didn't play was polo because he didn't like horses, but he played everything with a ball – he was a member of the Royal and Ancient at St. Andrews but he never spoke about it, I only discovered it by chance. He played a great deal of rugby football and cricket; he was captain of the all-Ceylon team.

He drank far too much but then practically everybody in Ceylon did, but he was very able, he was good at his work. At the age of 32 he found himself senior partner of a massive concern in Colombo, founded by his godfather Edward Aitken, which owned plumbago mines, tea and coffee plantations and town property - they were also Lloyds shipping agents - and he began to make a great deal of money very quickly, and this was just before the war broke out. Playing cricket one day he tore the muscle in his right arm right off the shoulder blade, and his arm was wrenched out of its socket. He wore a sling for about a year, his guns at Chilliper were Purdy guns that had to be specially made for him, and his coats had to be padded on the right side, but otherwise you wouldn't have known there was anything wrong with him. The war broke out just then, and he was told that he couldn't go off to war with an arm in that condition, his brother Jim went instead. Jim was divinely handsome, so my godmother once told me, blue eyes, straight nose, fair golden hair, but Jim I think would have been a problem had he not died gallantly in the Black Watch during the First World War. He forged his father's name on a cheque at Cambridge, criminal charges were pressed and papa had to rescue him, so perhaps it was not such a bad thing that poor Jim went in the way he did.

The Admiralty prevailed upon papa to stay in Ceylon to act as their agent, and he agreed. My mother told me how he used to stay in the office all night coding and decoding admiralty messages, because although he didn't pass on operational messages to the ships - at least I don't think he did - Colombo was a great naval station and commanded the southern Indian Ocean, and was the gateway to the Far East, and it was my father's job to keep these great ships supplied.

My parents, Walter and Ivy, met at a hotel, she was sitting at a nearby table, and it was love at first sight - the male variety. She was coming from London where she had been studying to be a concert violinist. I try to picture mother as a young music student in London but nothing appears; did she live in a rooming house? Could she have practiced on her own for hours? Could she have submitted to the dictates of a teacher? Clearly music wasn't mother's life for I never heard her play a note, although I did hear her telling someone quietly that the Wigmore Hall was built by her father. She was now on her way back to her parents' home, so Walter followed her down to Australia. He visited her at her parents' house in Perth, and proposed to her. In Australia, a fiercely individualistic sort of place, one dispensed with the father in this transaction, and she agreed to marry him. Papa had an hereditary title, by the way, he was officially Sir Montcrieff Paterson. Mother was quite frank with me about it from my earliest years, she told me that she didn't love him, and although she didn't say that she'd married him for his money and title, I had no doubt that she had. When I was born she announced that she would be bearing no more children, and later she assured me that I myself had been an oversight.

For the first six years of my life the three of us commuted between Edinburgh and Ceylon. Father hated the climate out there, he considered that he'd made quite enough money so he sold the house and returned to Scotland once and for all. He was just under forty years old and, according to mother, he was worth a quarter of a million pounds. He was born in Edinburgh where his name was greatly respected, people knew the family, and would have been glad to welcome him back, but he loved shooting and fishing. Edinburgh, beautiful city that it is, is set in a ravaged countryside with coal mines not far away, no proper streams flowing nearby and moors, in some cases grouse moors, quite good but very hard held by other people, so he struck north, far north to Aberdeenshire where he found a pleasant little estate called Place of Tilliefoure that had belonged to the Grant family, not very large, about 5000 acres, with a delightful house set in the most beautiful countryside you can imagine. Heathery mountains standing up behind the house and protecting it from the north winds, oak woods, and a lovely river flowing past the door. My mother hated the place from the first moment she saw it. He was rather naughty, he did what I've done once or twice; fearing that his consort would refuse to have anything to do with his dream he went off and simply made all the arrangements and presented her with the done thing. It's not a bad technique provided you're ready to face the music afterwards, my mother wept when she saw the house. It was not so very big as country houses go, it had 40 rooms which I suppose is manageable if you've got the servants to keep them clean. It was also a charming house with character and comfort about it. But my mother sat down and decided to be injured for the rest of her married life.

In all my childhood my father never kissed me, never put his arm around me, never said a kindly word. He didn't say unkind words either, he merely told me to pull my stockings up or wash my hands, or asked me why I was late. I believe that it was to do with mother. I was her creature, I adored her, to my young eyes she was as glamorous as a film star, she had me believe that she was a captive princess imprisoned in a gloomy house in a rainy land, oppressed by stuck-up local people, tied to a boring man who didn't understand her; she could hardly say that he didn't love her because that was too manifest. Perhaps he felt that she had turned me against him, that I was on her side; how could he properly trust me, when she and I were as thick as thieves? She may have wanted to separate us from each other in order that each of us should love her and her only. Perhaps she was worried that he might leave his estate to me, so she made it her business that he and I were not close.

I loved Tilliefoure so devotedly, as he did, that I could think of nothing in the world happier than to live there for the rest of my life. I remember dear old Smith, the head gardener, asking me when I was about eleven what I was going to do when I grew up – he'd been on the place for about 40 years – and I said that I was going to breed horses and live at Tilliefoure all my days. He was delighted of course and went off to tell all the employees that when the young heiress came into her property they'd have a good lair because she'd be sticking around all the time and looking after them, instead of gadding off. I remember so well one day asking father if I could go out with him when he was going on his rounds, usually he and I made our escape into the outdoors as quickly as we could, we always went in separate directions, he never invited me to go with him but on this occasion he allowed me to come. And as we were walking down the river drive, there was a great field on the left, I suppose about 40 acres or 50 acres, it was under rough grass and never had anything but scrubby cattle grazing it, and I said, 'do you think, father, that we might have a forestry enterprise here, or something of the sort? That field never comes to much, does it.' And he turned on me with his fine dark eyes, like an angry bull, and said, 'don't make suggestions like that to me, it's none of your business, understand, and you have nothing to do with it'. As if I was trying to trick him, or cheat him out of something. It's painful to look back on these things. In the course of my life a good number of people, generally male, took a dislike to me, but to be disliked by your own father is unfathomable.

It was only ever the three of us, there were no friends or family around, just Ivy, Walter and Lorna, triangular, and since we traveled every year by ship from Ceylon to Scotland, my isolation was complete. We were nothing like a family, our roles were indistinct, it wasn't clear how we felt about one another, we never talked about things the way people did in the novels I read, I never learnt to make friends. But I had my books, as many as I wanted, and this is how I accumulated information – I do not use the word 'learn' advisedly – about how other families behave. Although I had no idea how my parents felt about me, I felt the deepest attachment to them, and why should it have been otherwise? On balance I consider myself to have been lucky because although some things went wrong, I had this beautiful place to live in, and that meant more to me than anything, I could always escape into this land of peace and grandeur. I spent much of my time, even when the weather was bad, in wandering on the mountains and in the woods. There was a magic wishing well, it was called the Lady Well, the pool below it in the river Don was known as the Ladywell pool. And the drive, one of the drives, ran between the hillside in which the well was set, and the river. Deep and dark below, where the salmon lay. The little grotto itself was the most exquisite thing, it was set into a green hillside with hazel wood, a few little granite steps led up to it, it was completely natural, nothing man-made about it, a tiny grotto with ferns and flowers growing within and without, and a stream of the clearest, crystal water flowing over mossy stones into a tiny pool of gravel. It was a place where one wished. I offered one or two requests over the years, and one of them I remember was that I should ride horses and learn Arabic.

Papa must have had an extraordinary capacity for loving one woman, and mother incredible powers of persuasion bordering on the hypnotic, for he never left her although she was an abominable wife. I later discovered that the neighbors around Tilliefoure were not stuck-up after all, in fact many of them were very nice, but her manners were so bad that they couldn't stomach her, this was born in upon my poor father after a year or two at Tilliefoure, so that he refused to go out with her anymore. This became one of her great complaints, that she had to find another squire if she wanted to go to a ball or a dinner party because my father refused to take her. He'd have people to the house but he would not accompany her anywhere. After I was married and had my brief period of effulgence, my mother wanted to go with me everywhere when I was meeting interesting people, and although I loved her still and would have been glad to take her with me, I couldn't because she was quite unpredictable and might suddenly burst out with something thoroughly unsuitable. I'm quite sure that she was not interested in sex, she was interested only in admiration, and being blessed with that most useful gift, she only liked nice men, there were always a few nice men hanging about wistfully offering admiration and getting very little in exchange.

On one occasion, poor woman, she did fall badly in love – as far as her nature was capable of falling in love – and with an Orkneyman from the Island of Stronsey, a man truly fascinating. Although she comes straight out of Strindberg, I can't forebear to pity her in this particular affair, and I, all of twelve years old, fell in love with him also. For three years I loved this man, and would have died for him happily. He was tall and fair and gentle, he had the most beguiling voice, beguiling intonation that I ever heard, it made everything he said sound significant, he was a man of few words, very good-looking, I never saw him wear anything but a faded kilt. There was no carnality about it as far as I was concerned, I never thought of touching even the tips of his fingers, and I hardly ever saw him. Mother would drive 30 miles with me sitting in the car at her side to meet him, he farmed in Buchan, on the great windy plains where the black cattle roam. He had two sons about the same age as myself, and we children were sent away after about five minutes conversation with him, and we then played about and were happy together, and after about an hour or two we came back, and I'd have another five or ten minutes with him in which I could just look at him, that's all I could ever hope to do. I thought about him day and night and I wrote him poems, I remember, which I had the sense to destroy as soon as I'd written them, but one day I left one lying about and my mother found it.

My poor father got to know about this business due to an indiscretion of mine. My mother, as I said, used me as a stalking horse, she used to take me out with her saying that we were going to do this or that, you see, and one day she didn't brief me properly, and at luncheon I gave the show away, I'll never forget my father's look. Mother was not really frightened because she was not afraid of him, but she looked taken aback, he was stricken. In fact from this time until he died, about 25 years later she denied him his conjugal rights. She told me that she was going to do this, and although I was only a child of twelve, I was upset. I'd read enough, and I had enough imagination and common sense to know that this was a very wicked thing to do, and I remember saying to her, 'you can't, he pays for your bed and board, he gives you everything, and he's never done anything he shouldn't do, and he loves you, you can't do such a thing, and she said, 'disgusting little girl, I'm in love with so-and-so and yet you expect me to allow your father to make love to me?' And I said, 'yes I do', and I thought I'd better say no more.

In fact, I looked upon mother as a superior being, and placed myself firmly in her slipstream. In my child's eye papa was a great man because he was undisputed master of Tilliefoure, and were it not for my reading I would not have known that life existed beyond its borders. But mother commanded papa, she truly commanded all that she surveyed, it seemed so natural that she should drive a car without a driver's license – she did so until she died – because she wasn't a person who needed permission for anything, she could do exactly as she pleased. I don't recall ever hearing her apologize, even when she was patently wrong, or in the wrong, and as I achieved maturity, I could see that she was wrong about a great many things.

About this time, in the full flow of the affair, she took me for a walk down the drive, we climbed up into the oak woods and sat on a grassy knoll and looked out onto the river and hills, and she told me that her lover wanted her to go away with him, and that she wanted more than anything else to go, but she couldn't go and leave me alone with my father because he would not be kind to me, he'd probably divorce her, and keep me because he will be the injured party, and he'll marry again and have a family and I should be neglected, and he'll leave all his money to them – which is what it really came down to. But I was completely enchanted with the situation, I was no less in love than she. I said to her, 'don't think of me, mother', I said, 'go, I shall be quite alright with father' - I spoke truer than I knew, as a matter of fact I would have been quite alright with him - 'you go and forget about me because all will be well with me, I want you to be happy.' 'No, no', said she, 'it would be cruelty, I must stay with a broken heart', and she went on in this vein, and I, a smaller but truly romantic version of herself, lapped it all up. Actually she had no intention of leaving my father, Gordon Sutherland was a comparatively poor man and she would never have gone away with him unless he'd come into a fortune, but I had no inkling of that.

The only time that Sutherland and I were alone together happened when I was about 14, I suppose, and had loved him for two years, and he came to spend a night under our roof at Tilliefoure. I can't think why, because papa would normally never have invited him, but perhaps he was going to escort my mother to one of the balls; the Aboyne ball, or the Braemar ball after the Gathering. What a wonderful sight it was to see the men in their evening dress, their kilts. No woman, not even the most beautiful can stand beside a man in his full fig when he's wearing his evening tartan. Some in their velvet doublets of claret colour, or sherry, with lace cravats and ruffles at the wrist, some of them wearing the black doublet with the silver button and scarlet waistcoat. Yes, you have to be a great beauty to compete with even an ordinary man when he's wearing his full Highland dress. I don't know why this man was under our roof but I think it was for some such reason. I found him alone in the library and, gathering all the courage I could find in my adolescent frame, said to him, 'I have something important to tell you, Gordon, would you be kind enough to meet me in the small garden tomorrow morning at seven o'clock?' He gave me a most delightful smile which I took to be an assent, and I quickly left the room, my heart racing. Of course he was perfectly aware of me, I've never been able to hide my feelings.

It must have been late summer because these gatherings take place in September. I remember the night I spent hardly sleeping, and then at about six in the morning I got up and got dressed in my little brown tweed skirt, and brown woolen stockings, and jersey, and I went out by the back door into such a world! No birds singing because it was early autumn, but all the trees were rustling with green, and the dew on the grass so heavy that there were rainbows lying on it, and such a smell of sweetness, an idyll, quite self-contained. You may know that Scottish country houses make their gardens a long way from the house. I don't know why this is, it may be so that after a luncheon party you can take people out at half past two, that sort of blank hour, saying to them, 'would you like to see the garden?' You've walked them for a long distance, you've walked them back, it's time to put them into their cars at half past three and they can go away. It lay on the hillside carved out of the oak woods, fronting the southerly sun, and I went up at about a quarter to seven. Through the woods with the smell of moss and flowers, and the sunlight slanting down through the trees, and I, in ecstasy, I was going to see him, and see him alone, what was more.

The first garden I came to was the walled garden, and I looked over the gate and it seemed to be empty. It lay on a slant on the hillside with a great green ride up the middle, vast herbaceous borders on either side leading up to a curved white seat and cypresses at the top. There were fruit beds and vegetable beds on either side, with a rose and clematis walk that bisected from left to right. I went in and walked under the rose pergolas, and there was no sign of him. I went through the wall at the end into the flox border, as we called it, this was a sloping garden again with a stream running down the middle with little waterfalls and shaded grass on either side, and two great green borders about 15 feet wide, of floxies. In the early autumn people used to come out from Aberdeen on five shilling hops on airplanes and turn at the flox borders and see the great splash of colour lying on the hillside. It was very easy to discover whether anybody was in it, and he was not there, and my heart began to sink a little. I went through the cypress hedge, there was a big tall hedge about 12 feet high into the wild garden, this was a place where there were specimen trees and shrubs, rather neglected, a place where anybody could hide. I went all through it, I quartered it from end to end and he was not there, and I began to feel pangs of agony. Could it possibly be that he wouldn't be there at all?

There was only one place left and that was the potato patch which lay between the wild garden and the oak woods. So I went under the cypress hedges into the potato patch, a considerable area with bee hives on the left, and a ridged earthen area in front of me, and there it lay, all still in the morning sunshine. And he wasn't there. This, of course, my cup of anguish. There I stood, I looked across the ridged earth, and far away on the other side, where the wicket gate led into the oak woods, where all was green and blue, I saw the sunlight dapple on his kilt as he came out, and we met in the middle, devil that he was, he must have known that the greatest ecstasy comes after anguish. And then with great propriety he led me back, down to the house again. Every step, of course, a darkening of the joy, because every step meant a drop nearer separation. But we retraced our steps past the stables, past the garage and the gun room, and then the skittle alley, into the kitchen. He let go of my hand and followed me into the dining room where people were gradually coming down for breakfast.

These things enlarge one's horizons, one's feelings are lacerated perhaps, but I wouldn't have been without my devotion to Sutherland for anything. Even anguish can enrich one, and being a child I wasn't in anguish all the time. He jilted mother, he wrote her a letter and broke it off about a week after we left for Australia. I was very sorry for her indeed. I think part of her fury during our six months in Australia may have been due to this. If you're vain as well as in love, think of the agony, not only of your wounded heart, but your wounded vanity. Sutherland came to a dreadful end, poor man, *dreadful.* He died about seven years later at the beginning of the war, mad of GPI, in the pauper ward of Aberdeen lunatic asylum. He was consigned there by his cold-hearted wife whose name was Hope, whose own life was not without drama; she was in the process of divorcing him when she had him committed. She continued with her suit, not on the grounds that he was insane – that would have taken too long – but on the grounds of his adultery, and not with my mother, either. She was engaged in a race to divorce her husband so that she could marry her lover, Sandy Irvine, before he died – he'd been stricken by cancer. The Irvines of Drum are one of the oldest families in Scotland, Drum had been given to Sandy's forebear by Robert the Bruce, and Hope very much wanted to become queen of the castle, but death defeated her. At least she got rid of her husband, which she'd been wanting to do for a long time. Goodness, the blackness of the human heart!

I had always been an avid reader, I hadn't the distraction of other children. At the age of seven I used to sit under the piano and read Shakespeare for hours, I read all the classics and I could memorize poetry with great ease, I went through a succession of clever governesses, but mother sent me off at the age of ten to boarding school at Ascot. I didn't at all like being closeted with other children, I wasn't prepared for their society, I was queer, talked like a book and was bullied for it. I had been wrenched from my wild surroundings, and like any wild animal, I pined, I got whiter and thinner with every term that passed, cast myself before my mother and begged to be taken away, but she wouldn't hear of it. I spent all my private time in weeping, till fate who saw me tried too sorely, gave me not death but a disease, painless yet dangerous, exactly what was wanted. I got tubercular glands, very bad ones in my lungs, and they were discovered by my mother's good sense, she insisted that the doctors x ray me all over, and I was released from purgatory into comparative heaven. I was laid out like a fish on a slab, on a long chair on the south east coast of England, the air was so bracing it stiffened the hair on your head, and there for six months in the care of a hospital nurse I lay – I was not allowed to walk about – I lay and ate peppermint creams, and read trashy books. And I was happy except that I was separated from my mother because she left me there and didn't come near me for four months. I slowly got better, I had a temperature all the time, fortunately for me the TB hadn't entered into my bones, and slowly my temperature came down from about 100 to something near normal. Meanwhile I felt as merry as a brig and as fit as a fiddle.

Finally my parents came to visit me and decided that they could bear to stay with me for a month or two, and got rid of the nurse. I needed no nursing anyway, I merely had my meals brought to me on a tray and my book changed every day at the library. Tarzan I remember, I read every single Tarzan book, and a lot of sci-fi; my mind remained totally unimproved. And then they took me to the specialist again and he permitted me to go back to Tilliefoure, one of my former governesses of whom I was very fond came back to look after me, and I had a happy, happy summer. The specialist told my parents to take me to Switzerland the following winter, and my parents intended to leave me there at a boarding school so that I could learn French. Well, my father looked at me with a hint of pity in his eye because when he was 18 he was sent to Lausanne for a year by his father to do just that thing; to learn French. He told me that he never loathed a year in his life more. He detested all foreigners and considered them totally unsuitable acquaintances for a Briton. I was not at all enthusiastic about staying in Switzerland, I detested it from the moment I set foot in it, those horrible icy mountains with gashes of black rock, and the Swiss are the most boring people in the world, and utterly without humor, I was there for five months and formed not a single friendship. I was also feeling unhappy because that was the summer I fell in love with Sutherland.

When I was thirteen I was sent to a boarding school called St Leonard's at St. Andrews in Fife. It was an austere foundation, very wealthy, with a great tradition of scholarship. Most of the girls who went there were middle class, they came of able parents, they were serious, about half of them were Scots, the other half were English. Although boarding school has always been for me an ante-chamber to hell, St Leonard's was the very best of boarding schools, and if I was unhappy there I think the lack was in me and not in the place. I was sent to a good house, one of the three best, and I had a delightful housemistress, a wonderful woman, her name was Miss Pritten. It's as well to remember what sort of women were teaching in those days. She was a great big strong tall Englishwoman. She had the OBE and I must tell you how she got it. During the First World War when she was a young thing – I think she must have lost her love then, because she should have been the mother of a family – she drove an ambulance in France. And the story ran that one day she was transporting German wounded to a hospital accompanied by a medical orderly when they had to pass through a French village, and the inhabitants came to know that the men in her ambulance were not allies but Germans, and they surrounded the vehicle and threatened to lynch the occupants. So she and her orderly, taking in their hands spanners climbed out the cab and went round the back where the double doors were, and stood on the step, and told the Frenchmen who were preparing to tear apart their enemies limb from limb, that they would do it over their dead bodies, and that the first man who set foot on the British soil of a British ambulance would have his head cracked in by a spanner.

This splendid woman was about six foot tall, she was a valkyr, and she was broad in proportion, and I've no doubt the sight of her deterred the Frenchmen because they were able to hold the doors of the ambulance until a British column came marching through the town square, and rescued them. My dear housemistress was awarded the OBE by a British government for having saved the lives of so many Germans. Can you think of any country in the world except Britain which would reward its nationals for saving the lives of its enemies? She was a wonderful woman and I was very fond of her. We used to talk to each other, which was very uncommon in schools, as you know. I was equally lucky in my headmistress. Her name was Miss McCutchin and she looked like a Chinese mandarin, she was square from the neck to the ankles, and wore strange brown gowns and rows of beads and she had a flat yellow face, and within that unprepossessing body was housed a noble soul. Her mind had the keenest edge, she was a classicist from Cambridge and she was so kind to me.

When I returned to St. Leonard's after the trip to Australia, mother had got it in her head that I should try for Oxford, presumably to distract me from my new interest – she was not a great believer in education – and the school evidently thought I was up to it. My Latin was dreadfully bad so Miss McCutchin took me for extra tuitions, and we used to spend the time talking, I'm afraid, about many things besides Latin. She gave me the poems of the Silver Era, the Mediaeval Latin poets, to translate into English, but I usually liked the Latin so much that I didn't want to translate them into English. There was the dearest little poem about the springtime:

> *In hac vale florida*
> *Florius fragrate*
> *Intra caepta lilia*
> *Locus porporatus*
> *Dungeritus merile*
> *Dulcita ludit*

Philomena carmine
Dulcita concludit

We spent the whole tutorial, about 40 minutes discussing the meaning of the word porporatus. She was a word woman, you see, and she maintained that it meant the sheen on the breast of a swan, and I maintained that it meant the bloom on a grape.

I had a dear, delightful friend, who was a black Celt, the child of a south western Irish father, and a north western Scottish mother, I was fond of her, she was handsome and gallant and faithful, and she had the same sort of black humor as I did. She and I used to go out in the middle of the night in the summertime and sail boats out into the North Sea, fools that we were, we might have been carried off to Norway, we used to run the town and watch the sunrise from the castle at half past three in the morning.

My beloved Mary tried to kill me once, I was very lucky to escape, not with my life but with a serious wound. How wild are the Celts. Speaking as a Lowlander with a strain of Highland blood I feel an understanding for their absurd on-goings. I took her bath period from her and added it to my own on a cold winter's day, and when I came gaily out with my bath towel over my shoulder Mary sprang on me from behind a door with a great long knife in her hand, and she plunged it downward with great force and accuracy just where it would have pierced me between the collar bone and the shoulder blade, and possibly penetrated a lung, or conceivably my heart. But my guardian angel, that delightful person with a Hebrew name who I hope to meet on my deathbed, and who has worked so hard for me over the years, he fixed it that I'd put my bath towel over my right shoulder. Mary's knife was smothered in the folds, and I slipped forward, we fell to the ground, I mean, what force from the blow that a strong girl like I should have to fall flat on her back, and Mary on top of me, and the knife out flashing and ready for my throat this time. I was terrified, and I was convulsed with laughter at the same time too, this is a sign of nerves, nothing else. 'For God's sake get her off me', I said to the people who stood foolishly around. Of course they thought we were a couple of idiots, and did nothing to help, and presently Mary dropped the knife and walked away. Came up the head of the house. 'What's all this?' 'A bet', said I, 'which is the stronger of us', and I pocketed the knife and went after Mary and apologized to her for my bad behavior that had led to all this drama.

I'd just had my seventeenth birthday, it was that bleak Easter term which is the lowest point of the school year, I felt very cooped-up (I was engaged to be married), and Mary and I were caught canoodling. It was suggested to our parents that we might be better away from the school. No reason given, no suggestion that we were expelled, they were far too civilized for that. They wrote to my parents and put the proposition that I might be sent to Florence. I suppose they thought of Florence as a sort of festering Renaissance city full of beauty and bestiality, I wish I'd been sent there, I'd have loved to go but I was not sent there after all. I was not sad to leave St. Leonards. It was a school where they were trying to take to the women what had always belonged to the men, not only the academic records which they were quite entitled to ask for, but also the physical prowess which I think is fairly unwise for women to attempt, and so the pressure was always great. But even if that had not been so, even if there had been less Philistinism, I would still have been unhappy because I was away from Orde. There were memorable moments but it was not a fruitful time, I learned very little, the time of my learning and my training began when I got married. When my schooldays were done I felt such a lightening of the burden as I've never felt before or since. I said to my mother, 'whatever happens to me now in life, nothing can ever bring me back to school', and I've had no reason in all the sorrows that have beset me since, to feel the same relief or release as I felt then.

I had been expelled from St Leonards but Oxford was still on, and in June of 1935, with my mother in attendance, I went to sit my entrance exams at Lady Margaret Hall. Orde came out to visit me there, he arrived early on a Sunday morning, and we went out before breakfast on the banks of the Cherwell. I took his hand, I turned it over, I think I was going to kiss the palm, and I looked at it and my heart stood still because I saw that his line of life was broken in the middle, there was a gap of about half an inch, it was quite unmistakable. He noticed that there was something wrong, 'What is it?' 'You are going to die young' I said. 'When?' he asked. 'The break comes just after the half-way mark.' 'In that case, I think we should get married quickly', he said. I had already half-decided that I didn't want to go to Oxford after seeing how the women's colleges were treated, I thought it would be far better to marry Orde.

Chapter 3

My parents had taken an instant dislike to Orde when they saw us together on the Cathay; they wouldn't have been thrilled if he had been a boy of 17, but this! After Orde walked out of the Browns Hotel (without even looking in their direction), they frog-marched me up to their suite and swarmed all over me with questions and accusations. I told them simply that he had come to tell me that he had broken off an engagement to another woman, and that is all I knew with any degree of certainty. Mother screamed, 'But why did he break it off now, is it because of you? Did you have him in your cabin? Have undertakings been given? He meets a sixteen year old girl, talks to her for half an hour and then breaks off a long-standing engagement? How is this possible, what did you do?' Then, suddenly changing tack which was perfectly in character, she said, 'I knew there was something fishy about him. Don't you see, Lorna, you are being drawn into a very sordid business by a man you hardly know, and if you don't publicly distance yourself from him, your reputation will be ruined'. Papa's line had been, 'The man is a bounder and a fortune hunter and I forbid you to have anything to do with him, I shall make inquiries, I shall take the matter up with his colonel...'

In matters of the heart I was now beyond their reach but I was not beyond the reach of the law; Orde and I would have to wait for two years. During the school holidays I was incarcerated in Tilliefoure, my mother wouldn't let me take calls from him on the telephone, in those two years he never once set foot in our home. Finally mother said he could visit on condition that he wouldn't kiss me! I told her that I wouldn't insult him by repeating what she had said. The dramas at home were continuing intermittently, we were not fantastic characters from a novel we were ordinary people. I threatened to elope and have an illegitimate baby.

Papa and I were crossing Park Lane together one day, and he said, while the traffic swirled around us, 'you have been a great disappointment to me'. I looked up at him, his face was so sad, I was heartbroken that he could have such feelings for his only child. I'd been a good little girl in most ways, difficult from time to time, my utterances were the only unconventional thing about me, I'd never asked for anything, never run after men, never wanted a season in London, or a fur coat, never had rows with my mother as some girls have at that age. I was truthful – I sound a paragon, I was nothing of the kind – and I was not the sort of daughter that most fathers would find a disappointment. I suppose Papa wanted me to marry a man of means, I know mother wanted me to marry a title, she felt that I owed it to her.

Since we were not officially engaged, I was only introduced to Orde's people for the first time a month before the wedding. Orde drove me down in his Talbot, he was cheerful enough, it was a sunny day, the roof was down, and he was driving very fast through narrow lanes, this was something he evidently needed to do, and he was whistling a tune of a popular song:

Button up your overcoat
When the wind is free
Oh, take good care of yourself
You belong to me

That was all well and good, but I was not feeling very cheerful myself, the broken engagement was uppermost in my mind, it was a large blot on Orde's copybook, not the sort of thing that could easily be brushed off. I was frankly afraid to face his family, they were sure to hate me at first sight for bringing him to this pretty pass. They lived in the county of Surrey, in a village called Godalming which was a little over an hour's drive from London. The house was smaller and more ordinary than I had imagined, with very little in the way of ornament because of course they were Plymouth Brethren. The English are very good at putting a stranger at their ease by means of bustling about, absent-minded small-talk, gentle banter and such like, but the Wingates didn't go in for that. I'm sure the siblings didn't stand there with their feet apart staring at me – I couldn't tell without my glasses – but it felt like it, and I was terrified that one of them would have a fit of the giggles, which would have been mortifying, I might not have survived that.

My hackles were up, as I said, when an aproned woman with one eye marched up to me and planted a large kiss on my cheek, and hugged me in the most extraordinary way, whispering my name, then stood away from me, smiling and telling me how beautiful I was. This could only be Orde's mother, but why had I not been told that she had one eye?

There was an empty socket with skin drawn over it, and a moist horizontal line of eyelashes intertwined like bramble. While she spoke to me, keeping hold of my hands, and looking into my eyes and smiling, it was a battle as to which eye I would focus on, it had to be one or the other, at that range there could be no dissimulation. Fascinating as her empty eye was, her good eye was so completely animated that it drew one in, and within minutes of being in her company one not only forgot that she had only one eye, one wondered why one really needed two. She however did not forget, and the only photographs that I know of, of Ethel Wingate, are taken in profile, showing her complete side.

She lost the eye in a household accident as a child and in overcoming the loss became the woman she now was. With one eye she brought up her siblings and cared for her parents, and conquered the heart of Colonel George Wingate, and then made him wait for her for 16 years, not in spite of the eye, surely, but because of it. She must have taught herself to look a person directly in the face and command that person's attention to her good eye, and she did it by force of her irrepressible effervescence and charm and intelligence (and I, who am afraid to be seen with my spectacles on!). Orde's father, George, fell in love with his future wife when she was 14, she must have been a very remarkable girl. She would not marry him because she would not take leave of her father, Colonel Orde Brown, a great authority on armour. He used to take her with him as his secretary all over Europe to conferences in Vienna and places where they're keen on that sort of thing – he had a wonderful collection of armour too, and he wrote an interesting monograph about it. Ethel who was the eldest of seven children remained at home until her father died. George finally achieved her when he was 48, and Granville Wingate was born when he was about 60.

The Wingates lived frugally, the house they lived in didn't belong to them, Mrs. Wingate made their clothes and they used to give each other the most extraordinary gifts at Xmas or birthdays, like a pound of cheese, or something like that. Whatever surplus the Wingate and Orde-Brown families may have once had, they had given away to worthy causes; they were extremely high-minded. For example – and this is most curious as will later become apparent – William Wingate, Orde's paternal grandfather, walked away from a prosperous business in Glasgow to become an evangelical missionary to the Jews of Hungary. Who on earth would do a thing like that? The house had a large garden with a vegetable garden attached, and several greenhouses, and the children cleaned and gardened and helped with all the household chores because Mrs. Wingate had no servants, which surprised me greatly. Now, as a boy Orde – his name in the family was Ordey – fell far short of his father's expectations, I simply can't imagine why, and the Old Colonel beat his son quite savagely from time to time, and was often very unkind to him at table – where I suppose they saw each other – so much so that Monica, who was telling me this, sometimes had to leave the room because she couldn't bare to watch it. According to Granville, the beatings appeared to have no effect on Orde because he would just carry on doing whatever it was that had annoyed the old Colonel in the first place, understanding that his father's rages came and went, and he was there as a sort of lightening conductor for the rest of them. The Plymouth Brethren held that the Old Testament, the font of all wisdom and morality, should be the backbone of a child's education, to be read and re-read until a child could recite passages in his sleep. Orde learnt that God smote the Children of Israel from time to time when they deserved it, and so it was with his own father.

This was a prayer-driven family, they prayed for guidance for the smallest decision, every blessing came from Him, every ungenerous thought and deed was seen by Him, and so their lives were filled with terror and wonder, they were altogether on a higher plane than other families, and their lives richer and more intense.

When Colonel Wingate was in his eighties, he was asked by Orde to back for him a bill of 50 pounds at Lloyds Bank, and he refused. This was for his expedition into the Libyan Desert. I thought it was unconscionable, I felt very bitter when Orde told me this, after all it was a notable exploit for a young man, it could do him nothing but good, and bring honour to his name, and to be refused such a request seemed to me gratuitously cruel, but it didn't turn Orde's affections away from his father.

Orde told me rather dramatically soon after we met - cards on the table - that he and his family were under a curse, the curse of inherited insanity. I asked if any of his forebears had been mad and he said, 'no but after discussion he and his sisters had come to the conclusion that somewhere, perhaps through the malpractices of some poor soul called Torrance among their ancestry, syphilis had been brought into the family. This was just a theory, of course, but it was in order to explain why he and Sybil and Monica not, I gather, Rachel who seemed to be aloof from it all, were blighted by a recurrent malaise. He said that it was a very painful experience that occurred two or three times a year, and he told me how it came on and what it felt like while it was in process, and how it wore off. It obviously meant a great deal to him, this experience, and I gather that his sisters, like himself were almost obsessed by the fact that they were no sooner through one attack than they were preparing themselves for the next. Now the thing was in fact a chimera, a creature of darkness, perfectly real to the people who saw it, perfectly unreal to someone like myself. Something to be wrestled with, like Jacob and the angel, it strengthened him. But I think it was a group experience that the Wingates had decided to have together. They didn't know this, it was not a conscious decision on their part, but they would all suffer together; not in fact all of them because Nigel was in Kenya and he never complained about having these melancholic fits, and Rachel who was a woman of great common sense, remained apart. But Sybil and Orde and Monica, who all came together in the middle of the family, spoke about it, they discussed their symptoms with each other, they were dreadfully serious about it all. I mean there was an air of dread and darkness about this disability and in the end they started to wish this disability onto poor Granville who was a lad of 22. When I was there one day they were saying that they must take him to the mental doctors, and that it was beginning...'have you heard, Granville had an attack', and all this.

Sybil took me aside one day and told me I should never have any children because they would be cursed. I'd had an aunt in a lunatic asylum for years, everybody has madness in their families, and everyone has badness too in their families, what does it matter?

Orde was a basically most sensible man. I say basically, he was thoroughly sensible but every now and then, like all of us, he'd put on an act. Sometimes he did it to impress other people, to get them to do something by demonstrating, and sometimes he did it for his own amusement, or possibly for his own auto-therapy. I'm inclined to think that the dreadfully dark way in which religion was presented to these poor children played a part, and did in fact claim a real victim. The dark God that Colonel Wingate worshipped, and Mrs. Wingate, for all her gaiety and wit, she worshipped it too, it did demand a sacrifice and it got it too.

Tossie Wingate who was apparently the gentle, golden-haired one, died aged 25, a year before I met Orde, in a lunatic asylum, of melancholia. I'm told it's a dreadful disease, the patient wastes away in the utmost misery. It dies in a far worse state than people die of cancer, and this naturally had a powerful effect on the other children. Orde only ever had one serious attack in the years I knew him, and I put it down to the fact that he had a lot to get on with, and he was separated from his family; this was in Cairo during the war.

I've always thought that madness is something you wake up with in the morning and go to bed with at night. I did feel that there was something about it that was due for deflation. I felt that the whole thing was, in a way, rather like the Brontes, when life became rather dull it had to be hotted up, so I didn't give Orde the full mead of my sympathy, I was not unsympathetic, but I didn't take it all that seriously.

Orde and I had arrived for luncheon, it was a Sunday as I recall, and we were soon seated around the long bare table eating a gruel of some kind and, under the benign and amused gaze of their parents, the siblings engaged in a snarling and wrestling which is really the characteristic of a den of young wolves, and that is what they were conversationally, they were enjoying themselves hugely, and as they wrestled and tussled and bit each other, one could see that this was how they'd sharpened their wits, because the speed of the argumentation was dazzling. The strategy I had devised, prior to my arrival, for finding my place in the scrum of siblings was to meet their stares politely but without blinking, and to restrict my conversation to monosyllables in order to avoid a faux-pas or possible disgrace. However I had been so disarmed by the intensity of Mrs. Wingate's warmth that I entirely forgot myself. The subject at the table was some recent declaration by George Bernard Shaw, and I was sitting there quietly in my own thoughts when I heard my name called.

'Lorna, are you a great admirer of GBS?' It was young Granville who, I could tell by the attitude of the others was getting ahead of himself, and by his tone of voice it sounded like a challenge.

'Not at all, I dislike him intensely', said I without a moment's hesitation. Well, there was a short silence, and Sybil who did most of the thinking for that family, she was one of the brightest women I ever met, said to me in a tone of restrained disbelief and condescending fury, 'Are you very familiar with his work, Lorna?'. 'Yes', said I, looking at her directly, quite displeased with her hectoring tone of voice, and it was as if a flag had been dropped because all hell broke loose and soon I was howling and scratching and clawing along with the best of them, in this manner I earned my spurs as a Wingate.

Once I had been thus admitted into Orde's childhood, I discovered a number of rather endearing things about the man I was to marry. He wasn't considered particularly clever, the Wingate women were cleverer on the whole than the men, and yet things were expected of him. When he entered a room people would look up, not with admiration but with curiosity, as if something might happen.

Monica told me that they were once at the circus, and a team of horses were performing, and at the end the horses stopped their gyrations and came to a halt directly in front of us, and bowed. They were all convinced that they were bowing to Orde, he was all of eight but he loved horses. Whatever it was that distinguished this family, Orde had more of it than the others, he was the essence of Wingate, a best of show sort of thing, and he set a standard in the family for courage and determination, but he wasn't terribly bright as a boy.

The clever one was, as I said, Sybil. She was older than Orde by 18 months, and was at University in London when Orde left school, and she took a proprietorial interest in her brother and wanted always to keep tabs on him. She embraced socialism with great fervor, and after he left home to attend Woolwich Military Academy, away from her watchful eye, she took to popping-in on their favourite bookshop on the Charing Cross Road to ask old Mr. Henderson if her brother had been in, and what he had bought.

Orde found three heroes going into manhood, I would say, and they were still on him when we met. One was George Bernard Shaw, whom I regarded as a rather clever poseur and a phony, another was HG Wells who didn't interest me a great deal, and the third was Gilbert Murray, a man perfectly cut off from reality. Gilbert Murray was a classical scholar who was really the father of the League of Nations, or at least one of them, and he had a hold over a generation of Britons who wanted to find an alternative to warfare as a means of settling disputes between nations; they quite properly wanted to avoid a repeat of the Battle of the Somme. A sort of world government backed-up by the British Empire that, with the help of British arms and British money, would stop wars from breaking out; this was Mr. Murray's extraordinarily naïve program. Of course, Britain would share, Britain would be generous, and the nations of the world would applaud and be terribly grateful.

World government was on the lips of many young men and women of the day, such were the times, and it was being promoted by Orde's three paradigms, Shaw, Wells and Murray. I thought it was rather facile to imagine you could stop people from fighting, but the Wingates thought otherwise. Whatever the state of their religious belief, salvation was still the thing – salvation is a very big word, isn't it – and since God and his redeeming son had failed to avert the catastrophe of the Great War and its aftermath, an alternative was required, and this was going to be it; pure science fiction. Many years later, when Sybil recognized that Gilbert Murray was not the second coming, she rolled up her sleeves and bravely went off to fight with the Republicans in Spain. With or without God, the Wingates all managed to find a mission in life.

Having fallen in love with Orde because of his unique manner, abundant resolve and high moral fiber, all of which set him above the normal run of men, I was dropped now into a veritable nest of Ordes – why do I use nest; as in viper? Surely not, but nest persists – and each more purposeful and high-minded than the next. He had three sisters who would have happily chained themselves to the gates of Buckingham Palace, or thrown themselves under a passenger train in pursuit of a given purpose. If I appear to be laboring the term 'high minded', one must remember I had only my own family as a point of comparison, and furthermore, they weren't all of quite the same caliber; brother Nigel, who was so handsome I had to forbear looking at him, struck one as marginally bad when standing next to his sisters, of course he was nothing of the sort, but he was the least Wingatian Wingate. The youngest was Granville, he was just a child in my eyes, three years my senior, but he would never have become a missionary.

On the subject of my own family, my encounter with the Wingates, Mrs.Wingate in particular, had opened my eyes. I saw at once my own mother's manifest vanity and selfishness, and how much of it had come down to me. I think the Wingates may have thought badly of papa. It wasn't because he had made a great deal of money during the Great War, it was because he didn't seem to be doing anything with it. It wasn't snobbery of course, they were incapable of that particular vice, they judged people entirely by what they made of their lives, and not by how much money they had, or the manner of their birth.

I think that Colonel and Mrs. Wingate thought of me as an eccentric but decorative companion for their son. Mrs. Wingate would say to me, if ever I commented on something beautiful, a sunset, a lovely piece of china or something of the sort, 'dear little kitten, how extraordinary that you should notice such things.' I was only under Colonel Wingate's roof twice during his lifetime, and on both occasions when he led the family in prayer at the end of a meal, he alluded to me with something along the lines of, '…and thank you, Lord, for leading this lost little lamb to our home and table'. I was very touched, it made me feel warm inside. Anyway, Mrs. Wingate had a sufficiently high opinion of her son that if he had brought home a fan dancer she would have accepted his choice. Sybil told me more than once that I was a perfect foil for her brother, and Monica said, in a letter after he died, that Orde and I were like two peas in a pod. Yes, the Wingates were a great treasure and I was indeed fortunate to have crossed their path.

One of the constraints on Plymouth Brethren was a severe curtailment of social contact, which meant that the children were not allowed to mix with anyone outside their immediate family circle, and this engendered, among other things, a sense of unity and 'usness'. However Mrs. Wingate believed that at a certain point her children had to go out into the world, and so she put her sons into the local school which happened to be Charterhouse, one of the great schools of England. It had an extraordinary rule that brothers may not consort with one another, known as the rule of Hill Side, so when Nigel was of an age to join his elder brother at the school, at the end of each day they had to walk (aged twelve and nine) from the school to the house with a minimum of 100 yards between them. Who thought up this rule?

Orde, being the first up, was taken from a pious, disciplined, and protected setting and thrust into what must have appeared to him to be Sodom and Gomorrah, no less. Whatever his position in his family, he was now in the brutal world of adolescent boys who took one look at his narrow shoulders and sour face and he was instantly re-christened 'stinker', a very specific epithet which inferred that he had soiled himself. The boys would hold their noses as they passed him in the school yard, make cruel comments then burst out laughing. Other boys who might have befriended him were put off doing so, for reasons only adolescent boys understand. He was, he told me, the only boy in the school who had no pocket money, none whatever, and the school tuck shop which constituted an important and pleasurable supplement to school dinners, was for him out of bounds. In his first term, and at the end of each school day, he would walk down the hill and across the town to his home where his family eagerly awaited him, and he would be implored by his younger siblings to tell of his adventures at the great school on the hill, and he tried not to disappoint. He told them of his new friends, and the exciting games they played up there, and the wonderful classrooms full of light and knowledge. In reality, he had withdrawn completely, and managed to preserve his pride by speaking to no one, volunteering for nothing, and spending his recreation time in the library or in the chapel. This of course confirmed his status as a famous stinker, for nothing was more unmanly and degrading to a boy's standing than going to the library, let alone the chapel, when it wasn't mandatory. They thought it an act, and a very poor one, and it annoyed them, it could not have been a happy time for him.

After Orde's death I received many letters, one was a tribute from an Old Carthusian, and a strange tribute it was. The writer was Jocelyn Hennessy, a classmate of Orde's but from a different house, and I shall try to reproduce it from memory. He began in usual fashion, introducing himself to me, and expressing his heartfelt condolences etc, then he wrote, 'I wish to tell you a story that concerns your late husband, a story that I have never told anyone. I fancy this is not the kind of thing one writes to a grieving widow but the event in question was a watershed in my life, and I shall never forget it.' Of course, my interest was pricked, he wrote very well and in a clear hand. He went on, 'I was a new boy at Charterhouse, plump and gauche, and slow-witted, and subject to relentless verbal abuse and 'shoving' from a certain group of classmates, to which one had to submit, and I was extremely unhappy and, like many boys in my position, wondering what I had done to my parents to make them send me to this fearsome place. We were in class one morning, and the master was Mr. Fletcher, the school headmaster, a dull man who taught Latin to the younger boys, and he was a severe disciplinarian even by the Charterhouse standards of the day, so we were quiet and paid attention to what he was saying. Wingate sat where he always sat against the wall on the periphery of the class, having nothing to do with any of us, practically invisible. Mr. Fletcher selected me to stand up and recite a poem by Horace upon which we were later to perform a comprehension, and the boy immediately behind me, his name was Wickstead, leant forward and gently pushed a pencil into my backside where my trousers had collected, and there it remained sticking out as I fought to retain my composure while reciting Horace to Mr. Fletcher, with tears of shame running down my cheek. 'Come, come, Hennessy,' said the headmaster, 'surely Horace is not as bad as all that!' This occasioned much laughter, indeed it was amusing on many levels, and nicely judged, everyone thought well of Wickstead for having produced such a clever diversion and, imagine, tweaking Fletcher's nose in the bargain.

The bell rang, there was a slapping of books and banging of desks and the boys were settling down for a brief interval between Mr. Fletcher leaving the classroom and another master entering it. Now this Wickstead character; I was very much afraid of this boy, he was full of unpleasant tricks, and my best hope generally was that he would not notice me, so I never reacted to his goadings, and all the lesser boys in the class were deferential to him because he was a sort of leader, he did as he pleased with us, and he was probably having a very good time of it at Charterhouse, he was big fish in a small pond sort of thing, indeed he was large for his age. I remember thinking that I had come to the end of my tether, there were still x number of weeks until the term was over, I didn't know how I would get through the next day in this terrible place, I really didn't belong in this type of school. So I was sitting in my chair, unable to control my sobbing and therefore doubly humiliated, when suddenly there was a movement immediately behind me, chairs and books and pencils scattered left and right, for a boy had leapt over the two or three rows of desks and thrown himself bodily at Wickstead who himself fell backwards heavily onto the floor, banging his head, no doubt as surprised as everyone at the extreme violence of it. It was all over in an instant. Wingate picked himself up off the pile and returned to his desk slowly, taking the long route past the master's dais, and not looking back at the chaos on the floor, because Wickstead was groaning and cursing, and by the time Wingate was back at his desk with his book open in front of him, felled Wickstead still hadn't risen. I went over to the stricken boy, the entire class was gathered around him, I had to clamber onto a desk to get a look in, and it became apparent that the reason Wickstead couldn't rise was because not only was he bleeding from his head where he had struck the corner of a desk, but he had a pencil sticking out of the middle of his bottom through a hole torn in his trousers, with blood seeping out onto the floor. I looked over at Wingate in disbelief and he was reading his book exactly in his usual position, not a hair out of place, as they say. It was a very shocking thing in the particularity of it, and in a situation as unusual as this, one tended to look the other way, which is what we all did.

The matter was taken no further, there was no higher authority in a dispute of this nature, this was another rule of Charterhouse, so Wickstead went off and reported to matron with his wounds, and the rest of us were left to reflect upon the meaning of what we had witnessed, and the change it had wrought in the hierarchy of the class. Stinker Wingate was henceforth known as Wingate, and I was no longer the object of Wickstead's attention. Wingate continued to brood in his corner, and Wickstead seemed to settle down, and in due course became a scholar. Wingate and I never became friends but I always liked to sit near him in class or in chapel because I was afraid of many things and he was afraid of nothing. No one, before or since, has gone so far out of his way on my behalf as your late husband did for me then.' I wrote back to this dear man to thank him for his kind letter and to tell him how moved I had been by the writing of it. Of all the letters from the great and the mighty that I have lost and burnt, Hennessy's letter is the one I most regret. Nigel of course didn't have to endure bullying at Charterhouse.

Orde held fast to the religion of his father, and remained necessarily removed from the other boys, but for one romantic attachment he formed, as one does at public school, which was deep and lasted two years. However these were unusual times at Charterhouse, because a very terrible war was in progress, and it wasn't so very far away, less than a hundred miles across the Channel, I refer to the Great War. Once a month on Sunday at evensong, Orde told me, the chaplain read out the latest tally of fallen Old Carthusians. There were of course great fluctuations in the numbers from month to month, but over the period it averaged out at about sixteen. Many of them would have been known personally to the boys, all were known to the masters. The boys of the OTC were straining at the bit to get at the Bosch to avenge the blood of their schoolmates – I'm sure it was the same in Germany – but in the face of this unfolding, accumulating, unparalleled calamity, it raised the question in older people's minds whether the British race was still the apple of God's eye, and Orde was surely touched by it. In 1914, any or all of Colonel and Mrs. Wingate's offspring might have been destined for a life of service to God. By the time I came on the scene, not one of Orde's siblings could call themselves a true Christian; they all professed a belief in God out of profound deference to their parents, but the truth was they had dropped Him. Somebody wrote something very true.

> *[We] had been taught to believe that the whole object of life was to reach out to beauty and love, and that mankind, in its progress to perfection, had killed the beast instinct...All poetry, all art, all religion had preached this gospel and this promise. Now that ideal was broken like a china vase dashed to the ground.*

This horror, of course, marked the end of an entire way of life, and this is what Orde had to contend with when he emerged from his childhood; a deeply ingrained belief system dashed whole, and trampled into the ground.

Chapter 4

Orde had an old friend from Woolwich Military Academy called Derek Tulloch. Derek will return again and again to my story, so it would be as well to introduce him properly, and in so doing, throw some light on the character of my soon-to-be husband. If you were to ask, say, a French person to describe the typical young Englishman of his day, it would be Derek. Soft-spoken, frightened of women, pressed trousers, well-mannered, hard-working, tends to blush, not overly imaginative, anxious to not give offence, indecisive and loyal. He was Orde's only constant friend. They say that opposites attract, do they not? Orde was frightened of nobody, he liked to raise his voice, he had a flair for the theatrical, anything you could do he could do better, he could be utterly charming but never hesitated to give offence when it was called for, terrifyingly decisive, and loyal. For all the above reasons, neither man was sociable in the sense that they might belong to a clique of friends, no clique would have them; one was too diffident, the other too fierce. But they had been thrust together at a young age, both in the same profession, both liked horses very much, and both needed a companion who would overlook the other's social defects.

Orde never belittled Derek, never brought him to a blush, never asked more of him than he could give. Derek accepted Orde exactly as he was, that was the compact. So when Orde cruelly jilted Peggy, whom Derek had known for six years as 'Orde's girl', Derek would have said to himself something along the lines of 'I'm sure Orde had his own reasons for behaving that way, I don't greatly approve (British understatement) but it does not shake my friendship for him.' By now Derek of course was married to Mary, and Mary, Peggy's soul mate in the affair, might have said to herself, 'the man is quite depraved, the poor, poor girl, he shouldn't be allowed to get away with it.' When, about a year after I found Orde, he introduced them to Peggy's substitute, Derek saw before him a self-assured, pretty, lively, happy girl, he blushed when he shook my hand, wondered how Orde had gotten away with it, was warm and correct with me. Mary saw a clueless schoolgirl with crimson lipstick, a shameless hussy, a home-breaker, and was cold to me from the first moment.

It was clear that Derek would be Orde's best man at the wedding, there could be no other. Because both families disapproved of the match, and because everyone felt uncomfortable on account of Peggy, it was always going to be a smallish affair, but at least there was good-old-Derek as best man. Two days before the big day, Orde casually let slip to me that Derek couldn't attend after all as he had promised to go on a partridge shoot, and to be perfectly honest I didn't think twice about it because I was just too excited.

The guard of honour was there in regimental colours, but no Derek.

Mother came to the church dressed in black from head to toe and silver fox furs, she wept the whole time, and announced that she would not be giving us a gift, she had to make her point. The Wingates were out in force, there were about forty of them in the church, it was a three line whip and no excuses, and even though the church and vicar weren't quite their cup of tea, they sang at the top of their voices. It's not that they didn't feel for Peggy, it was just that they were fearsomely clannish, it was family first. I was aware of no cloud, it was the happiest, most perfect day of my life, I felt triumphant. I remember we were standing side by side and the vicar was doing something at the alter, and presently Orde leaned towards me and said something very funny and I giggled, then I leaned towards him and said something else and he giggled, and afterwards Kitty Wingate who was dear Rex's nasty wife, took the family aside one by one and said that it was the most shocking behavior she'd ever seen that the bride and groom should start laughing and talk to each other.

Our first home was in Bulford, and it was also my first taste of the real world away from mother and papa, as it were, for I had no experience of normal, ordinary people and how they got on with things. My companions at the camp were naturally the other wives of serving officers, and I was struck how difficult and narrow their lives were. Their education was often imperfect, they were beset by worry, financial worry usually, and the terrifying possibility that their husbands would not make the next grade in the middle ranks, would not for example make lieutenant colonels having been majors into their middle years. With children at boarding school, black penury lay before them should they fail in their exams, should their confidential reports not give them that further boost, and these women,

I mean, their faces were ravaged by anxiety. I felt the greatest sympathy with them while finding them of course boring, boring beyond belief, and it made me wonder if the army was really the place for us to be. Would I end up like those women? I expressed the revulsion I felt by being conscientiously gay, careless and loud-mouthed, the little bête noire of the compound, and I made a point of not sucking up to the wife of Orde's commanding officer, a thing that the wives of junior officers were expected to do. We had a charming army-issue house with a tin roof, I refused to do any housework, I certainly didn't enter the kitchen. The house was tiny and extremely congested with bric a brac, one had to climb over things to get around, and Orde seemed as happy as a lark with his newly-minted wife, we sparkled together.

Very soon after we moved to Bulford, I walked into the small living room one morning and I found Orde in the middle of a mental attack, he was extremely pale, he shook all over, his teeth chattered on the rim of a glass, he sat huddled in a chair, he was obviously in great distress, he looked like he was having a nightmare, it was a terrible sight. I decided that there was nothing I could do for him except give him a couple of aspirin and a hot drink, so I told him I was going to leave the room and let him have some peace and privacy. I thought that if I was to tell him how sorry I was for him he'd probably feel worse not better. Later I asked him what it felt like to be in this state of mind, and he told me that he felt that he was wrestling with a cloud of darkness that descended upon him, accompanied by horror, and the feeling that God had withdrawn the light of his countenance. He said that his remedy was to hold on to his belief that there was a God and that the universe is good, and that all would come good in the end; a very courageous and proper attitude to take. That was the first and only time I witnessed the Wingate Curse.

Derek and Mary had built themselves a brick house, it was the only house with a proper fireplace in the street. We often used to go there for dinner because everybody was busy in the middle of the day, and they always welcomed me with a nice smile, Orde with affection and cordiality, then we'd sit down and for three hours, perhaps more, the three of them would talk about horses. During the winter months of course there was hunting and in the spring steeple-chasing, and these three people used to go over every fence and discuss where every horse had put each foot, what the hounds' performances had been, then when they'd finished with their own steeds, and Orde had four of five (not so very unusual for an artillery officer) and Derek and Mary had at least two or three, they would then discuss the horses of their friends. From time to time I used to make a tentative remark, not connected perhaps to horses, and when I did there was a pause, everybody smiled kindly, and when I'd finished they went back to talking about the horses, just where they'd left off. In fact I was a horsewoman in my own right. From the age of about five I was cracked about horses, as little girls are, I'd thought about horses, I'd read about horses, not flashy books like Muriel and Mousy but solid stuff about horse management and about stabling, and about diseases of the horse and various kinds of seat, and how foreigners ride, and how the British carry on the management of the horse. I knew a lot because I was taught by some of the best instructors in Scotland and later in the schools I went to. I might have shown more enthusiasm if anybody had taken the trouble to talk to me about them, instead of always turning their backs and talking to each other, so my feelings for Derek and Mary were rather cool. We were not good friends in any sense of the word.

One of my greatest pleasures was watching Orde working a horse because he had a gift. He used to take me into the riding school at Bulford, which was a properly constructed one, and there he trained me in minor acrobatics riding Martrene, his enormous thoroughbred mare, the only one of his horses that had the temperament for a lady - the others were half-broken or half-crazed or both. She was 17 hands from the ground, falling off her was no joke, but he had me riding bareback with my arms folded on my chest like a circus girl.

His charger was a magnificent creature called Hannibal, the most beautiful living thing I've ever seen. Hannibal was a dark bay with dapples, and he had black points, that means he had black stockings on his legs and black mane and tale, and he was a candidate to be described by that good Jewish word *meshugga*; he was gallant and he was mad. One morning Orde told me he was going out to school Hannibal, and the German military attaché who'd come down from London to spend a few days at Bulford, and no doubt to find out whatever our army had to show his, was going to accompany him. I asked permission to ride with them, on Martrene of course, and so before breakfast we rendez-vous'd in the field where the obstacles were. I remember so well, on a dewy summer morning, the German military attaché, who was a Nazi, because this after all was 1935, he and I sat side by side on our mounts, I stole a shy glance at him from time to time, he was a horrid man but quite impressive. He was a Junker, very tall, very pale, very square about the head, very cold, as a matter of fact I think he was a queer because the only time I had to entertain him in Orde's absence, he immediately went over to the bookcase, took out a book, sat down and refused to speak to me, when I said something to him he didn't answer.

He was a horseman alright, and as we sat there we watched Orde bring Hannibal up to a most extraordinary obstacle, a sort of St. Sebastian's grid, no St. Lawrence was the poor chap who was put on the grid, Sebastian had the arrows. I expect it's well known in the horsemanship schools, it consists of a great iron ladder laid down on the ground with thick iron rungs supported on V pieces which stick up about, oh, I don't know, a foot, something like that, and the rung is laid across them in the crutch about, if my memory serves me, four feet apart, about a dozen of these pieces of iron laid out, one above the other, parallel with the ground. Now the object of the exercise is for the rider to bring the horse up and to pitter it over rung after rung, so that its forefeet always go together, and it gathers its hind feet up, and brings them forward, and so on like a rocking horse. It's a skill, and rather an impressive performance when it's properly done, and it calls for great coordination between horse and rider. Orde went first and he took Hannibal who was only half broken, I may say, and given to curious outbursts of craziness, he used to jump over fences onto the roofs of passing cars, things of that kind, and I watched him, he was very fond of Hannibal so there was a rapprochement between the two, a rapport is the word I suppose, - why does one use so much French? Because one doesn't know one's English – and they went over. Beautiful, I've never seen anything more impressive. Hannibal never put a foot wrong. I should have thought that a foot wrong on a contraption of that sort would have meant a nasty fall for both horse and rider, and then I looked at the Nazi attaché, just a glance of course, and I saw an expression on his face, it was very revealing, it was a great tribute to Orde. A slow smile curled his lips, cold white face; pure admiration. Then he in turn – he had a rather different seat I remember, he rode with a very long stirrup, he took his horse over, he did it perfectly well, nothing wrong with it, but it hadn't got the neatness and the grace of Orde on Hannibal.

This man, this German got on very well with Orde, they liked each other. In those days of course we didn't know much about Hitler, we had no Jewish friends, the news of his atrocities had scarcely penetrated to Salisbury Plain in the summer of 1935, his intentions were quite mysterious to us, and Orde one evening invited this man round to play chess with him. Now, apart from Derek and Mary and their hospitable house, there was one other household that I was always glad to visit. They were much kinder to me and more friendly than Derek and Mary, they were some people called Fildes, the man Denny was the son of a very famous Victorian and Edwardian painter, President of the Royal Academy called Sir Luke Fildes, and Denny who I think had private means, painted pictures, semi-professionally. He painted all the lovely girls in the county families round about, and as a wedding present to Orde, a very generous one I think, he painted a picture of me. It was a large picture, three quarter length I remember, he was particularly good at doing the dress. Well now, Denny who was rather a weak man but a very nice one, was married to a tough little creature, an Australian called Marge, and Marge and he were childless and they made their house a gathering point for all the young things both male and female in that area, and they were kindness itself, so gay and so generous.

On this particular night, when Orde had settled down to play chess with the Junker, I knew that neither of them would speak to me for the rest of the evening, so I said, at about nine o'clock, 'I wonder if you'd mind if I left you now and went to spend the evening with the Fildes, I'll ring them up and ask them if I can come'. 'Excellent idea', said Orde, returning to pawn to king three or something, and I duly set out in our car. I arrived at the Fildes' delightful neo-Georgian house in the dear little village of – I can't remember the name, it begins with 'A' and Queen Guinevere died there, about five miles away from Bulford. My brain is softening, good gracious.

I went upstairs and found Marge and Denny sitting on either side of the fire, and nobody else in the room. I took off my coat and sat down on the sofa. And then Marge said, 'did you go to the cocktail party at the so-and-so's this evening?' And I said yes. She said, 'did you see anyone interesting there?' 'I saw lots of interesting people there'. 'Did you see Harry Slesser?' 'Yes', said I, 'I saw Harry in the distance, he was slightly drunk'. Now Harry Slesser was the general's ADC, General Burnett Stewart, an excellent man, and Harry was exactly like every ADC, tall, good manners, just the man for putting place cards on the dinner table, and I heard a kind of snort or giggle from behind the sofa, and peering over the back, I saw a man crouching on the ground, Harry Slesser no less. I didn't think that this was a funny joke at all, everybody else did, Harry came out from behind and settled down beside me.

We had a pleasant evening, and at about 11 o'clock or a little later, I asked if they'd mind if I left, and Denny went off to find my coat. No sooner had he and Marge left the room for this purpose than Harry who was still somewhat intoxicated seized me, though quite gently, flung me on the sofa, and flunked himself on top of me. Now I was 18, and had never known how to cope with any man at all, and I didn't know what to do. I was very cross, so after a good deal of pushing and pulling, I managed to wriggle out from under Harry, and fall on the floor. I got up, very ruffled, Denny came back with my coat, I put it on, not having enough sense to say to him, 'take care of Harry, Denny, he's just made a fool of himself', I went out; I didn't want to get Harry into trouble, that was the whole point, and away I went back home, getting there at about half past eleven or so.

When I arrived of course the attaché had gone, and Orde and I prepared ourselves for bed, and then he looked at me and he saw something, he said, 'you look very pale, is anything wrong?' And like a fool I told him the story, no embellishments. Horror! He immediately flew into a towering rage, seized the telephone (this was about midnight), rang up Marge and asked her what the devil she meant allowing his wife to be insulted by Harry Slesser. She, being Australian and not accustomed to mince her words, flew back in another rage, and after one or two searing minutes, they put the telephone receivers down. Well, by this time I was shaking with alarm and apprehension but it was too late, the ball had started rolling. The next day Orde went round to see the Fildes, he demanded an apology from both Denny and Marge. Marge refused to give it, and accused me of having made the whole thing up in order to excite Orde to a sexual frenzy. Well. Nothing could have been further from the truth. But, now comes this business about far-reaching consequences. A really horrid situation developed. Orde demanded the apology and said that Harry must write an apology to me, he went to his colonel in the end. Harry wrote me an abject letter of apology, I wish I'd kept it, it was very long, very nice as a matter of fact, I give full marks to poor Harry, and at last Orde hauled Denny in front of the colonel and made him do the apologizing. But Marge was going about and spreading her story, and it permeated the whole army.

When we left Bulford we went to Sheffield and Orde became a Territorial Adjutant there, and this was a happy time. We were removed from regimental soldiering, I think he enjoyed it very much, it took me a short while to adjust. I was greatly pressed upon by people, the whole place was a hive of personalities and social activities and so forth, but we went to a dear little village about eleven miles from Sheffield and there we had privacy and freedom to roam, yet a framework of duty which was very good for both of us. We never got up until midday in our delightful pub, out in the depths of the country at the gates of Chatsworth Park, then we went down to a very frugal luncheon. Orde went off at about 4 o'clock in the afternoon to Sheffield to meet his delightful manufacturers of knives and forks who were his territorial brigade, they were very nice people, I liked them. I was left behind, sitting in front of our little sitting room fire, reading books, until he came home at around one in the morning. He would then go down to the bar which never shut, have drinks with the locals, eat pickled walnuts then come up and he would tell me all the tales that they'd told him, and then of course, sleep until midday, and so on, this was really a very pleasant way of life.

I imagined Sheffield to be a grey place. In one's ignorance, one thought that people lived in a place like Sheffield because they had to, and they would be putting money aside in order, one day, to leave Sheffield and move to London or the home counties. Well, I was entirely mistaken, the people I met there regarded London as worse than Paris or Brussels, dirty and corrupt, remote from the center, and not entirely safe to live in, a hotbed of anarchists. Sheffield quickly grew on me, I liked the food they ate and I should have been perfectly content to acquire a small house in the better part of Sheffield, a house full of age and character, for very little money, and quietly lose myself running a second hand book shop. People would come from all over the world to 'Lorna's' to find only the rarest military books and documents, I should write monographs in my spare time, and send letters for publication to the Manchester Guardian.

It is extraordinary how well-suited Orde and I were in some matters. We both had periods of energetic employment, and periods of complete indolence, and we were seldom out of step one with the other. Likewise, while we both enjoyed the plain and simple, we also had a weakness for things of beauty.

Our second Christmas as man and wife we traveled by train from Sheffield to London in a third class compartment, both preferring the working class ambiance to the stuffy first class, it was no hardship whatever. On arrival in

London, we walked three or four miles through the center of town to save money on a taxi, and then as we were walking down Jermyn Street, Orde suddenly wasn't at my side, he had disappeared into a dark doorway, and following him I discovered that he had dived sideways into Sulka, on an impulse. Well, he paid two guineas for a pale blue silk shirt for himself, and I, not to be outdone, forked out three guineas for a pair of silk men's pajamas for myself. I don't think we ever stopped to discuss these choices we were making about when and when not to spend money. I cannot recall any discussion or argument about money in all the years we were married; why that was I cannot say. My people had money, Orde's people had none, and because mother had placed an embargo on us for having the temerity to get married, we lived on a soldier's pay, and the shirt alone represented one month's earnings. Of course, now that I'm older I take a different view, but in these first years together we acted as if we hadn't a care in the world. I wore my silk pyjamas through the war, during my confinement, and beyond; it was money well-spent.

From Sulka we continued our journey by train to Godalming, third class, and of course we were chattering and arguing with one another without pause throughout the journey. I can picture Orde in my mind's eye, having arrived at the Wingates, chaffing with Sybil, and so very pleased with his silk shirt, opening his jacket fractionally for his family to glimpse, and his sisters scornfully laughing at him for the waste and idiotic pretention. Orde had on a green tweed jacket, a pair of threadbare ginger-coloured plus-fours, and black town shoes, socks around his ankles, and a trilby. I see now that this was a ridiculous ensemble – I wonder now, as I write, if he didn't buy the shirt as a provocation, and a much appreciated one – but at the time I thought him so very attractive and elegant in himself that I didn't ever notice what he wore, until the day he donned the uniform of a British General. The Wingates – bless them – didn't care about how one dressed at all, 'You Are What You Wear' was not the family motto, this was not a fashionable household.

If Orde had come from a wealthy family with a generous father, I think he would have been exactly as I found him, not only because he would have carelessly run through his fortune by the time I came to him – money meant nothing to a true Wingate – but because money would only have got in the way of his vast ambition. With all the levity and pleasure-seeking and steeple-chasing and constant chaffing and his great human warmth, Orde had at his center a cold hard black verruca of ambition that made him into such an unpredictable, interesting and dangerous creature, and that is surely why I was so powerfully drawn to him, for without it he would have been like all the other men one met. Orde felt born to command, and he didn't just want to command an army, he wanted to take it out on great and impossible missions, to beat the longest odds, to astound humankind. Every schoolboy dreams of being Jack the giant-slayer, but Orde was long past his childhood and still he wanted to slay giants. He wanted to be better than any other commander, and different from every other commander. And because he was a Wingate, he wanted to be also the most righteous commander. The army he commanded would right wrongs, would fight for justice, would protect the weak, and Orde could settle for nothing less. So he put up with the lethargy of the British Army and its hidebound methods, biding his time, waiting for his opportunity.

All the things that Orde wanted for himself, I also wanted, and whatever ambition I had of my own I placed at his disposal. I was his sparking plug, a thing of no use whatever on its own, but when properly installed, will transform a sleeping engine into a thing that roars and drives forward. So Orde and I prowled around Salisbury Plain, and the back streets of Sheffield like two sleek, black, hungry cats, waiting for dinner to appear. This is a very large metaphor, we weren't grave-robbing or emulating Jack the Ripper or anything of that sort, but we were not your average British military couple. In fact, in Sheffield we were much in demand as dinner guests; I could be a show-off, and Orde ten times worse than I in this regard, if not twenty. When we became bored, as happened in certain company, we might decide to be loud-mouthed and contradictory, in order to stimulate and shake things up. If we were with people whom we liked, we might be soft and affectionate, or for the amusement of a certain host and hostess, I could become dusky and sultry, and he and I would execute a verbal tango. And if we found ourselves with people we needed to impress or persuade, and this did come to pass from time to time, we could be winning and coherent, for we worked well together, our timing was excellent, we knew when to let the other speak, we were a veritable double act. When we were alone, of course, we fought frequently – I don't mean argue – and sometimes I felt the need to throw things at him, or kick him very hard, because he himself was dominating, and often tedious with it. I think this was not only due to a certain cast in his nature, but very much due to the sort of upbringing he had amongst his six brothers and sisters, their conversational manners were abominable, and they gloried in it, it amused them, and one could see this in him. The use of rough language, discourteous, steamrollering tactics as no normal person would put up with. Sybil, for example would, without batting an eyelid, blurt out 'you are a fool and I shall tell you why'.

Orde could be a pompous ass, he would make a statement a propos nothing, 'a weapon should never be used for sport!' I couldn't let that pass. 'My father shoots and it gives him a good deal of pleasure,' I answered. Of course, Orde hadn't given it a moment's thought, he did it all the time.

'How can I know what I think until I have heard myself say it?' was something he said, and there was truth in it. He would routinely subject me to a dissertation or an exhortation which would last an hour, and if I tried to make a point, he'd raise his voice, and if I raised my hand and said, 'I want to speak', he would say, 'don't interrupt me', or 'what I have to say is worth far more than anything you could have to say'. This tended to get on one's nerves, and finally the only way to get the man to shut up was to pick up a plate and cast it at his head; I became a proficient lancer of the small object, and ceramic pottery was my choice because it shattered and sprayed so well when my aim was true, or at least on the wall behind him. He was a mental bully but not a physical bully, we wrestled from time to time but he was as gentle as a lamb in the clinch, and no harm would come to me. Of course no son of Ethel Wingate could ever raise his hand against a woman.

Orde was due for an overseas posting, and in September he received orders to report for duty as a staff officer in Palestine, Northern District, under the command of bloody nose Montgomery. Montgomery had no wife, poor fellow, and he didn't believe other people should have wives either, so he issued a veto, 'no wives'. Orde's ship sailed from Southampton somewhere in September 1936, there were 30,000 troops in Palestine at that time. He was assigned to General Dill as an intelligence officer with special knowledge of Arabic which he had acquired in the Sudan. While on board he gave a couple of lectures to the assembled staff of 300 on 'Arabs and how to treat them'. Orde had a high opinion of General Dill.

I went out clandestinely in October on a so-called Prince Line steamer, there was a cargo line which called all its boats by the name of a prince; Arabian Prince, Cypriot Prince, and so on. Delightful ships which carried twelve passengers, made no concession to them, and took about twelve days to get to Alexandria and, believe it or not, it cost me twelve pounds to get there from Manchester. We sailed down the Manchester ship canal and we made our way to our port of destination which was Alexandria, and when I arrived there Orde came on board, and I noticed that he looked terribly pale and frightfully wrought up. He was in such a state that we didn't kiss each other when we met, we shook hands. I said, 'what's wrong?' He said come and sit down and I'll tell you'

He knew that I was arriving on a certain day on a ship called the Arabian Prince, and he came down from Palestine to meet me, he went to the shipping office for Prince Line steamers and he said when and where does the Arabian Prince get in? They said she arrives tomorrow at such and such a berth at time so and so. So he arranged a taxi, and the next morning he went down to the Prince Line dock and the taxi driver gestured towards a ship that had the word Prince on it and the gangway down and said, 'there you are sir'. So he went up the gangway, went on board and found everything to be fairly quiet, he went down to the passenger accommodation and found a steward. 'Will you show me Mrs. Wingate's cabin', said he. 'She's not there' said the steward, 'she got off in Cyprus with Sir Colin McKenzie'. It's rather a dubious commentary on me, but Orde believed every word of it. He rushed off to the general post office in Alexandria, and sent a telegram to Mrs. Wingate, c/o Sir Colin McKenzie, Nicosia, Cyprus, 'UNLESS YOU IMMEDIATELY COME TO ALEXANDRIA, ALL IS OVER BETWEEN US', and one or two other pungent remarks. He then went to the Prince line office and said to them, 'what the devil do you mean not telling me that the Arabian Prince called at Cyprus?' 'But sir', said they, 'it didn't. The

Cypriot Prince called at Cyprus, the Arabian Prince has only just docked. He came down to the dock and there was another Prince Line steamer busily loading and unloading, the gangplank down, up he went, 'where is Mrs. Wingate's cabin?' 'there, sir', and there was I.

Chapter 5

Orde now took me off on a sort of honeymoon to the home of a man he knew called Jennings-Bramly who dwelt among the Arabs in a remarkable castle called Burg el Arab, quite literally in the middle of nowhere – well it was somewhere, somewhere in the western desert but it wasn't marked on any map. He had built it himself and it was his life's work. He had a love for the Arab, and he had come to it long before T.E. Lawrence, and although Jennings-Bramly was a devout Christian, as was his wife, and he had built a small chapel into the outer wall of his castle, he would not preach to the Muslims, and would have nothing to do with missionaries who did. He wanted only to introduce the Arab to modern advances in education and medicine and such like to improve their lot, I suppose.

This dear man, having achieved his life's ambition, was, I think, lonely and wanted us to remain with them, he liked

Orde very well and told us that he would build a house for us within the compound if we chose to remain. Now this was a most beautiful and romantic spot, something really out of Arabian Nights, and I would have thought that Orde might have been inclined to accept, he had been steadily grumbling about the army, why should he not resign his commission and join this older man in his very rewarding work? I thought it was a good idea, indeed, it felt like the realization of my wish at Lady Well as a child. I think I should have been satisfied if we had grown old in Burg el Arab, I should have bred horses. But Orde declined immediately, this was nothing more than a curiosity for him, a treat for me I suppose, for he had business to attend to in Palestine and he was agitated to return there, and so we set out for Alexandria. Something significant had happened to Orde since he'd arrived in Palestine, all he could tell me, cryptically, was 'I am going to show you something'. What could be more compelling than Burg el Arab?

We traveled from Alex to Port Said, and then by rail along the coast of the Mediterranean Sea, a dozen shades of blue on one side, and an endless golden desert on the other. We detrained in order to visit the brand new desert town of Tel Aviv which had been built entirely by Jews! I was most taken aback. I remember thinking to myself, 'aren't Jews the flashy types who hang around London's West End? What are they up to in Palestine? Is there any money to be made here?' But this town was pristine! I had never seen the like, I imagined that the train had left the Haifa Egypt railway track and, having gone off into a siding, was taking me through the Earls Court Ideal Home Exhibition. When we arrived at the terminus at Haifa, Orde took me to our new apartment. He had moved out of the Army hostel where wives and mistresses weren't allowed, and had rented a flat high above the port, with a little balcony overlooking the bay of Haifa, charming place, and this was to be our home for the next three months.

Haifa, also built by Jews, was no less beautiful and modern than Tel Aviv, except that it was perched on a steep hill commanding a view of a huge bay. He showed me round our lodgings, and from a window pointed out a neighbor who was hanging washing on a line – Jewish men did that sort of thing – and he told me that the man was an intelligence officer in the secret Jewish underground army, and that we were under observation! Orde called out to him, the man waved back and smiled, behind him the glittering bay with the ancient fortress town of Acre in the distance, how marvelous! I felt like a character in a John Buchan novel.

Presently Orde took me on a tour of the country in his badly-behaved Studebaker, the engine of which boiled over every thirty miles. We had a Bible and a loaded revolver on the bench seat between us. Life in Palestine was almost normal, very little in the way of fighting, in fact just as I arrived a large number of troops were being sent home, and those that remained tended to keep themselves to themselves. Orde was dressed in mufti, driving around in a private car, speaking Arabic with an English accent, he might have been an archaeologist or some such thing, so he deemed it safe to bare his wife into the Arab villages and into the countryside at large. We spent most nights in villages where we were received warmly by the Arab Mukhtar, and the occasional night in the Jewish farming settlements which were called 'kvutzot' where we were received with courtesy and curiosity, and at every stop Orde would open up his old Bible and find a reference to the place as if he was reading from an A-Z, he had a superb grasp of topography and the like, and always seemed to know exactly where we were.

As we drove through the wild countryside he would point to such and such a house in the distance, and tell me that an arms cache was known to be under the kitchen floor, or another house in which lived a useful informant, or a hillside where two wanted Arabs were killed by our troops six months ago, along with every particular of the encounter, he was very thorough. Although this was mid-winter there were many warm, sunny days, we bought things to eat in the villages and stopped for a picnic whenever we felt hungry. And of course Orde wasn't neglecting his own business, he had an exercise book in which he was busy making notes, and keeping nothing from me. Orde was at pains to show me what the Jews had achieved in Palestine, and it was quite monumental. I understood immediately that something profoundly important had happened to Orde, and that he had caught fire, he was burning with an enthusiasm and I was instantly and uncritically infected. This was the thing he had been looking for, this was his cause, his reason for being. Now, enthusiasms come and go, an enthusiasm can be a hobby or an interest, but this clearly was more than an enthusiasm, and more than just a passion, Orde had changed, he was no longer the same man, and soon I would no longer be the same woman, we were changed people.

Orde had discovered Zionism, a word I'd not heard before, it denoted bringing the Jews who were scattered all over the world back to the Promised Land, and this apparently was what the trouble in Palestine was all about; the Arabs were not at all keen. He had quite fallen under the spell of the thing, which as an intelligence officer in the British Army, he wasn't supposed to do. He had placed himself firmly in the camp of the Jews. I had never seen him in this state of animation and naturally he wanted to run it all by me, try out his theories on me. One of the reasons for this interesting and most enjoyable drive across Palestine was to demonstrate to me – and to himself - that the Jews had the right of it, that this was indeed their patrimony. All his years as a child his father had drilled him in

Old Testament wooden-bench Christianity till he knew it backwards (or take a beating), this was for him like passing through a landscape that he has seen clearly in a dream. The restoration of the children of Israel to the Land of Israel! I knew nothing about Jews, I had never met one as far as I knew, and I had never discussed the subject with Orde, one heard vaguely uncomplimentary things about them, and I knew that they were connected in some way to the Israelites of the Bible, and so I was completely unprepared for what followed.

My first encounter with a real Zionist took place on our return to Haifa, we were invited to dinner by the young man hanging his washing, whose name was Emmanuel Wilenski, a small, neat chap with excellent English, an engineer by profession. We ate our dinner, children were duly kissed and put to bed, out came the scotch, I don't think Orde had planned what he was going to say, but he was always a man who could think on his feet. He started off by divulging to our hosts details of his work, his precise mission in the north, the name and rank of his commanders and colleagues, and then reeled off the exact same details as they pertained to Emmanuel, and I noted that he had taken the trouble to learn the pronunciation of the Hebrew names, I am sure our host made note also. There was a long silence, the polite smiles on the faces of our host and hostess had gone out of the window and were probably half-way to Cyprus, and Emmanuel coldly asked Orde what it was that he wanted. He said, 'I would like the privilege of helping the Jews achieve an independent state in Palestine'. Emmanuel burst out laughing, I was quite taken aback myself, I looked at Orde out of the corner of my eye and his expression was unmoved. Emmanuel was still amused. 'What makes you think that the British will grant us such a thing?' asked Emmanuel. Orde answered, 'The British government will never grant you a state, there is no chance of it, and that is why you will need my help.' Emmanuel didn't say a word, he was dumbfounded and embarrassed at the same time, he had no idea what to make of this, and I was rather taken aback, I would say.

This was our Rubicon, and it had all happened so quickly. At first the Jews wanted nothing to do with him, they thought he was mad, or a spy, which was understandable. At the same time he was making himself thoroughly unpopular at GHQ on account of his outspoken pro-Jew views, but he didn't seem in the least unhappy with his predicament, quite the contrary. Orde conquered Emmanuel's heart and mind, and in due course we started to see a great deal of the Wilenskis and many of his associates. On my mantelpiece downstairs is a card from Emmanuel; one arrives by post every year from Haifa on my birthday with a warm, dear message.

David Hacohen was the first Jew to properly understand and recognize Orde. He met him just once, and announced (with wonder) to his compatriots that this British officer was truly 'one of us'. Hacohen was rich and extremely able, but for some reason considered young and foolish by the Zionist inner circle, and at first his assertion was dismissed with mockery. Nevertheless, one by one the Jews discovered this miraculous man, and indeed, by the time Orde was done in Palestine, there was not a single Jew who harbored doubts or reservations about his loyalty in any manner or form; consider that.

According to David, it was the manner in which Orde chastised his own people that was so utterly remarkable. Admiration for Great Britain in the inter-war years was so great that it tended to paralyze. One was completely convinced of Britain's natural superiority; the casual saunter of the British officer, the authority of the BBC, the integrity of the British courts, the sheer size of the Empire; its manpower and its wealth! Both Jew and Arab sought to dress like the British, talk like the British, walk like the British, shave like the British (Hitler's moustache was an attempt to look British and therefore statesmanlike; the entire world was at it!). Then along comes Orde Wingate in 1937, and tells the Jews that the leadership of Britain has lost its way, its courage fled, a shell of its former self, and not in any way a proper role model for young Jewish men and women. The Jews must find inspiration in their own glorious past (from the very book that had once been the spiritual foundation of British power). It was as if Orde had come down from the mountain, the effect of this knowledge on certain Jews was shattering, and of enduring importance. He wasn't only preparing the Jews psychologically for their struggle with Great Britain at this difficult and terrifying time, he sought to imbue them with a belief in themselves.

The Jews were in deadly earnest about returning to Zion but their conception was, I noticed, quite different to Orde's, and it was extremely complicated. The Agency treated the thing as a large-scale transmigration, an enterprise with shareholders that they were building from the ground up, with books and ledgers for so many dunams of land, so many boatloads of refugees, so many tons of steel, with strict control over the money that paid for it all, in short, it was dry; dry as a bone. And the religious Jews of Palestine who lived in quarters, like Jews of old in ghettos, had been warned by the Rabbis not to touch Zionism with a barge-pole, the Messiah had to come before they could restore Israel, so they piously read the portion from Genesis or Leviticus as if it concerned Poland or Argentina, and not the ground under their feet. And the young Jews were filled with Marxist indignation, and the women were struggling for emancipation, the land was buzzing with isms, but for Orde it was like being at the opera, a thing full of colour and sound. When he looked at a young Jewish farmer, he saw before him a Maccabi, he'd have him blowing a ram's horn for good measure, and standing with me at Ein Harod, he fancied he could hear the prophet Samuel whispering in Saul's ear. And when he sat opposite Dr. Weizmann, he felt himself in the presence of King Solomon. He described Zionism to me in the following manner:

> 'If the Greeks today were to throw out the orthodox church, restore their ancient temples and rites, teach themselves the language of ancient Greece, establish Socratic schools, it still would not match the improbable miracle of the rebirth of ancient Judah, for Greece did not disappear from the map of the world two thousand years ago, her temples were not pulverized, the language did not cease. Do you think that Greeks in exile would have stayed true to their ancient Gods, suffered persecution through the ages for doing so, and prayed to them every year for a return to Hellas?' .

And it was true. I stepped out of our apartment in Haifa and I heard a dead language, more ancient than Latin, being spoken at breakneck speed by little children running between motor cars and shinning up telephone poles. And so I too became a Zionist and a very happy one.

Orde's thoughts about Palestine were crystallizing rapidly, and around January of 1937 he sat down at his desk – we were by now in Jerusalem – and wrote a letter to cousin Rex in Cairo. Rex (or Reginald) Wingate was a well-known Arabist to whom Orde regularly turned for help and advice, and I think Rex was very fond of his sprat of a relative. A Royal Commission headed by Lord Peel, which was in Palestine gathering information, had not come to Orde for his advice (understandably), so he offered it instead to cousin Rex. He proposed a complete about-turn for Britain's imperial policy in the Near East, it was a rollicking report, it took a day for him to compose and for me to type up, it was like a torrent for its force and incisiveness, a massacre of all the stale, stultifying, preconceived ideas that obtained in Jerusalem at that time.

Orde always wrote as he spoke, with absolute directness and without frills, qualifications or riders, he would have made a very bad lawyer. He was strictly a subject-verb-object sort of man, he had no use for metaphors or similes, they just got in his way. Let me give you a taste of his style. '…the officials here are third rate…the High commissioner is incompetent…the Arabs are unfit to govern their own affairs, so hand over Palestine to the Jews…plant here in Palestine and Transjordan a loyal, rich and intelligent nation with which we can make an everlasting treaty, and which will hold for us the key to world dominion without expense or effort on our part…I tell you that the Jews will provide a soldiery better than ours, we have only to train it. They will equip it…the potential military strength of the Jews is the equivalent of two British Army Corps.' And then he ended the letter, '…for pity's sake let us do something just and honourable before [the war] comes. Let us redeem our promises to Jewry and shame the devil of Nazism, Fascism and our own prejudices.' I think there was a beginning of a metaphor in the last sentence.

I took it to the post office, and after about a week we got a fairly perfunctory reply – evidently Rex didn't agree with it – but with his note was a letter of introduction from Rex to his old friend Arthur Wauchope, and this was a great prize for us. A black watchman of old, known also as Butcher Wauchope because he slaughtered a number of Turks during the First World War, somewhere up North; the story was that he was so shocked by his own barbarity that he was never able to take a strong line with anybody again. He was a very nice man for all that, little and shy, you know, as soldiers so often are when they retire. He was now the High Commissioner in

Palestine and he invited us round to dinner at government house on the eve of the great hunt ball – a jackal hunt ball. Government house was a delightful place, and she was all dolled up for a great night out. We found that there were a lot of people there for the dinner party, and we were introduced to a splendid looking man, tall, about six foot two, kingly bearing, small beard, dark eyes, aged I suppose about 60 or more, a wonderful deep plum pudding voice, a Russian voice, and his delightful wife. This was Dr. Chaim Weizmann, and he and Orde immediately took to each other. His wife was sweet and delightful to me, not only then but for the rest of our association together which covered many years. We had a short talk before dinner, then we had to sit down to the meal, and then at about nine o'clock the ball began. All the hundreds of people who hadn't been at the dinner party came flocking in, you know, the entire official world of Palestine.

At this point Orde and Weizmann vanished, they went to some private corner and they talked, I was left behind somehow, and of course Orde and I had already made it plain that we were on the side of the Jews and not of the Arabs. And I think it was sufficient commentary on the official attitude that, although I was a pretty girl of 19, for three and a half hours not only did nobody ask me to dance with them but nobody spoke to me. It was a grueling experience, I think that even now I would be gruelled by it, it was very painful at the time. At about half past twelve the Inspector General of Police, who was an old friend of my parents – he used to come to stay at Tilliefoure and pat me on the head when I was one and a half – he was the master of the jackal hounds and was organizing the ball, he came up to me kindly and asked me to dance with him, but nobody else did. But meanwhile, much more important than that, Orde was talking to Weizmann. When he finally collected me at about one in the morning and we went home, he told me something of his talk and how immensely impressed he had been by this great man.

We were soon invited by the Weizmanns to their beautiful house in Rehovot among the orange groves south of Tel Aviv, and we went to stay with them there many times, a glorious place indeed. There was no one whose company I enjoyed more than theirs and I think the feeling was mutual. Of course Chaim loved the English and he was quite used to being loved and admired by them in return. And what a relaxation we must have been to him in the midst of his great exertions and struggles with his own people! We presented well, exuded contentment, and we had fallen passionately in love with the thing closest to his dear heart. Look, if it had been Orde alone, Chaim might have been forgiven for dismissing him as a crank, but there were two of us; Vera understood me as a woman, and could see that I had a mind entirely of my own; as much as I cared for Orde I wasn't in thrall to him. The two of us were greater than the sum of our parts. So this is how it was with us; from the first day, I felt more at home with them in Rehovot than I had felt anywhere else in my life, they took us in, there were moments I could imagine that I was talking to my own parents, and they treated us both as their children. I shall call it an embrace.

Historians seek to understand why H.M.G. in 1917 issued the Balfour Declaration, and a number of perfectly valid reasons are given, I shall not repeat them. To this list of reasons I would add the Weizmann embrace. I believe that Arthur Balfour, not a known philo-Semite, fell under Chaim Weizmann's spell. I have no idea if Mrs. Balfour met Vera Weizmann, but my guess is that she did, and that both Mr. and Mrs. Balfour experienced what Orde and I experienced. Chaim and Vera exuded power and gentleness in a unique way. Mahatma Gandhi had it also, but with this difference: Gandhi represented a vast and proud nation, an entire sub-continent, he could call on hundreds of millions of followers, and Chaim represented a scattered, despised remnant with not an inch of land to call their own, let alone a sub-continent. Another difference between Weizmann and Gandhi was that Weizmann was a very attractive man, even in his sixties. He was tall, and well-built, his eyes were dark and beautiful and wise, and his voice sounded like it came out of a deep well or cave. Mother had been clamoring to be introduced to the great man, and finally one day I brought her to meet him, and it was the strangest thing and at the same time the thing most normal; he liked her very much, and was drawn to her. Mother was still an attractive woman with an excellent bust, far better than my own, and entirely available; and there it was, for a season at least.

I have referred to the bias on the part of the Mandatory in favour of the Arab. Remember, Palestine was governed from Cairo and London, each center had its own priorities and idiosyncrasies. There were four broad reasons for this bias, and they need to be adumbrated in order for Orde's experiences in Palestine to make any sense.

The first was that even if one doesn't like the Mohammedans, there are a devil of a lot of them and they have the oil; this was more London than Cairo, it's the kind of thing that marvelous fellow Henry Kissinger would have understood so well. The second reason is what was known as the Lawrence factor. The impact of the writings of T.E. Lawrence can not be exaggerated, he posited a spiritual – not to say erotic - bond between the noble Arab and the fearless Englishman; so if you want to be a fearless Englishman, go and find yourself a Bedouin, QED; is this not what brought a good many Englishmen of that generation to service in the Near East? The third reason was the terrifying determination of Jews, there was nothing those people couldn't do. It brought to mind the relationship between a Polish lord and his Jewish administrator, the problem was that we had our own administrators brought in for the job and the Jew was showing them up badly. And finally they didn't like Jews, and why should they? Jews don't drink, they don't play rugby or cricket, they don't laugh at the things we laugh at, and they are extremely stand-offish; they don't invite one into their homes. And they are so, so intense all the time, in short, they are not amusing to be with. What a coincidence! Orde could be most un-amusing, he also didn't play ball games, he was frighteningly intense, he was determined, he considered Lawrence to be an absolute charlatan, and when he placed God and His covenant with the Jews on the scales against the Mohammedan masses and their oil, he made up his mind to be a Zionist.

For my part I was in love with a Zionist, and that was more than enough to secure my allegiance to the Jewish cause. I acknowledge now, and with some remorse, that I became something of a fanatic. I always try to be honest about myself and about my motives. There was another reason why perhaps I espoused the Jewish cause in opposition to British 'interests'. I am a Scot, and not just a Scot. My great-grandmother was a MacDonald of Glenco, directly descended from McGian's eldest son John, from whom I get my black looks. McGian was the chief who, along with 40 unarmed clan members, were butchered by troops in the service of King William III of England. We Scots have long memories.

Towards the end of our first year in Palestine, the Arabs stepped up their attacks, there wasn't a day I didn't hear gunfire somewhere in Jerusalem. Our soldiery went about in convoys with machine guns pointing in every direction, while little Jewish boys and girls in blue knickers on bikes used to scoot about all alone amongst the brigands and the terrorists. Early one morning at about 8 o'clock I took a taxi from our flat to go and see my doctor, she lived in the

Jewish quarter. Now Jerusalem in those days was separated, all the quarters were separated by delightful wild areas. We for instance lived in the Catholic Arab quarter and we were surrounded by scrubby olive groves, neglected, full of outcrops of grey stone, green grass and full of wild flowers in spring. Lovely, a place to roam, wander in. The German quarter which had been built up by the Christian Germans who'd come under a religious impulse to settle in Jerusalem, a very pleasant place with white houses and red pan tiles and pleasant gardens – delightful – this again was ringed around by countryside. The modern Jewish quarter, nice enough in its way, low-rise flats, well-constructed, unimaginative perhaps but all very tidy and pleasant, was separated from the main part of the city by green grass and flowers and wild trees.

A couple of days before I set out to see my doctor, a poor old newspaper seller, a Jew of advancing years had been slaughtered by some Arab gunman at the top of our street. On this particular morning I was passing through one of these green belts, and there, lying on a grassy knoll by the side of the road, was a body so I told my taxi to stop, and I got out. The murdered man was young, he was an Arab, he was no more I'd say than 25, he was a peasant, he'd obviously just come into the town, he was wearing the long shirt that comes almost down to the ankles, grey striped garment, and he was wearing the agal and keffiah, the black camel hair circlet and the white headpiece, he was lying on his back, he was quite dead, only just been killed, ten minutes before, I didn't hear the shot though again, no sign of blood, no wound at all and he looked so peaceful. You know one of the extraordinary things about the few bodies I have encountered is that those who died violent deaths look so peaceful. I suppose it's because they don't know what's coming to them, provided it's quick, it's merciful. Now I was seized by an overpowering sense of anger, this lad had been killed by a couple of Jewish boys as a reprisal for the murder of the old newspaper seller but when I saw him lying there, the first dead man I'd ever seen, my feeling was he was poor, a simple lad, he had nothing, he owned nothing in life except his own vitality, his life, his existence and it had been taken from him, uselessly. It taught me a great lesson, and all in the space of ten seconds. When you hold a gun, when your finger is on the trigger, you will think very carefully because what you are taking away from the creature at the other end is all that he truly possesses. Anyhow that was my first dead man.

We had been in Palestine for six months and now had a small circle of not only Jewish friends but also Arab, and even a few from British officialdom who seldom arrived during daylight hours. Our flat became a salon for every kind of agitator and thinker, we seemed to attract interesting and colourful people. Preparations were underway at the Agency for the visit to Palestine of an important American called Arthur Sulzberger. America was at this time something of a backwater in international affairs, Britain still ruled the waves, but one could see that America might one day become the next thing, and so there was a lot of interest in this man's visit, everyone wanted to put their best foot forward. Sulzberger owned the New York Times, he was a sort of Lord Northcliff, and he was a Jew, evidently a Jew could own a newspaper in America. One would have thought that he would throw the weight of his newspaper behind the Zionists, what could be more natural? The work the Zionists were doing in Palestine was surely for the good of Jews everywhere, and what is the point of owning a newspaper if not to give public currency to your own point of view, the British press barons were famous for it.

A reception was being held for the great man in Jerusalem at the new university, and Chaim had written to us, enclosing two tickets to this reception, he would be abroad but he thought we would be interested. Interested be damned! Chaim wanted Orde to go up to this man and speak plainly to him, because we were now a part of the political game in Jerusalem. Everyone knew where we stood, on the entrance door to our house was a ceramic plaque saying in Hebrew '*Po Beito shel Captain Wingate*', which means 'this is the house of Captain Wingate', but there was no English translation on the plaque. I had ordered it from a small local factory, it was hand-painted on a Prussian blue background with the most exquisite floral display around the edge, and this left the visitor to our flat in no doubt as to where our sympathies lay. Orde decided not to go, as he was working flat-out producing a report for his superiors on Arab smuggling routes, and was out of Jerusalem for most of the time. 'Would you give me permission to go in your place?' I asked. He replied, 'yes, that would be a good idea.'

Since my arrival in Palestine, I had read every book I could lay my hands on concerning Zionism, and everything in the way of novels and history that had been written by Jews in Palestine. I now took myself to the American Colony Hotel, about a quarter of an hour's drive from Hallak House which was the name of the house in which we lived in Talbieh, and asked them if I might sit in the lounge and read Mr. Sulzberger's newspaper which arrived at the hotel about two weeks late, and there was a good pile of them to be had. This was a very thick newspaper, one needed a briefcase to carry the thing; who had time to read it, and why are things in America so big? Is it because the country is large, and everything has to be done to scale? I arrived in time for breakfast at the hotel, and I took lunch and dinner there also, and once I had done what I came to do, I returned home directly to share my discoveries with Orde. Was Arthur Sulzberger really a Jew? His newspaper had little enthusiasm for Zionism, it seemed so very strange, did he in fact own the New York Times, or was there someone above him?

I knew quite enough about Mr. Sulzberger's newspaper, and I had made inquiries about the man himself, and I considered myself fully primed for what I intended to do. Come the day of the reception, I arrived at the university campus which was built on a dusty, golden hill commanding a view of the Judean desert on one side, and Jerusalem on the other, and I was shown into the hall where people milled. I took up a position in the center of the room and stood there with a generally interested and intelligent expression on my face, a glass in my hand, waiting until some kind soul would come and talk to me, because I had just had my hair cut short in the style of the Jewish girls and I wondered if anyone who actually knew me would recognize me. A very presentable young man approached me with a wolfish grin on his face, as if we were at a dancehall and not at a diplomatic function, and before he could get into his stride I said to him, 'I am as blind as a bat, I wonder if you might point me in the direction of Vera Weizmann.' The young man took hold of my hand directly, and led me across the room, marching up to Mrs. W. who was in the middle of a group of American ladies, and announced, 'Vera, I found this creature in the woods, she had a tag around her neck and your name was on it.' Everyone found this fairly amusing.

Vera embraced me warmly and introduced me to the other women, one of whom happened to be the wife of the guest of honour, 'this is the wife of the young captain I was telling you about', she said, and this fine woman whose name I forget, and I, quickly latched on to one another, which had fully been Vera's intention, and I wasted no time in asking her why her husband's newspaper was not enthusiastic about Zionism. Well, she made some anodyne remark about how the newspaper tried to present different points of view, and then, because I had done my homework, I was able to demonstrate how this was not at all the case, and I quoted a succession of hostile reports and the names of the responsible correspondents, whereupon this excellent lady exclaimed, 'Oh my, is this a complaint from a subscriber? I will take you straight to the man in charge.' By now I was on to my fourth glass of Champagne, and although, pound for pound, I could carry my alcohol as well as any man, I now approached the owner of the New York Times, a little the worse for wear. I was introduced to him as a friend of Vera Weizmann, so he turned round to face me, and looked me up and down, and there was an expression on his face which said, 'How can I help you, little girl?'

I was certainly the youngest person present in the room, not including Vera's nephew who might have been younger than I, and at twenty one years old I looked about sixteen. He had been in conversation with the head of the university, an American gentleman whom Sulzberger addressed as rabbi, and then one of those curious things happened. It's happened to me two or three times in my life, not very often, you get some access of power, you have a feeling that now is the time to go into action and if you do, you will be wholly successful, nothing to worry about, it's a lovely feeling, I wish it were not so rare. I looked Mr. Sulzberger straight in the eye and said, 'why is your newspaper against Zionism?', and I may have raised my voice slightly, because there was a palpable turning of heads. This was surely the question on everyone's lips, and the question that no one wanted – dared is not too strong a word – to put to him. He cast his wife a mildly reproachful glance, and said to me, 'OK young lady, you have two minutes, make the case for Zionism.' I was entirely unprepared for a question as direct as my own, so I had to rack my brains, and then I thought, 'yes!', and said to him, ' I can do it in less than one minute', and repeated what Orde had told me when we were fresh in Palestine, the thing about the modern Greeks returning to their ancient religion (page 84), which had made such a very strong impression on me at the time.

Sulzberger stared at me, I don't know if I can properly say that he was lost for words, but he didn't say anything, the rabbi on the other hand cleared his throat and said to Sulzberger, who was obviously an old crony of some kind, 'may I, Arthur?', and receiving a nod, turned to me and said,

"Mrs. Wingate (he knew my name and I knew his. Jerusalem was but a hillside village), Mr. Sulzberger is not anti-Zionist, and neither am I. Supposing the Greeks, upon returning to Hellas discover that it has been settled by another race which is peacefully farming the land and tending their sheep, are the Greeks to displace this race in order to realize their 'Hellenism', or live peacefully side by side?' I answered, "Do the Arabs wish to live with the Jews side by side? I think the Arabs do not want the Jews here at all (I actually said 'us' instead of 'the Jews'). It is unfortunate, is it not, Dr Magnes?". The discussion was brief, there was a small crowd gathered about, and Mr. Sulzberger remained silent. I did not like Dr. Magnes, he was a sanctimonious bore and if he had no stomach for the settling of Eretz Israel, he should have returned to America from whence he came, and this was not only my opinion.

If Vera had not interposed herself in timely manner, I might have become quite acerbic. Snubbing Magnes, I held out my hand to Mr. Sulzberger, gave him my most winning smile, and withdrew, my other arm firmly locked in Vera's elbow. The young man found me again, plied me with more Champagne, and finally put me in a taxi. Vera telephoned me the following morning to thank me for speaking so well, and told me that I should make a career of it. However my performance had been duly noted, and now all Jerusalem officialdom knew beyond doubt that Mrs. Wingate was a Zionist fanatic.

A Green Rose

The New York Times didn't alter its editorial policy one iota as far as I could tell, and there was no mention in subsequent editions of a 'brilliant and attractive young advocate for Zionism who sprang from a Jerusalem glade'. I'm sure Sulzberger thought his newspaper a very important affair, and essential to the well-being of his fellow New Yorkers, and that his fellow New Yorkers thought well of him for providing them with his broadsheet, indeed he was an important man, hence the elaborate party that had been thrown in his honour. Did Mr. Sulzberger imagine that if the New York Times came out in support of Zionism, Father Coughlin would take his newspaper away from him, and that he and his wife and his children would be put out on the street, and be spat at by little urchins? I came away from this experience with a deeper and more somber appreciation of the Jews. Orde was constantly saying, 'they are not a people'.

For the first 18 months of his time in Palestine he traveled the country and beyond, and together with Anthony Simonds, with whom he shared an office, established a network of informants in the Jewish and Arab villages of the north. He gave Jerusalem HQ no cause for complaint on this score, I would say that he was doing a very good job. Meanwhile the Arab gangs had stepped up their attacks, and the death toll on both sides was rising steadily, and it was becoming apparent that the army's response was inadequate. Bernard Montgomery, for example, sent armoured formations chasing back and forth along the northern border but could not get to grips with the enemy. Orde sat down and wrote an excellent report proposing a new approach to the problem, and in it one can find the embryo of his revolutionary theory of warfare that resulted in LRPG five or six years down the line. The Arab was evolving his own method of fighting the British, and the British had to respond, they couldn't just go on doing things by the book, fresh ideas were needed. This was an insurgency, and it called for counter-insurgency.

Orde was not at this time a combat officer, he essentially had a desk job, but he could not sit still. If, at this point, Orde had approached his superiors for permission to lead a formation of British soldiers to take on the gangs, he would have received them in less than two days, no questions asked. There were thousands of perfectly good ones lying around in barracks, drilling in courtyards, and doing guard duty up and down the country who would have been delighted to go into action, and everybody would have patted him on the back for it. What prevented him from doing this? Why did he insist on using Jewish soldiers? Not only were the Jews not lobbying Wingate to employ their young men, they were against it, and when, finally and against all Mandatory logic, Orde obtained permission to raise a Jewish force, he encountered stiff resistance from the Haganah chieftains. They were willing to allow their Jewish boys to fight under British command on purely defensive operations, but didn't want to provoke the Arabs with operations of the type Orde had in mind. The Jews didn't want it, they couldn't begin to visualize such an undertaking, and the Mandatory of course wanted the Jews to sit quietly and behave themselves. Why did Orde insist on taking this hard and dangerous road when an easy one was open to him?

Having set himself the task of helping the Jews to achieve a nation in Palestine, and having observed that the Jews were not a unified people but a 'rag tag of interesting and contradictory notions', he concluded that the Jews must go to war. Nations are forged in war, and war was coming to Palestine whether the Jews wanted it or no, so let it at least find them prepared when it arrived. He wasn't interested in dazzling his colleagues in Jerusalem with brilliant actions against the gangs, of which he knew himself capable. He was interested in rousing the Jews from their slumber, and training them in the art of modern warfare; preparing them, moreover, not only to take on the Arab armies which would soon appear over the horizon, but to defend themselves against British armed forces, if and when such an outcome became necessary. He had thought about these things thoroughly, and had done so alone; he didn't represent a school of thought, there was no one on the Jewish side who thought as he did, and of course none on the British. From his earliest days in Palestine, in 1937 until his death in 1944, Orde had but one driving ambition that eclipsed all other desires and interests; to lead a Jewish army in the field preferably, but not necessarily, in the service of the British Empire. Throughout those years, as his own fortunes waxed and waned, he never wavered for one moment from this single objective. You see what a lone furrow this man ploughed.

Orde had produced a report, as I said, in which he proposed a formation of Jewish soldiery with a stiffening of experienced British NCOs, to defeat the Arab gangs which were becoming bolder and more disruptive with every month. Arming Jews was anathema to the Mandatory, and his report was not being taken seriously. Then the Arabs changed their tactics, and began to target the Kirkuk-Haifa oil pipeline where it passed through Palestine. They started dynamiting it, resulting in stoppages whose economic effect was felt both in Cairo and London. As in all military undertakings, one never knows where a thing will lead or how it will end. An urgent and unequivocal message came directly from Whitehall, 'stop the attacks on the pipeline, *by all available means*'. Now the Arabs were not fools, they had expected London to react sharply, and were prepared to engage any British formation, employing their guerrilla tactics as they had been doing successfully for a number of months. They calculated that the cost to the British of defending this long and vulnerable oil pipeline would go some way to convincing Whitehall to bend to Arab demands, and this was what it was all about. The gangs acted hand in glove with the political echelon, the Higher Arab Monitoring Committee, which was trying to convince the British to stop Jewish immigration into Palestine. It is not unreasonable to suppose that British officials were quietly advising and helping the Arabs in coordinating this effort, as they too wanted to see an end to the flow of Jewish refugees into Palestine; Jerusalem was a hotbed of intrigue in those days, Orde was not the only one playing a double game.

The Arabs and their British helpers had reckoned without Wingate. Orde saw the pipeline attacks as a unique opportunity, and he seized upon it. He adjusted the thrust of his report into a plan to protect the pipeline, but with such speed! He wasted not a minute before he was on top of General Wavell who had personally received the Whitehall directive, and placed the solution in front of him; 'I shall stop the attacks on the pipeline, and at little cost to the Mandatory', and Wavell, quite overwhelmed by Orde's initiative and self-confidence – none of Wavell's other subordinates were badgering him with ideas to stop the sabotage, they were scratching their heads – said 'go ahead, but quickly'. Within four weeks of that meeting, Orde was leading the first Jewish formation out against the enemy. He fashioned his formations which he named 'Special Night Squads', entirely on his own, there was no textbook for what he was about to do, no mentor to whom he could turn for advice. Until the eleventh hour he was arguing and cajoling the Jewish leadership, and his own superiors, neither were keen on his plan, obstacles were thrown in his way, no one believed in him apart, for some reason, dear old Archibald Wavell. And Orde knew that he hadn't a moment to lose, it was surely a matter of time before there would be a change of heart in Whitehall, Wavell replaced (it happened almost immediately), a withdrawal by the enemy, or any one of a hundred possibilities that would result in a cancellation.

He dressed, armed and trained Jewish boys who had next to no formal military experience, and had them operational in the field within, as I said, four weeks; it was unheard-of. Orde felt that his destiny was upon him. The training was rigorous, the information-gathering comprehensive, the disinformation campaign elaborate, Orde punished carelessness among his Jewish soldiers with a beating, they were given to understand that they were no longer at school, and the Jews proved equal to the task. The little battles they fought were decisive even if they didn't always go according to plan. The SNS operated in the hours of darkness, they ambushed, crept up upon, killed and captured dozens of Arab fighters with no operational losses on their side. Orde exposed himself to danger in every action, was wounded, and was in fact awarded the DSO. The squads left their calling cards throughout the northern region of Palestine, 'the Jews have now taken the offensive' was their message.

The Arab fighters had been adept at avoiding the British formations, now they didn't know when and where the next blow from the Jews would fall; *al-yahud* had always been an Arab curse, now it was a cry of fear. The night no longer belonged to them, and with their defeats, they lost face with their own people, they walked with less swagger. Arabs – not only Arabs – had always considered the Jews to be an easy target, it had always been thus, objects to massacre, no better than women, living under the protection of someone else's Army. Now the Arab fighters started to fear Orde's Jewish auxiliary more than the British soldier, he was less predictable, deadlier, appeared to enjoy his work.

The Jews were acquiring a taste for real battle. When was the last time Jews had gone out in a military formation?

1800 years ago? Long-forgotten martial skills were returning, and with it, pride and confidence. Just as I know what it is to be a Jew, I also know what it is to be a man, and the longing to prove oneself in battle. You cannot take the warrior out of the man. The only people who ever attempted it were the Jews, and that is exactly the condition in which Orde found them when he arrived in Palestine in 1937, and which he made it his job to reverse. The young Jewish fighters earned the grudging respect of their British NCOs, they lost their fear of the night, they began to look as if they owned the Land of Israel. The Arab High Monitoring Committee then placed a price on Orde's head, but it was too late for them, because even with Orde dead, the genie was out of the bottle.

Did Orde shoot prisoners? Much was made of this in the press after his death. The answer is yes, he did on two occasions shoot a prisoner, and he also tortured a prisoner without killing him. He described to me the process, and the feeling that accompanied it, it was hateful to him. He never allowed a Jew to do it, he merely wished to teach the Jew to be a warrior, and to show him how it's done. And one of the lessons of war, the most important in my view, is put the fear of God into your enemy by any means available. It spares you trouble in the short term, and obviates the need to kill many of them in the long term. Orde was very particular about the proper treatment of civilians and prisoners, and wouldn't tolerate gratuitous violence or drunkenness, and none of his boys ever indulged in pillage and rape, there was never a suggestion that they did, although the same cannot be said about the other side. But sometimes in war, as every soldier in every nation knows, the shooting of one prisoner can result in the saving of dozens of lives on both sides. Intelligence is the key to warfare, the British know this better than any nation, and one will go to any length to acquire information and disseminate disinformation.

War is a method of selection, a trial of strength, and men are born to it. If you establish your ascendency rapidly, your enemy will put aside his enmity and go back to ploughing his field. It cuts both ways. If you are given a demonstration of the power and determination of your enemy, you may save yourself a lot of trouble, and stop fighting him, and get on with whatever it is you have to do in order to feed your family. General Sherman taught us that a war must be brutal, otherwise it will never come to term. If the stronger party holds back, the war drags on, inviting pestilence and famine and misery for the general population. History is littered with long wars that kill off entire populations of non-combatants; if there has to be a war, and there will always be wars whatever Orde's sisters want to believe, it is the work of the soldier to make those wars short.

I have dealt with Orde's 'brutality', now I shall address his 'quirks and oddities' of which far too much has been made. Lawrence and Tarzan were two British inventions which opened up unimagined possibilities to young Englishmen; to take one's leave of Clapham Junction, and disappear from civilization into the vastness of the distant jungle or desert, and then to return with honour and fame! Orde despised Lawrence not just for the multiple deceptions of his life, but for having anticipated his own deepest desire. I think it highly unlikely that Orde ever read Tarzan, he was nonetheless intimate with the both Tarzan and Lawrence myths. They were a part of his Englishness along with Hundred Acre Wood, Long John Silver and Barchester Cathedral, and I believe that I am right in saying that he was as touched by them as any other man of his generation. Both suggested a means of escape from the suffocating hierarchy of British society in general, the British Army in particular. Escape into the desert, escape into the jungle, both places rendered hospitable in the imagination. And of course they should dress-up for the part! A suede loincloth for the apeman, flowing silken robes for the duneman, the English do enjoy their pantomime. Orde's famous Wolseley helmet was out of fashion among young officers in the 1930's, it was a throwback to an earlier age but he didn't care. It was lightweight and beautifully made, and if you had a mass of men milling around, and a soldier or an officer wanted to know if the commander was in the vicinity, he had only to raise his eyes and look for the helmet. Orde wore it into every battle he ever fought for the benefit of his soldiers and the enemy alike.

Themes of rebellion and escape repeat themselves uniquely in British history; Clive of India, Wolfe of Quebec, Horatio Nelson, Lord Byron, Walter Raleigh, the list of men by whose acts of disobedience the nation was enriched and ennobled is a long one. Britain's love of eccentrics has its source in this calculation of profit, other nations lack the confidence to honour disobedience in this way, for disobedience is known to be contagious and can give rise to social upheaval, in France the Reign of Terror, the Civil War in America, let us not talk of Russia and Germany. I apologize for this pedagogic interlude in my story, but I'm coming to the point. Within the bounds of this rich tradition, Orde would occasionally interview colleagues while in the nude. Poor old Sykes couldn't get over it, he even had a picture in his book – well a sketch, actually – of Orde in his birthday suit. When the heat in Palestine was oppressive he would strip down in the privacy of his room, and if a male visitor knocked on his door, he did not scamper around to find his trousers, he told him to enter and waited for him to state his business. He did not have a beautiful body, or a large member with which to impress other men, and he certainly was not an exhibitionist; he was a lean man with rounded shoulders, nothing at all to write home about I can assure you. A man not afraid to be seen naked is a man with confidence, personal courage.

A Green Rose

When Orde was at Woolwich, studying to be a soldier, he couldn't have been more than twenty, he was subjected to a ritual of a kind known primarily to institutions of learning in the English-speaking world. In Woolwich it consisted of making a fellow run naked between two lines of fellow-cadets and be whipped as he ran, and then be thrown into the lake at the end of the run. It was meted out to the new intake of cadets, a rite of passage, accompanied by much mirth and cheering, and the 'runner' invariably took his punishment in good part; he was made to run on that particular night, and he would make others run on other nights. Well, Orde didn't care for this game – he played no sports whatever apart from riding – and he wouldn't go along for these 'runs', and refused to be run himself. He was not a popular cadet, and his refusal to be run rankled with the others, so one night a group of seniors dragged him from his bed and carried him to the place where the running took place. One imagines the atmosphere might have been rather tense, because these boys – well they were men – were intent on teaching Orde a lesson, they didn't like him. He was white with fury, but facing a mob. He removed his pajamas, and stepped forward to the starting line naked, as required. The thing was to run the line of cadets as fast as possible to outrun the speed of the whipping, as it were. Well, Orde walked extremely slowly, robbing the affair of its tempo and entertainment. He stared at each cadet as he passed, and after the first quite severe whippings, the boys lost their enthusiasm, there wasn't a lot of cheering, and the assault petered out. When Orde got to the lake, since no one made a move to throw him in, he dived in neatly, swam back to shore and returned to his bed, naked and wet. Orde never mentioned this story to me, it came from Derek and a few other soldiers I ran across over the years who were present; Orde's comportment had made an indelible impression. He challenged his tormentors with his nakedness.

On another subject, he believed in the medicinal properties of raw onions; the fitness of his men was of paramount importance to him, and if chewing those things in public helped to drive the point home, then all well and good. The alarm clock strapped on his wrist? Punctuality with a theatrical flourish! Orde was a great teacher, his training methods were second to none, and in this manner he taught his men the value of personal comfort, health, and punctuality. It wouldn't have gone down well in the American army or in the German army, but Orde's British and Jewish soldiers lapped it up. Possessing a fearless, eccentric commander in a dirty uniform (when he wasn't stark naked), insignia of rank hanging by a thread or just plain torn-off, topped by the old Wolsey helmet, made them feel special, and when one feels special, one feels safe.

The battles he fought have been properly described by Sykes and many others, and I have nothing to add on the subject. They were small chaotic affairs with young men on both sides undoubtedly wetting themselves, for many it was a baptism of fire. The only thing that mattered was that victory was to the Jews. I was absent during these momentous days, I was with mother in Aberdeen, on my back, recovering from an abortion, my second such mishap, and mother paid for my boat journey, unwilling to leave me to bleed to death in the heat and dust. I decided to terminate these pregnancies because I was entirely without the mothering instinct. I had of course asked Orde what he wished me to do and, knowing my state of mind he answered that I was very young, and that we would make a family only when I was good and ready. How many men of his generation would have been capable of such consideration? The fact is that other people's children left me cold, I preferred to read books. This is a terrible admission and when I think of all the women who are unable to have babies, and the sense of loss it engenders in them, I feel like the worst ingrate. Perhaps the answer was for me to make babies and give them to women who can't. It wasn't a matter of my being too young, or being unsettled, or us not having enough money. I wanted to be a soldier, I wanted to fight, or at least be close to the fighting. If I couldn't carry a sword, let me at least carry a shield but, please, not a baby. Throughout our time in Palestine I believe that I was jealous of the young, handsome boys who were gathered around my husband, adoringly; was I not his armour-bearer? Was my place not in my lord's tent, at his side? What, was I to knit? In fact I wanted to command those handsome boys myself. Women have led men in battle, have they not? Queen Boudicca led the Britons against the Roman invader – she had her daughters with her in her chariot, I shouldn't have done that. And of course, tragic Joan of Arc. I would not have flinched under fire, of that I am certain. But I had married a great soldier as Karum Bux said I would, and I would have to settle for that.

I was laid up in Aberdeen, and letters and telegrams started pouring in – I can't think what the postmaster imagined was going on – from all our dear friends in Palestine, with news of Orde's little victories. If I had depended on British newspapers I would have known nothing. What my friends didn't tell me, in order, I suppose, to spare my feelings, was that Orde had been shot up and hospitalized. The one aspect of the affair that pleased me the most was the fact that the Arabs had put a hefty price on Orde's head. What acclaim!

Chapter 6

I had just returned from Aberdeen, Orde was convalescing from the effects of one of his battles and had been ordered by the excellent Brigadier Evetts to go away for a few days. He was completely run-down when I caught up with him, in fact he looked like an ill man. Morale in the encampment was high, several of the young Jews were coming forward in a promising manner, they were out practically every night. Orde could be spared so he left them to get on with it, and we drove down to Rehovot.

This was a most important visit, and it took place on the day that Neville Chamberlain was in Munich with Herr Hitler, Vera and I were tuned in to the BBC, it affected all of us deeply; I thought the cheering crowds in London inappropriate and lacking in backbone. Orde and Chaim talked into the night, as they say, and the bits one heard were mostly Orde going on and on about a Jewish formation.

One must remember that there was not a true military mind among all the Jews of Palestine at that time, and why should there have been? There were a great number of very brilliant men and women – one likes to state the obvious – but none who had devoted their lives to the study of war. At the same time there were several very colourful and gallant commanders like Isaac Sade who could undoubtedly lead men in battle, but they were quite unschooled in modern warfare. Orde, fresh from action, plaudits coming in from every quarter, was the nearest thing the Jews had to a real military figure, and although he didn't come out and say it, this was certainly Chaim's view at the time. Orde firmly believed that diplomacy was not going to work with the British, and only an army would. Chaim didn't agree with this, Chaim was a man of peace, and he no doubt told himself that this young man was a warrior, and would naturally wish to use the instruments which he understood best. He instructed Orde in the ways of diplomacy, telling him what they were doing on that side, Orde gave Chaim his view of the military side, and the great man appeared to listen.

About a month later, a confidential message was delivered by the Agency from Dr. Weizmann in which Chaim wrote that he needed Orde's presence in London urgently, would he and I consider traveling to England by plane at the Agency's expense to perform an important service. This was an extraordinary request, all things considered, couched as it was in the most affectionate and flattering terms. It was a time of intense diplomatic activity, things were going badly for the Jews everywhere, and we didn't think twice, we packed and left. Orde was due for army leave, but he didn't have time to complete the necessary paperwork, imagining that his superiors would look the other way. It had been a while since he had seen his family, Mrs. Wingate was bursting with pride over Orde's DSO, and rightly so, therefore we did not leave Palestine with an altogether heavy heart. But as things turned out it would have been far better if we had not left at all.

The mood in London was one of despondency, and talk of war was on everyone's lips. If a Nazi were to have strolled through the West End, he should have been most gratified. There was a palpable anti-Jewish feeling in London society and in the newspapers, and it revolted me and terrified me. How did they find the time for it, I asked myself. Ben Gurion and Chaim, both in London for meetings with British decision-makers, were barely talking to one another, and no one senior in government would talk to either of them. Orde ran himself ragged for the two older men, we had them at all hours of the day and night in our flat in Welbeck Street, Orde purloined maps of Palestine from the Geographical Society, the living room became a map room, he arranged meetings for them with the high and the mighty, begging favours from friends, colleagues and family, because this was a most critical moment for the Jews. The Peel partition thing was now a dead letter, a new plan was in the pipeline which we knew was going to be much worse for the Jews, so we were trying to cobble together a map – essentially ceding still more ground to the insatiable Arabs – that would satisfy our masters in Whitehall. This was an undignified moment for Chaim, he was almost cap-in-hand and I couldn't bare to watch it. For a man who had been received with honour by Britain's greatest statesmen for over a generation, this was a painful reversal of fortune. Orde told him that he would get nothing from Whitehall by conducting himself as he had in the past; Whitehall had nothing to offer the Jews, they had opted for the Arabs, no hard feelings. He begged him to stand tall, behave like a monarch. 'You must walk into the office of Macdonald and Chamberlain, shouting, and bang the desk with your fist and threaten to resign! Refuse to be used in this way! Be indignant! Tell them 'there is nothing for me in London,

I shall return to my people in Palestine', and then march out'.

Ben Gurion was taking it very badly himself and, I think, behaving badly; arriving late for meetings, refusing to participate in discussions, I didn't take to him at all. One particular meeting which Orde had stretched himself very thin to arrange, was with Lord Lloyd. Here was a man who could make a difference. Lloyd agreed to see Ben Gurion, but asked for Orde to accompany him, he wanted to get a look at this Wingate fellow, so the two of them were ushered in. Ben Gurion spoke for five minutes, Lord Lloyd spoke for the next five minutes and then they walked out. Ben Gurion was beaming, he thought it had gone rather well, Orde told him it had not gone at all well. The sticking point, as ever, was over the having of Jewish soldiers under British overall command. At the flat we all played a game of coming up with different names for a Jewish formation that wouldn't alarm the British, I remember 'Empire Croquet Club'. Finally we had the Desert Defense Force, it had a good Lawrence feel to it, Desert Border Patrol was another, which also sounded more Arab than anything. The words to avoid here were Palestine and Jew.

Whitehall's aversion to Jews defending themselves at a time when Jews were being attacked and killed both in Europe and Palestine should really have tipped Chaim off as to how the land lay. The British were against having a Jewish formation because they understood that it might pose a threat to them in the future. It was as if they feared a future Jewish army more than they feared the existing Italian or German armies; not because it would be harder to subdue than a German army, but because the British would then be making common cause with Herr Hitler against the Jews, and a lot of people in Great Britain would not have stood for it. With the exception of the rump of the Tory party, but not all the Tory party, Parliament was strongly pro-Zionist. Chaim and Ben Gurion had many disagreements at that time, but one thing on which they were united was that they could not – dared not - alienate Great Britain. This now became the bone of contention between Orde on the one hand, and practically the entire Jewish leadership in Palestine on the other.

Our time was almost up. We spent our last evening in London with my papa and Orde's mother, he took us to eat at the Embassy Club, and I could not but painfully reflect how much the better woman Mrs. Wingate was compared to my own dear mother. My father's attitude to Orde had changed, I could tell, but he still didn't like him, and kept a distance. It was touching to see how hard Orde worked to make a favourable impression on his mother, I took advantage of the moment to get him on the dance floor for the first and last time in his life.

While still in London we had intimations of trouble awaiting Orde back in Palestine. On arriving there just before Christmas in 1938 he was peremptorily given to understand that he must remain in Jerusalem, and that he should report in to GHQ every day except on Sunday. His first day in, he got filthy looks from practically every officer in the building and their secretaries. He got a ticking-off from his commanding officer for having left without formal permission, for having overstayed his statutory leave, and for having met the Secretary of State for the Colonies, and discussing with him matters unbecoming his rank. General Haining was livid, not only for the above reasons, but because of Orde's insufferable high-handedness. Orde was entirely prepared, coming from London, for the next blow to his standing. The SNS was to be shut down and the Jewish soldiers, having turned in their uniforms and weapons, sent back to their settlements; this was not actually Haining's doing, the orders had come directly from London.

The Arabs could not have been expected to reciprocate by laying down their arms and going home; the violence continued unabated and had to be addressed. Orde's deadly little formation of 200 specially trained Jewish and British soldiers was replaced by 15,000 British troops shipped in for Montgomery to do the identical job Orde had been doing, in the way Montgomery knew best.

From the Arab perspective, Montgomery's elephantine exertions could be endured because on the 17th of May 1939 Whitehall, casting-off all pretence, formally revoked the Balfour Declaration. At this point in time Orde could have retired himself from political intrigue, it really would have been the intelligent thing to do. Reports of his work with the SNS were filtering down through the British Army, had been noted by Liddell Hart, he had supporters in the War Office, Dill, Ironside, Wavell etc. He was even known to Winston Churchill, and he had his DSO; they weren't handing those out in 1938. If he had put his feet up, and waited for his next posting like a good boy, he would have got his perfect report from Haining and he would have been commanding a division in one of the main theatres in 1941, if not before, and Montgomery might have been his second-in-command.

A report about the SNS had been written in his absence, which contained a careless remark about Jewish soldiers. It wasn't offensive but Orde decided to take umbrage. He wrote to Brigadier Evetts and demanded that the remark be struck from the report. There was no mechanism for doing so, the report had been written and signed off, it was a done thing, but Orde persisted. To my amazement, a few weeks later he received an apology from Montgomery! – a task that Monty could not have relished. From my vantage, I could only wonder at my husband's blithe disregard for the antagonism he was creating around him. I encouraged him in the way a small boy encourages a large boy to throw stones at a still larger boy, while standing behind him. But I knew also that there was method to Orde's madness. It wasn't that he couldn't charm and lie the way one does to get what one wants, he was capable of great charm, and was an excellent liar. Orde read people very well. His ability to know what moves people was surely the key to his genius as a commander. If you want to bring a man to your point of view, you can argue and wheedle and persuade, and at the end you may get him to waver. But if you show him that you hold to your view utterly, and will die for it, then he will follow you to the ends of the earth, the view be damned. Orde believed that Britain had a sacred duty to enable the Jews to return to their ancestral home, he held to it utterly. He had followers and he had enemies, there was no one in between.

As punishments go, the travel restriction was quite mild. He was in His Majesty's Armed Forces and not on the floor of the House of Commons, one cannot but sympathize with his superiors in this matter. I believe, moreover, that both superior officers, Haining and Richie, valued Orde, and were taking the line of a stern headmaster teaching a gifted but unruly schoolboy a lesson for the benefit of school discipline; they were not at that stage in any way considering expulsion. But they had, to all intents and purposes, already lost the boy. They could not fathom the level of indignation that Orde harbored, righteous indignation, at the attitude of H.M.G. towards the Jews of Palestine. He didn't care tuppence for the King's regulations, he was ready to hand in his papers.

Orde and Chaim were increasingly drawn into each other's orbit, it was as if Chaim was the only man he needed to talk to in all of Jewish Palestine, and Chaim increasingly saw in Orde a key weapon in his diplomatic struggle. The problem was that Chaim was in London, and Orde was not only prevented from leaving Palestine, he was now under constant surveillance. This was a period of great unhappiness and frustration for us, we were stymied, as they say, so Orde submitted to the travel restriction by refusing to leave the flat. The Colonial Office was, I think, fully aware by now of the close relationship that existed between this inflammatory British officer and the Jewish leader, and the danger contained therein. Weizmann was for the British a means of controlling the Jews, and they felt – correctly as it happened – that Wingate was filling his head with ideas. So Orde and I became 'interesting subjects' for the people responsible for Palestine. We remained in our lodgings and amused ourselves as best we could, and for two months we fell into a delicious (for me) reverie, it was like being back in Bulford one hundred years ago. We lay on the rug and played gramophone records, we had a lot of modern music from America, but Orde always ended up with Beethoven because it was the only music that completely satisfied, he said it made him swell. Whole chunks of day dissolved in this delightful manner, I luxuriated in his inert proximity, while he gloomily contemplated his future. In the evenings our flat became a magnet for all sorts of interesting people.

Here I have to mention the strange case of George Antonius who was a frequent visitor at Hallak House. At that time he was probably the best-known Arab intellectual in all the Near East, he had just published a book that everyone was reading, and naturally we were flattered by his attentions. He would leave his wife at home, a thing he seldom did because she was a great charmer, and arrive uninvited, laden with boxes of the most delicious-smelling food and sweetmeats - it was known about town that Lorna never set foot in the kitchen – and he wouldn't leave much before dawn. George was a Christian, respected and with a large circle of friends, who was known (at GHQ and at the Agency) to be close to al-Husseini, the moving force behind the Arab Revolt. I was sure that George had been sent to spy on us but we didn't discourage his visits, he was too amusing and too generous. Then one day someone threw a bomb into Orde's car while he was driving away from the house. It was a home-made thing and it didn't go off, but it shook me out of my reverie, thereafter we saw much less of George.

We knew for certain that Britain was going to abrogate Balfour, and abandon the Jews, but we could not persuade Chaim that this was the case; he would not accept Orde's view, and the more Orde argued the case, the less Chaim trusted his judgment. Chaim was obdurate, he was so enamoured of British charm and British power, so grateful to her for having granted him *personally* the Balfour promise, so utterly beholden to her, that finally he betrayed his own people. His position in Zionist circles was unassailable, and as long as he assured the Jews that he had matters in hand, they left him to his own devices, and this was a fatal error.

The fact that Orde was no less beholden to Chaim, and could never betray him was academic because there was no alternative leadership in Zionist circles. If Ben Gurion had ousted his older rival in 1938, he would not have taken up arms against the British, by his own admission; he wasn't beholden, he was overawed. I had a low opinion of the revisionists, and anyway they didn't count, but if there had been just one man in all the councils of the Jews who had been willing to resist this disgraceful British swindle, I should have gone directly to him, I cannot speak for Orde.

As soon as Chaim and Vera arrived back in Palestine in mid-April 1939, Orde sent them a message that he needed to talk urgently and a secret meeting was arranged at a flat in Tel Aviv for the following week. We were under surveillance, and, as I have mentioned, our relationship with the Weizmanns was known, so this was something that could be damaging to Orde. We arrived after dark, and the two men were together for about an hour, while I made the acquaintance of the charming English occupant of the flat, a young woman whose name was Mary Fyvel.

Orde had come to the conclusion that the Jews had to act now; policy was being formulated in London, and therefore Chaim, as leader of the Jews, had to deliver an ultimatum to Malcolm Macdonald, and he had prepared a draft for that purpose. This was a most important conversation for which Orde had been preparing for two weeks, and he recounted it to me on our drive back to Jerusalem.

At first Chaim would not read the draft Orde had prepared, and reiterated that he had had meetings in London, and that he had received certain assurances from Whitehall, whereupon Orde scolded him, and said that he didn't understand what an Englishman meant when he used the word assurance. 'When an Englishman intends to do something, he says, 'I will do it.' And when he says, 'I assure you I will do it,' it means that he wishes with all his heart that he could do it but he cannot. The word 'assure' or 'reassure', is used when speaking to a dying man, or to someone who has just lost his life savings. So when you start getting assurances from an Englishman, you should know that something is seriously amiss.'

Chaim was a very proud man and, like any of us, didn't like to be told that he was wrong, and certainly didn't feel himself in need of an English lesson, and so he now scolded Orde and accused Orde of behaving like a zealot. Now just as 'assure' means something very particular in our culture, 'zealot' means something very particular in Jewish culture, because it was the zealots who took up arms against the Romans and the Greeks before them, and brought upon the Jewish people the destruction of their commonwealth many years ago. So you will see that this was verbal swordplay between two great masters, and the fact that Chaim became belligerent – so out of character for him – and left the apartment abruptly, tells one something about the outcome of this contest. Chaim could deceive himself about Jewish diplomatic prospects and he could deceive his colleagues, but he knew that he couldn't deceive Orde, and this was the proof of it.

At one point in this quite heated exchange, Chaim said, 'And once I have delivered my ultimatum, what comes next?' and Orde answered, 'Stand back, and let the British ask themselves the same question, and while they are doing that, I will have resigned my commission, and the Colonial Office can take note of that also, and there may be other defections.' Chaim said that the Jews would not declare war on the British Empire, and this is when he introduced the term 'zealot'. This was a very foolish historical parallel, because Rome was a dictatorship permanently geared-up for war, and liked nothing better than to field an army and blood her generals, whereas Britain under Chamberlain absolutely dreaded war, and was in a low morale, certainly in no fit condition to make difficult choices in Palestine. Neville Chamberlain was not Nero, and was not about to send the fifth and the tenth legions to Palestine under Vespasian – Montgomery, say – to butcher the Jews. Orde was pulling his hair out. He told me after this exchange, again, 'the Jews are not a people, they do not think like a people or act like a people'.

This meeting took place on April 18th of 1939. We arrived home after midnight, I went to bed and Orde sat down and wrote a report; it started out as a report to no one in particular and it turned into something else. Chaim had an imperfect appreciation of London's intentions and no appreciation at all of Jerusalem HQ's capabilities, so in his writing he addressed himself exclusively to the latter. Palestine was known to be the least popular military posting in the empire, the political interfered with the operational, one didn't know who one was fighting from one day to the next, political directives from London were at odds with the ones from Cairo, and subject to constant change, it was all confusion and this was deleterious to the morale of the officers. Palestine was the last place an English civil servant would wish to be posted, consequently the quality of the British personnel in Jerusalem was lower than that of the Sudan or India, this was generally known; the fact that Palestine was filling up with Jews did not add to the luster of the posting.

Orde argued in the thing he was writing that the Jews could, under the correct conditions, seize control of Palestine, and this is the message he sought to convey to his friend and mentor, Chaim Weizmann. Time was extremely short, Orde was expecting to be sent back to England any day, and therefore he decided to force the issue with Chaim and it needed to happen before the publication of the White Paper which was due in less than a month. As with all his reports, he went at it hammer and tongs, we banned all visitors, I took to locking the front door, drawing the curtains and ignoring people knocking, whistling or throwing small stones at the front window. Mother was due for a visit, I cabled her to delay her arrival by three weeks – I meant indefinitely but I thought our letters were being opened. We had food delivered by our corner shop, ate out of tins, and drank gallons of freshly squeezed orange juice for which I had bought a marvelous locally-made orange-squeezing contraption. Twice Orde put on his cleanest uniform to go to his office, he took his lunch in the officer's mess, a thing he hadn't done since he arrived in Palestine, and conducted himself in a civil manner, and came home in the evening with files and papers stuffed in his briefcase.

One night Tony Simonds accompanied him home bringing a small overnight bag, and they worked together solidly for two days. Tony was a tall and gallant English officer, a colleague in the intelligence department, they got along very well, and Tony was on the same side as us. He had a

Jewish girlfriend called Hava which is Hebrew for 'Eve', she was as short as he was tall, and they were frequent guests at Hallak House. I shouldn't say that Tony was a Zionist, but he didn't care for the pro-Arab bias in the service. He was the type of Englishman who liked to see fair play and, as I said, he was very fond of Orde and had a high opinion of his abilities; Tony remained a trusted friend to Orde until the end. He told us quite early on that he had been assigned by someone high-up in military intelligence to keep an eye on Orde's doings with the Jews, and said that he had decided to act as a double agent in this matter, and keep Orde informed of what was going on behind his back. Tony was Orde's sounding board in this affair but not, I would say, co-conspirator. He was able and intelligent, and a very hard worker, but a born rebel which is probably why he never rose in the army to full general.

A few days before the completion of this report, we were jolted by an official envelope with notification of Orde's transfer to England, and he was left in no doubt that the order had come from London, and that he was being thrown out of Palestine. We had no intention of leaving

Since I hadn't left the flat for ten days, and Orde only twice in order to go to GHQ, we felt that if we could slip out unobserved, we might not be missed for one day. We left Hallak House very early one morning and made our separate ways to the house of Dvora, my excellent and loyal doctor in Rehavia – I am now back in my John Buchan novel with a vengeance – and we drove in Dvora's car with two copies of Orde's report, with maps, rolled into cardboard tubes, wrapped in oilskin and concealed in the chassis. I was silent on the journey, lightheaded with dread, and listened to Orde speaking quietly. One of the things he said, and I'd heard it from him before, was, 'we judge other people's motives from their actions, we have no other way, and we judge our own actions by our motives, and so we must examine our motives; is this a selfish undertaking? And I whispered back, 'no, it is not a selfish undertaking, Orde'.

We drove to Rehovot, arriving at about 3pm on the Friday preceding publication of the White Paper. On arrival at Chaim's residence Orde announced himself to the Jewish guard at the entrance, and after a brief telephonic conference the guard informed him that Dr. Weizmann was not at home. Now Orde had not been in touch with Chaim since the previous occasion, and he knew that Chaim was not anxious for a repeat of what had gone before, so he was fully prepared to storm the castle. He pushed past the guard with me in his train, and hammered on the front door. The poor guard got back on the telephone, practically in tears, and a good two minutes elapsed before Vera opened the door in person, and let us in with a grimace, and we were shown into Chaim's office where he sat, rubbing his temples. Orde went straight into the attack, shouting, and warning him that this was the last time he would ever come to him, and since this was their final meeting, he would present certain demands, and would not remove himself from Chaim's office until he had received Chaim's assurance that those demands would be met in full.

Vera and I stood there watching Chaim closely, 'I notice that you don't bang the table, Orde', said he, which I thought was a nice answer, for indeed Orde was behaving in an almost insulting manner. Orde replied that this was no time for pleasantries and asked him for permission to present his demands, to which Chaim assented. Of course this was pure theatre, Chaim knew Orde better than any man alive, he could have had him thrown out with the press of a button, with the blink of an eye, but he chose to go along with it out of regard for the lunatic who stood before him – and also curiosity – and so he nodded gravely for Orde to continue.

Orde told him that he had drawn up a plan for seizing control of the levers of Government in Palestine, and that Chaim must undertake to show the plan to various individuals each of whom were in Palestine at that time – and here Orde produced a list of six Jewish notables including the two top Jewish soldiers – and only after discussing every aspect of Orde's proposal with these men, deliver himself of a decision, which Orde would accept unequivocally. We waited while the two tubes were removed from the car and brought to the house, then Orde recited a passage from Shakespeare:

> *'There is a tide in the affairs of men*
> *Which taken at the flood, leads on to fortune;*
> *Omitted, all the voyage of their life*
> *Is bound in shallows and in miseries.*
> *On such a full sea are we now afloat,*
> *And we must take the current when it serves,*
> *Or lose our ventures.'*

He then marched out of Chaim's office, I gave Vera a hasty kiss, and followed my husband out.

Powerful men must at regular intervals subject their motives to scrutiny. If they don't, they are liable to go off the rails, one sees it happen all the time. They're under pressure, the steam is up, they're actually under speed, going forward, you see, you've got to keep an eye on your direction, and he, without having any morbid interest in himself, was very conscious that he was a weapon of power, and in order to navigate, he had to examine his motives, it was a constant process. What precisely was my role in this affair? I supported Orde in everything he did, I didn't think that he was going too far in his support for the Jews, in fact I might have encouraged him to go further. Looking back I ask myself why I was so fierce. I loved the Jews, everything about them, I felt as if I were a part of them, and I still do. Like Orde, I felt that they had been wronged for too long; it's never too late to make amends. But I try to dig deeper, and deeper still to find my motivation; I think it's true to say that the female has a tendency, it is probably an instinct that goes back to pre-historic times, to make her mate cleave to her. Did I allow, even encourage Orde to go out on a limb because out there, in the wind and the cold, he would have greater need of me? I think the answer is yes.

I do not intend to set out Orde's plan, although I remember it in every detail, I have no desire to revisit this country. I would only say that it was quite unlike the plan that Leonard Mosley would concoct sixteen years later in his book about my husband. Mosley stated that Orde intended to blow up the oil terminal in Haifa; that would have been a foolish act indeed. Orde knew every British disposition in Palestine from the border with Lebanon to the border with Egypt, he knew every arms dump, every military vehicle, every weapon at the disposal of the British armed forces, and above all he knew the competence of the serving officers and the morale of the enlisted men. Orde's arrangements in the event of a failure, or any other necessity, tells us something essential about the man. He would surrender himself to British forces, and stand trial in London, in order to act as a lightning rod to anti-Jewish sentiment in the country, and in order to provide himself with a platform from which to denounce Malcolm Macdonald and the Colonial Office to the British people, and to the world.

When we returned home, we threw open the doors and windows and invited all our Jewish friends to come to us for drinks and we had a party that lasted several days, the sort of thing one does when one imagines that the world is coming to an end. Together we waited for the arrival of the White Paper. When we finally read it, it was worse than we had anticipated, and we had anticipated the worst. It was a brutal thing, I don't know how Malcolm Macdonald had the gall to put his name to it. Orde was elated because this would surely convince Chaim to adopt his proposal, but Chaim did nothing of the kind. He sent a car to collect Orde and bring him to Tel Aviv, and Chaim told him that he had met his demands in full, there had been a comprehensive discussion of the matter, and the outcome was negative. He added that both copies of the proposal had been destroyed, and the matter was now buried, never to be referred to again. The two men embraced, there was a full and tearful reconciliation, and that was that. Within a small number of years, not only would Chaim witness Britain's utter abandonment of the Jews, as Orde had predicted, but he would have proof positive of Orde's genius, and that Wingate, of all men, might have succeeded in achieving a state for the Jews in 1939.

This therefore had been Orde's apotheosis. Nothing Orde did in his life made me prouder of him than this moment of personal failure. He not only offered himself as a sacrifice to the cause he believed in passionately, he conceived a plan of subtlety and daring that, had it been accepted and executed, might have altered history. Churchill said, when Orde's death had been announced, that Wingate might have been a man of destiny. It wasn't death that robbed him of this mantle, it was – forgive me Chaim – the vanity and pusillanimity of the man in whose hands the Jews had placed their fate.

There was nothing further Orde could accomplish in Palestine, it was time for us to go. General Haining had determined that his usefulness in the country was at an end, and Orde's presence in Palestine now disturbed Chaim's equanimity. Orde and I wondered how much the intelligence services knew about our activities, I'm not even sure which department should have been interested in us, we seemed to fall into so many categories.

A Green Rose

But British intelligence in general has always been second to none, and now as I write, I wonder if they didn't even have listening devices in Chaim's home. We always thought it unlikely that we should be arrested for what we were doing, because they had so many other means at their disposal for curtailing our activities, but Chaim was less sanguine, and worried about our safety to an inordinate degree, and also for the effect a scandal involving Orde would have on his own standing with the British. So Chaim was glad, I would say, to see us out of Palestine. Orde understood that this was the first step in the ruin of his career, it was a very painful time and I was deeply unhappy, and so was he.

Orde put himself under great stress, and sometimes did curious things, I think they were a part of his character, I found them quite acceptable. One of the things he used to quote was a Napoleon utterance, 'Women are the occupation of the idle man, the relaxation of the warrior'. Not a bad idea, really. I think when men are under stress, particularly in time of war, when things tend to be so materialistic, the whole of the gentler, personal side of life is really swept aside, obliterated, there should be some relief from time to time. Now the Jewish girls in Palestine were some of the most marvelous specimens, but of them the most outstanding were the girls of the kvutzot, they walked around in baggy khaki shorts with their bronzed limbs,– English girls were discouraged from losing their pallor – and little shirts that only just contained them and had their hair cropped short, and they were fearless and did as they pleased, and appealed to me greatly. They seldom had the sort of looks one associates with Hollywood glamour girls, but they were full of sex appeal, and I could not but notice these vivacious creatures casting appreciative glances in the direction of my husband – possibly also at me – and I was, I think, perfectly resigned to the idea that Orde might eat of the fruit, as it were. Then I found out that Orde had been sleeping with, not one, but two Jewish girls.

One of them was a certain Doreen Silver, and I was not pleased because she was not a simple camp-follower or dairy maid, she was a highly intelligent girl whom I considered a friend. I found traces on his pillow one day, and casually asked Orde if he was sleeping with another woman – I had no intention of making of this a cause célèbre – and of course he answered promptly and in full. It transpired that he had not only slept with Doreen but had also spoken to her. Now I'm entirely in favour of bringing up the mistresses with the marmalade, but this was a different matter. It is one thing to sleep with the occasional admirer, and quite another to discuss with her philosophy, and although, as I said, I didn't make a great fuss about it – there were more important things on one's mind – I was upset. When he had faithfully completed his confession, I stood up, pulled the six or seven HG Wells first editions that Orde had on his shelves, and set fire to them in the kitchen sink which was foolish of me, there was ash everywhere in our flat for days. The reason for this action was that I placed part of the blame for Orde's blatant behaviour at the feet of HG Wells who not only made no secret of the fact that he couldn't keep his fly buttoned, but advertized it in the manner of a religious cult, and wrote monographs on the subject, he was a very foolish and foul individual and I informed Orde that if I ever caught him with another book by that reprobate in his hand I should plunge a knife into his ribs. Having got that out of my system I returned to my rational self, and accepted this thing as a fact of life, I certainly didn't walk about moping.

He was lucky in me in more ways than one. I say more ways than one, I can think of two ways in which he was lucky to have me as a wife. One of them was that I was a very masculine little girl. Not masculine in the sense of having a deep voice and a large muscle, in that I was very feminine, but I took much more of a young man's view of life than a young woman's. It took me a few more years, until I was 27, to appreciate that I actually was a woman and must live a woman's life. The second way he was fortunate was in my hermaphroditic sort of state of mind, which might have been rather a hardship for me sometimes, but it was no trouble to Orde. If I'd been more of a wife and less of an armour-bearer, I might have noticed his behaviour, and even objected to it, but it was no hardship to me to overlook some of his stranger happenstances – what a lovely American word, I don't know what it means exactly, perhaps it's a happening and a circumstance all mixed up – well, I didn't have to consciously be generous or forgiving or any of these things because I didn't really think that any of these happenstances mattered. In that I think he was lucky.

Orde and I were really animals of the same kind. Spots shouldn't marry stripes, and he and I were a couple of stripy animals although one of us was very much bigger and better than the other. And when we were together, we wrought each other up into a sort of frenzy at times because we were so alike. I responded to passion quite happily, I was not in any way frigid, quite the opposite in fact, but the affection, the tenderness alarmed me as I'd had none of this as a child. I think people who live a happy family life with loving parents and brothers and sisters, uncles and aunts, are initiated into this business of receiving affection, so that when they come to the great open seas of love they can swim. They start paddling, then they're promoted to the deep end, and finally they breast the billows, I mean you do it by degrees. Loving parents, a delightful family, warm-hearted friends, I'd had none of this, and when I finally found myself with a creature as warm as Orde, the affection and the tenderness alarmed me. I had a vision of a life engulfed by something about which I knew too little. I think I was not cold so much as I withdrew, I used to walk away. He took some time to grasp this I think, and by the time we got to Palestine where the tension built up immediately, he had come to accept it – I'm quite sure he didn't brood upon it and sit about biting his nails; asked himself whether his wife loved him or any of that nonsense, he was far too busy and far too interested in other things – he just, I imagine, shrugged his shoulders and treated it like the weather, you know. One day it's snowing and blowing so you do something else. The sun comes out and you enjoy that. But of course I realize now that if I had had the understanding that has come my way since, or if I had been a normal creature and not a deformed one, a three-legged tiger, I would have been able to accept and enjoy the full content of his affections, instead of backing away from them all the time. I've thrown away diamonds and pearls, I know, it's very unfortunate.

Chapter 7

We were given three or four days in which to gather ourselves together, I was tired and anemic and thin and pale, and I'd had, as I mentioned, one or two personal shocks in Palestine before we left, I was an unhappy girl of 22, but I was alright, riding the waves. My legs had swollen up like bolsters, it was the only time in my life that it's ever happened because I stood on them for about 48 hours without stopping, I had nothing else to do than turn night into day.

We got on board a train which took us very, very slowly though the Sinai desert and down to Port Said. It was hot of course, *hamsin* weather, and when we reached Port Said, we went to a hotel, kept by an Englishman and his wife, I remember the name of the place it was Bodel's – sounds like a Channel Island name – and there we lay on our iron cots and listened to the bells of the great hideous Catholic cathedral which stood just outside our windows, and waited for the advent of the troopship which would take us back to England. We walked once or twice along the grey muddy shores of the Mediterranean at Port Said where a few bathing huts looked like a grotesque travesty of Brighton, no human beings visible, only this decayed shore. And then we returned to our hot little room, and presently we were told that the troopship had docked and was ready to take us on board.

Now the British troopship, like the Queen Mary and the Fighting Temeraire, has faded down the river, and I don't know whether she has had her tribute paid to her in song or story, perhaps Kipling, but I don't remember any of his tales connected with troopships or dealing with life on board them, so let me tell you the story of this one.

We boarded the Dorsetshire and were assigned to cabins. It was very crowded as troopships always are, I imagine, I was fortunate in being given a cabin with only one other woman, Orde had to join at least three other men if not more. The ship was under the command of a colonel, of course the nautical side was managed by a merchant marine captain and his crew. We ourselves being somewhat late arrivals were set down at a table which had been allotted to the Queen Alexandra Imperial Military Nursing Service, the QA as they called them in those days. There were five exceedingly stalwart women wearing their delightful uniform, starched white headdresses and scarlet and grey cloaks, sitting under the cold blue eye of their senior officer, she sat at the head of the table, Orde and I humbly took the foot.

If you imagined that Orde's passion for the Jewish cause had run its course, you would have been mistaken. He determined to spend this time at his disposal, the time between Port Said and Southampton, nine days, on preparing a treatise on the situation in the Near East, and Britain's role in the immediate future, nothing could have been more vital. During the day Orde sat at the dining table which had a green baize cloth, in the saloon, he borrowed a typewriter from somebody, and he properly applied himself to writing this most impressive treatise. I read it at the time, it was quite long, it was not over-long, he had a trained mind, and the army training in exposition is second to none because it's so orderly, and he applied all his talents to the composition of this document.

I was living somewhat the same sort of life as I am now, I suppose this is partly due to my nature; in the end it's not really the circumstances of the beast, it's the nature of the beast that counts. I was fortunate in my roommate because she was a delightful young wife called Penny, so tall and fair and kind and gentle, and she left me alone to lie on my lower bunk and, as usual, I read my books, but every now and then I had to go out and walk about the deck. Now Orde was much too busy to walk about the deck with me, and somehow the word had got round that we'd been disgraced and were leaving the Near East under a cloud, these things are very quickly picked up in a tight community like the army. Most of the people on the ship had come from India. There were no tremendously senior people on board but it was a very full house. I didn't speak to anybody and nobody spoke to me except two men, that is, apart from my roommate whom I liked very much.

One of these men was small and thin and brown and he had the saddest expression on his face I think that I'd ever seen. It was permanent, you see, he had the same expression all the time so that it was noticeable. One day as I lay in my deck chair in the sunshine, and he happened to be sitting in a deck chair beside me, I turned to him and said something and he began to talk to me. He was an army doctor, I suppose he was about 40 years old, something of that kind, he told me that he had been stationed in Quetta in India. Now Quetta is where the Indian Staff College is, or was, I've never been there or heard much about it but I imagine that it's quite a sizeable place, not only did it have stone cantonments of a permanent variety but it had a large native population, well fairly large. In 1935, which was only four years before, there had been one of the most dreadful earthquakes in modern times. My doctor had been out on a call – unfortunately this earthquake in Quetta took place at night which meant that most people were in their houses – and when the shock took place he'd come back to his own house and found it a heap of rubble. He said, 'I worked among the stones for hours, my wife and two children were under them, they were all dead. I looked down at my hands in the early hours of the morning and I saw that all the flesh had worn off my fingers and the white bones were showing through. I hadn't even noticed, so I went to the hospital to see if there was anything I could do for anybody else'. Now apparently the hospital hadn't been quite so badly hit. I don't know what he was able to do for others but anyway, at some point he sat down on a bench outside the hospital on a veranda, and a woman whom he knew came walking in the light of dawn and sat down beside him. He said, 'well?', and she said, 'all dead', then he said, 'you've broken your leg', and they both looked down and through her cotton dress, the splintered bone of her thigh was protruding through flesh and fabric. 'Oh', she said, 'I had never even noticed', and she'd walked in two miles. Well, you see, this is how life is really lived and this is what happens. The human creature is infinitely variable, you may say it's infinitely strong, it's also capable of a good deal of suffering, I won't forget the look in his eyes. He and I spoke to each other two or three times, he was a good man, he was brave and he was gentle.

The other person who spoke to me, the only other person, was rather a different sort of creature, he was a captain of engineers, fair, square and quite good looking, and a boxer I would have thought from his shoulders and his chest. Because he was an engineer he was intelligent, and not only because he was an engineer. Orde and I spoke to him once or twice, we were introduced to each other, I never heard his name properly and I certainly can't remember it, but I liked him, he had a little fair moustache, close clipped, and he had an air of controlled strength, which is always attractive. Now I spent nearly all my time in my cabin, I never went to the saloons, I didn't join in whatever junketings there were on board ship, and when I took the air, it was always alone and no one ever approached me, but one day I was lying out in the sunshine on this deck chair with my eyes closed because I didn't want to speak to anybody, when I heard a voice say, 'Mrs. Wingate'. I kept my eyes closed and hoped the voice would go away. 'Mrs. Wingate', it said more insistently and I opened my eyes to see this delightful man sitting sideways and leaning towards me, 'I should like to give you a pair of gloves', he said. Good Lord! I was amazed, what on earth could he mean. 'How kind of you' I replied. I didn't say that I had enough gloves, I just thanked him and left it at that. After a few moments he got up and went away. Well we hardly saw him again after that, I think it was when we were standing by the rail watching the docking of the ship, I don't think his wife was there, she was a rather twisted looking woman, not very cuddly or lovable I would say, and Orde was certainly somewhere else, I said to him, 'there's a war coming, and that's what every professional soldier looks to for his advancement, what do you hope to do?' and he said, not looking at me, 'well, I suppose we all hope to become CIGS', and he turned away, and we never saw each other again. After the war I was in Canada and a delightful Canadian who was being most helpful and kind, did me the honour of asking me for my hand. He came to me one day and said, 'what size do you take in gloves?' so I said, 'I don't know, seven', and he said, 'I should like to give you a pair of gloves', and he said it very earnestly, looking at me with deep significance, so I said, 'my dear so-and-so, it's awfully good of you but actually I have enough gloves, I don't need gloves, I don't wear gloves very often'. 'What?' he said, 'don't you understand what I mean? If a man tells a woman that he wants to give her a pair of gloves, it means that he's deeply in love with her and he wants her to marry him'. 'Good God!' I thought, 'surely that poor man on the ship couldn't have meant any such thing.' I've never heard of this before. Wonderful piece of Morse code.

The last story connected with this troopship is perhaps more interesting than any of the others. I had passed by, and had a few words with a Major and Mrs. I-don't-know-what, the poor woman was only memorable because she looked so ill, so worried, she sat huddled up on her deck chair with her arms crossed over her front, her husband was totally insignificant. We learned their names I suppose, but we learnt nothing about them, and I don't think we ever saw them again. On the day that we docked at Southampton, we had our last luncheon aboard ship, we were sitting at the table with the QAs but two of them were absent. Halfway through the meal they bustled in, the senior one looking very red, and rather slab-faced and fed-up. 'I've just been delivering a baby'. She said this like a sergeant major who's seen a row of dirty buttons. 'Mrs. Snodgrass (the major's wife).' Then she said, looking around fiercely, 'you know that nobody is allowed to travel on an army transport within three months of delivery, they have to sign an undertaking that their pregnancy is not going to come to its term within three months of their taking passage'. 'Oh?' said we, raising our eyebrows. 'Yes, the major is at this moment with the colonel.' We had a dreadful vision of what the colonel was saying to the major. Then she added with a kind of ruminative look – and this is the point – 'It's a boy baby, and the sailors are very pleased'. We looked at her expectantly. 'You see', she said, 'I'm told that this ship is a killer, it killed a man in Southampton when they were leaving on the outward voyage, ground him against the quayside and crushed him to death, and as we dock, it's brought back a man, and the sailors say that it's just as it should be'.

One criticism of Orde by his detractors, both during his lifetime and after, was that he was ambitious – as if that should be a criticism; ambitious like Cassius, I suppose. If he had been an ambitious man, placed himself and his career before all other considerations, he would surely now have turned from the Jews and their interminable difficulties and attended to his own future. War was coming and this was a time when all professional soldiers were busy making phone calls, writing to long-lost relatives, or school friends who happened to be on the staff of one senior general or other, jostling for a good staff appointment. Not everyone wanted to go out and get bloodied, but everyone knew that this was going to be their chance to advance in the army and make a name for himself, not to mention a nice pension when it was all over.

There were opportunities for a man with Orde's gifts if he would but grasp them, why could we not just leave the Jews be? Did they require anything further from us? It seemed to me that the opposite was the case, in fact I think Chaim had seen quite enough of us. Why did we feel so deeply for the Jewish cause? Was this not some form of displaced religious fervor? Where did this passion come from? Was it all due to Orde's extraordinary upbringing? We didn't ask ourselves these questions at the time of course, but I ask myself now. Although his religion had been swept away, his God was real and present, he believed that every man and woman was His instrument, born for

His special purpose. Orde had groped for a purpose all his adult life, everyone who met him or knew anything of him has commented on this restless search. When he stumbled at the age of 33 upon the people of the Bible in the act of reestablishing themselves in the land of the Bible, to his eyes as helpless as the newborn lamb, it instantly came to him that his purpose as a soldier and as an Englishman was to shepherd them to safety. How could a successful career in the British Army compare to such blinding moral clarity?

Any thoughts we might have had about turning our backs on the Jews was dispelled on our return to London. In this season of preparation and uncertainty, the tide was now running forcibly against the Jews. Cinema newsreels of broken shop windows and Nazis laughing while elderly Jews were made to clean streets with toothbrushes generated a great deal of anger and disgust towards Germany but, strangely, no sympathy at all for Jews. I have already alluded to a degree of anti-Jewish sentiment in London – I'm not even talking about Mosley and his people. Well, Chaim maintained his composure wonderfully, and continued to speak publicly of his great optimism for the future and his enduring faith in Great Britain, but privately he was at his wit's end. He asked for meetings in Whitehall with special requests for immigration permits, appeals against court decisions in Palestine, and all the endless details that he had been handling for twenty years on behalf of the Agency, and he was now coming away from these meetings empty-handed; this started to affect his standing with his own people in Palestine. I heard from a number of sources that British ministers went to great lengths to avoid having to meet with him at this time, for Chaim was a living, walking rebuke. Orde made the observation that Chaim was reduced to playing Shylock on a world stage: 'An oath, an oath, I have an oath in heaven' When Chaim with his sad face and tombrous voice invoked 'Balfour', which he often did, was it not one and the same thing? 'Balfour' was probably the last word in the English language that the Secretary of State for the Colonies wanted to hear in 1939.

Ben Gurion was also in London and faring no better than Chaim, nevertheless he was the younger and more vigorous of the two, and he was breathing down the old man's neck, wanting his job, one imagines. Orde's view, as I have mentioned more than once, was that the only thing that mattered was the fielding of a Jewish formation, at this stage in the game one that would fight alongside the British in the coming conflict. If we obtained that, surely everything else would follow. In one discussion with Orde, I remember, Ben Gurion asked him what he thought would happen to the Jews of Palestine if the Germans won a future conflict. How would Hitler behave towards them? Would Hitler not use Palestine as a dumping ground for his own Jews? Would that not be preferable to the White Paper? Orde replied that such an outcome was out of the question. Hitler didn't have the substance to defeat the British Empire. He wasn't saying that British couldn't be defeated by German arms, only that Britain couldn't be defeated by Hitler, the man was unstable and hysterical, and therefore the Jews should not place any side bets on a German victory. This was not spoken by Orde in a defensive or partial manner, he was merely giving Ben Gurion an evaluation, and because Ben Gurion had ample proof of Orde's bona fides, I believe he took his words to heart.

Orde found it extraordinary that the Jews were behaving as if they were powerless and the Arabs were blustering as if they were the masters of the world. Why was this backward race such a master of statecraft, and the civilized Jew so inept? The Jews with no army stood in corridors waiting on events. What did Stalin say of the Pope? 'How many divisions does he have?', laughing no doubt. Thus it was with the Jews. No divisions, no talk. The only circumstance under which the War Office would agree to arm the Jews was if Britain and her empire stood under immediate and dire threat. An ill wind blowing in the direction of Britain brought hope for the Jews. Britain had placed a loyal and valuable ally in this false position due to a faulty and treacherous policy in Palestine. So when Mussolini invaded Albania in 1939, and growling noises were heard from Rome, the War Office wondered if the vast Italian army in North Africa might move on the Canal, and suddenly remembered the loyal Jews of Palestine. For an instant we thought that a Jewish formation was in the offing, but it lasted only for five minutes. The invasion of Poland, the Fall of France, Rommel's success in North Africa, all raised the hopes of the Jews that the War Office would relent, but the British didn't lose their nerve, and finally the Jews were made to endure the entire conflict unarmed and unprotected.

Orde never let up, he continued to press his case with every Jew and Englishman he met. We went to see Leopold Amery who was a very powerful figure in Parliament, and Orde made a fine and impassioned presentation. Amery was in favour and thought Orde a very fine fellow and took us out to dinner that same night, a most attractive and brilliant man. Through Leopold we met a number of young Labourites and, taking Leopold's lead they responded warmly to Orde, I think he was their little discovery; a British officer who could quote from Das Kapital and had read Beatrice Webb, with his little bookworm of a wife, and our passionate Zionism sat well with them. We became quite popular with this new set, and accepted invitations to dinner parties in Chelsea and Kensington, sitting next to brilliant thinkers and writers and having a very interesting time of it, but not accomplishing a great deal for our friends.

Orde was still an officer in the British Army, and whatever his indiscretions there was work for him to do. The war got off to a very slow start, as you know, and on our return to England he was posted to an Anti-Aircraft formation in Sidcup in Kent, with the rank of brigade major. I don't know why he was assigned there, but he was an artillery man and these were fairly large guns so I suppose it made sense. The important thing from the army's point of view had been to get him out of Palestine so I'm sure that anything would have sufficed.

Some of the new anti-aircraft weaponry was fresh off the drawing board, and of course no one yet knew how precisely it would work when the time came. Great stone emplacements were being dug on the periphery of our airfields and other places where the German bombers were likely to attack, periphery being the operative word because the concept was a defensive one; to hit the intruders before they reached their target. Orde studied the problem and decided that we were doing it all wrong.

The Sidcup batteries were protecting the south-eastern approaches to London in what was then called 'hell's kitchen', all pointing up at the sky with camouflage nets thrown over them, and he tried a few of them out, absolutely deafening they were, and after a few weeks of playing with this new weapon, Orde called up his superior officers and said, 'You had better come over and see something, the guns are all pointing the wrong way'.

A car filled with brass arrived the next day, or very soon after, and Orde took them to a room where he had built models with a great deal of string and wire, and told them that the guns should be pointing inwards over the target and not outwards at the periphery, and here he had grasped the brutal heart of the matter. There was little chance of hitting enemy planes as they approached because they could spread out and vary their approach in order to avoid our guns, and you weren't shooting at individual aircraft, often you made no visual contact whatever, and the best you could hope for would be to spoil their aim and bring one or two of them down. It would be far better, he said, to have the guns pointed inwards, directly over the target, at a killing zone or belt through which the intruders had to pass if they were to drop their bombs on target, and concentrate one's fire. Draw them in and shoot them down. Not very pleasant for the people down below, but if the enemy loses enough aircraft and crew, perhaps he will think again; Orde made the switch from static defense to ambush.

His innovation was accepted and implemented, and within a period of time, our fliers returning from missions over Germany reported that the other side was now doing the same thing with their guns. Of course, we now know what a vicious war our bombers fought, the carnage in the air and on the ground, and I don't think anyone should be in a great hurry to take credit for this particular idea, but I mention it nonetheless to show how Orde could be presented with a military problem and turn the thing on its head. There were dozens of able officers working with this new weapon, but it was Orde, arriving fresh, who consi-dered the matter and produced the innovation.

He also thought that women should man the guns, and sent a memo to General Pipes, arguing they wouldn't have to move across vast distances with an army of men and machines, and expose themselves to capture by the enemy, they could work from home, and be in no greater danger at the guns than they would be in their own kitchens, but they would release men for more arduous duties, and it would be good for morale. Pipes threw it in the wastebasket, but several months later when manpower was getting a little tighter, women were allowed to do this job, and one of the first batteries operated by women and men on an equal basis was commanded by Granville Wingate. Granville was very pleased with his girls.

One freezing morning in the early spring of 1940, Orde and I went to see Derek and his wife Mary in their quarters, a curious kind of pseudo-Tudor house in an outer suburb of London, I've forgotten where. Derek was attached to fighter command I think, it may have been bomber, and that was why he was living in this unexpected place, he was doing a very interesting job, he was concerned with ground-to-air liaison, in fact the use of the airplane as long-range artillery. At that time France had not fallen and the startling success of the Stuka bomber had not made plain to everybody that this was a new weapon, or extension of an old one, and Derek was one of a very small number who were studying it. Orde and I, as I say, went to visit him and Mary remained in the house for some reason, and I followed the two men out into the icy garden, all dripping and cold, and listened to them discussing Derek's work – very kind of them to let me come – the reason why we talked about it in the garden was because Orde now had a thing, and a very sensible thing, about bugging devices and he would never discuss anything that was of real priority, whether it was with his Jewish friends, or with Derek, unless he was outside, preferably in the middle of a field; he was a very thorough man and he was absolutely right, of course, and that's why I heard them on this subject, in the garden. I believe that Orde's later ideas on ground-air cooperation originated in this conversation with Derek, and from his work in Sidcup. This was a time of scientific and mental innovation, there were a great deal of extremely clever people in Britain in the war effort, and Orde was completely in his element.

The lightening attack on France raised the specter of an invasion of England, and Orde was called off the guns and into a most fascinating project. What would happen after a successful German invasion of Britain? Orde's work in Palestine was known to the War Office, and so they sent for him to consult on the running of an insurgency against a future German army of occupation. The idea appealed to him rather, he felt he could perform this task, because he had studied the work of the Arab gangs in Palestine and felt that he could probably do a far better job of it. This episode in Orde's career lasted for about six months until the threat of invasion receded, but it was a most interesting one, and it took us to Ireland, Yorkshire, Lincolnshire and to many parts of this beautiful Isle I would otherwise never have ventured. In writing up a preliminary training manual, Orde asked a Jewish acquaintance of German extraction to provide the likely German rendering of 'British gang leader', and that was what I was supposed to call him in bed; it was a very long word and occasioned us some mirth.

In September, the month that the blitz began, Chaim summoned Orde round to the Dorchester. When we went into the sitting room of their suite, Chaim opened his arms and said, 'Orde, we've got it. We've got the Jewish army. And it came to pass, apparently that Eden and Lloyd had been persuaded, even though they were hostile, to allow the formation of a Jewish force of one full division for actual combative duty in Egypt. It was going to be organized in two parts. Orde was going to gather together a cadre of officers in Britain, he was assigned Hampstead Heath to train them on – very suitable really – and there he was going in double quick time, he was going to cram his young lions and then he was going to take them out to Palestine where he would train the force to fight. It was to be a volunteer force, of course.

He was not to be the commander-in-chief because he was too junior, he was only a major, the man who was going to command was field-marshal Sir Gerald Templer, in those days he was of course a major general, a very intelligent man. I remember seeing him sweeping through the drawing room of Sigmund Gestetner, the duplicating person, at his country house when I was staying there. He went down there for conferences on how to command a Jewish army. He was very impressive, I was told he was just as impressive in private as he was in public. Orde was to be the chief-of-staff, and Templer was to be commander, and everybody else was going to be Jews. This was the greatest news we'd had, ever in our lives. But this entire business was nothing but a charade. The War Office had no intention whatever of levying a Jewish Legion, it was intent only on killing the project. I shall present the facts as they appeared to me.

Orde was just getting started with planning and recruitment, I remember he was in the throws of making a list of Palestinian Jews to be called up, and devising the training program, when he was summoned to the office of the CIGS, Sir John Dill, on the 17th of September 1940. He fully expected to receive his new appointment with Templer, but to his astonishment, Dill told him that he was being sent to Abyssinia. Dill was genuinely taken aback by Orde's strong reaction to this news and suggested he go to the War Office for more information. It was already late afternoon, so we came directly home. We analyzed the situation together and decided that it was probably another army cock-up, the left hand not knowing the right hand etc., and it would all be straightened out in the morning, for which reason we did not bother Chaim with it. But I did not sleep all night.

The following morning I drove Orde to the War Office and we waited in the car until 9 o'clock, and then he went in and presented himself. When he came back to the car he was in a shocking state. I took the papers that he held in his hand and read them and it stated quite clearly that he was being posted to Cairo for deployment against the Italians in Abyssinia, leaving England the following day! And attached was another piece of paper, King George's note paper with the seal at the top, typewritten, a few lines which said, "I hereby undertake that under no circumstances will I set foot in Palestine or any other country north of the canal".

He had been presented with this note by a man called Mallerby, he might have been Director of Intelligence, who had said, "I have nothing to do with this, I'm very sorry that I've got to offer it to you, but I must ask you to sign it." We now drove straight to Great Russell Street, and Chaim received Orde in his office while I sat outside with Chaim's wonderful secretary, a woman called Doris May who was actually a Catholic and a gentile, the dearest and most intelligent human being, and she and I waited with bated breath because we knew what was happening within. Presently both Chaim and Orde came out, Orde was terribly pale, he looked distraught really, and Doris and I sprang up in time to hear Chaim say to him, 'go out into the world, Orde, in another field, and then come back to us', then vanished back into his office. Orde and I took our leave and went out into Bloomsbury Square and started to make our way towards the British Museum which is just along there, and as we walked slowly along, he told me what had happened inside Chaim's room.

He told Chaim of the document he'd just received, and Chaim stood up and came over and placed his hands on Orde's shoulders and told him that shortly after he had been offered the Jewish Legion, he was informed that Wingate could have no part in it. Chaim had known for several days, but had kept Orde in the dark because it had to be that way. Orde said, 'don't you find it strange that these men should wish to levy a force at great expense but deny it its most able commander?' He told Chaim that it was a trick, that he understood these men, and knew for a fact that Eden and Lloyd could *never* agree to a Jewish Army, they had always stood against it, and that their undertaking to Chaim would be withdrawn the moment he (Orde) was out of the way. Orde put the whole thing as forcefully as he could, but Chaim refused to believe him. He said, 'nobody, no honourable nation such as Britain would first offer this that we have gone so far towards realizing, and then destroy it all under our noses, and go back on their promises.' The more one disagreed with Chaim Weizmann, the stonier he became, and finally he said, 'even if they do destroy us, which I don't believe for a moment, it's my duty to accept what they decree. You will have to go and we'll go on from here without you'. When Orde had finished this account of his meeting, I was so completely shattered, I remember I stopped and turned my face into the filthy railings of the British Museum, it has a vast forecourt there, so nobody could see me and wept and wept – I sound like an awful crybaby when I talk about these things, but of course these outburst were separated by many years – and when I turned back, Orde was very sweet, he took out his handkerchief, I never had one, he mopped me up and wiped all the grime off my face, then we went on again.

Orde still wasn't done, he wanted to see Ben Gurion one last time, and we went to him only a few hours after Orde's interview with Chaim. The meeting took place in Benzion Khounine's car at Orde's request. Benzion was a doctor we'd met in Palestine, who made himself available to us time and again, an invaluable friend. This was a remarkable meeting because, as we drove through Hampstead the sirens went off for an air raid, so I suggested we go to Primrose Hill to get a better view, and it was an unforgettable sight. The docks were being attacked, great orange flames rose in the air placing the City of London in silhouette, white beams of light dissected the night and explosions rent the air, a truly Wagnerian moment. One felt that there would be nothing of London left standing by morning. I don't know why Orde had asked for this meeting, his relationship with Ben Gurion was unlike his relationship with Chaim, they were closer in age, and Orde felt no deference. He told him that the British were making fools of the entire Agency, that the Jews were being sold down the river and none of them had the intelligence to see it or the guts to resist it. He didn't raise his voice, but he wouldn't allow Ben Gurion to speak, and finally Ben Gurion quietly asked Benzion to take him back to his flat, and he got out of the car having barely spoken, in fact, I thought his composure was remarkable, and we drove off.

On our last night together we surveyed our options, and we had none. One may not refuse a posting during wartime, he either sailed on the morrow or deserted. And the following day Orde was gone and I was on my own. Mother came down from Aberdeen to keep me company, and from the moment she arrived I wept for two days. I reasoned that Chaim had encouraged Orde to wreck his career on behalf of the Jews, but hadn't been prepared to listen to what he had to say; he had turned him down once too often. Of course it wasn't like that; Orde needed no encouragement from Chaim, but I was emotionally wrought up. I went to him in his room at the Dorchester, and I stood in the middle of the floor and told him what a wicked thing he'd done, and how he'd betrayed his people and all sorts of nonsense – not nonsense but it was shocking bad manners – and Vera sat and wept and mother sniveled and Chaim was very angry with me and I was very angry with him. Afterwards mother persuaded me to write him a letter of apology. I didn't feel in the least apologetic but he was an old man, and a great one, so I did, and he wrote me back a very interesting letter, very closely written I remember and masses of it, and in green ink! I remember showing it to Benzion Khounine, and he said 'this is an historic document, I hope you'll keep it carefully, Lorna'. I think that from that moment forward until the end of his life, although we saw much less of one another, my friendship with Chaim deepened. In due course Whitehall buried the Jewish Legion, exactly as Orde had predicted. Templer was hastily removed to a more hygienic post, no more was heard of cadres of officers on Hampstead Heath, and 10,000 Jews were very grudgingly allowed to enlist in the transport corps. If Whitehall was prepared to go to such extraordinary lengths to keep Orde out of Palestine, I would have thought it would have been simpler and kinder to have had someone push him under a bus.

Chapter 8

I knew nothing about Abyssinia, so I started reading. Abyssinia, like Libya, was an Italian colony and because Mussolini had had the temerity to declare war on Great Britain, Britain was going to take Abyssinia away from him and add it to her considerable list of colonies in eastern Africa. This was the conception of Generals Platt and Cunningham who were each leading a prong of a two-pronged British attack on the Italian Colonial Army in Abyssinia. Each General had at his disposal two proper divisions with artillery and aircraft, twenty or thirty thousand soldiers apiece. They faced an opponent who was very well dug-in – the Italians had had a number of years in which to do it – and they also had good roads and railways and had gone to the trouble of building an excellent port with which to supply their colonial army, and although the modern Italian didn't make the very best soldier, honour and prestige played its part and it was thought that they would put up a good fight on the day. Compton Mackenzie has a good account of the Savoia battalions at the Battle of Keren, if you are interested.

The British had an ace up their sleeve in the person of Haile Selassie who had been the Emperor of Abyssinia before the Italians threw him out. He was a small man, thin with a wispy black beard, extremely regal and, above all, fiercely intelligent. He had been living in exile as a guest of H.M.G. in London, he was no jumped-up major who had seized power. Haile Selassie was the legitimate ruler of Abyssinia and he was thought to command the loyalties of most of the tribes of that country, now more than ever. The Italians had made themselves particularly unpopular because they had used poison gas on the natives.

Whitehall created Mission 101 whose job it was to bring the Emperor back to Ethiopia and make his presence felt by all concerned. It was thought quite correctly that just by sitting him on a chair within the borders of his country, 50,000 enemy soldiers garrisoned between the Emperor on his chair, and the capital Addis Ababa would be tied down, relieving some of the pressure on Generals Platt and Cunningham.

Mission 101 was actually a creation of SOE which stands for Special Operations Executive. It was a hush-hush body, a sort of dirty tricks department, I know all about the SOE because I was working for them in London. Mission 101 had a number of excellent people working there, mainly old Africa hands, and these people felt that in order to ferment a rebellion of the tribes against the Italians, it would be desirable to have the Emperor advance with much fanfare, albeit slowly, into the interior of the country, in the general direction of Addis Ababa. And once Generals Platt and Cunningham were ensconced in Addis Ababa, the Emperor would sign a treaty with Great Britain and, then

– and only then – he would be invited to enter Addis Ababa himself. This is how things were done in those days, and why not? The cost of throwing out the Italians, quite apart from the number of British and Commonwealth soldiers who would need to die in its attainment, was measured in tens of millions of pounds. Mission 101's budget alone was a cool one million. Britain wanted to recoup its expenses, this had always been the guiding principle of the British Empire.

The man in charge of this entire operation was Archibald Wavell. He wanted this thing to succeed because Britain had been in the war now for almost two years and hadn't chalked up a single victory against the Germans, he hoped to do better against the Italians. He needed someone to lead this 'procession' into Ethiopia and he asked London for Wingate. He knew Wingate because it was he who gave the green light for the SNS in Palestine. I imagine that Wavell had Wingate down as a fomenter of rebellion. How right he was.

Naturally, while other officers made the journey to Cairo by air in two days, the War Office sent Wingate by the long, slow and dangerous route by sea to Cape Town through the Southern Atlantic and then up through Africa to Cairo, a ten week Odyssey.

Orde finally arrived, and here was a fresh opportunity for him to make new and powerful enemies among his countrymen. He requested several colleagues from Palestine to join him, including a Jewish SNS boy, Avraham Akavia, and dear Tony Simonds. His letters to me at this time – all hand-written – were full of day-to-day things, but telling me nothing about his tremendous battles. I refer to his battles with the British generals.

The first thing Wingate did was to get up the nose of old Platt, the General commanding in Khartoum, under whose wing he was supposed to mount his campaign in Abyssinia.

Orde was putting it in train and was himself in Khartoum, and Platt courteously invited him to spend a weekend on the River Nile on his houseboat. One evening as they sat drinking their whiskies and soda, he said to Platt, playfully, 'all generals over 50 ought to be shot', and Platt replied, that he was 56, and he never forgave him. Of course Platt should have said, 'my dear boy, I'm 56 so watch your step', but evidently he hadn't got the sense or the humour.

When Orde arrived at Mission 101, it was just a place where people were milling around, it was not yet an HQ, and he went directly to introduce himself to Haile Selassie. He was a very famous man by this time, practically a household name, so Wingate knew a great deal about him, most notably his Christian faith, for Haile Selassie was a devout believer, and this was a very solid foundation on which to build a relationship. Indeed during the next two months the two men came to know one another well, the circumstances were propitious. Haile Selassie told me many years later that from the first moment that he met my husband, he knew that this was a man whose word he could trust absolutely.

Wingate took Mission 101 by the scruff of its neck, turned it upside down and came up with a new plan and a new name. Mission 101 became 'The Patriot Campaign'. He named his formation 'Gideon Force' of which the Emperor approved, and he decided to march directly to Addis Ababa by the shortest route possible. He had 50 junior officers, 40 other ranks and about 2000 native troops. They traveled over land which had not been properly mapped, and they endured great hardship. He fought off his colleagues who challenged his decisions, he ignored orders from his superiors, and he led the Emperor in triumph into Addis Ababa. With a tiny, badly-equipped force he fulfilled his mission, killing 3000 enemy soldiers and capturing 18,000 prisoners and a large amount of weaponry for good measure.

He came in early and vastly under budget; I believe that the final bill for the Patriot Campaign was in the region of 320,000 pounds. This was all, by any standard, an outstanding achievement. Many of those in Gideon Force who had grumbled and opposed him at the outset were, by the end of the campaign true believers, and many volunteered to follow him into his next campaign. Wingate's overriding tactic had been to deceive the enemy into believing that he was facing a much larger British force, and this deception was sustained over an advance covering 300 miles, involving four significant battles and several dozen skirmishes, during a four month period. This campaign of disinformation reached its peak at the battle of Agibar. Facing Wingate was a force of 12,000 Italian and colonial soldiers under the command of a Colonel Maraventano. The Italians were defending a fort in an impregnable position, they had artillery, machine guns, three million bullets, vehicles, but they were short on food and medical supplies. Wingate had an exhausted force of Abyssinian auxiliaries in filthy, ragged condition with defective radios, inadequate supplies, but one operational mortar section. Ignoring orders from his superior officer to withdraw, he advanced to within sight of the fort, and commenced his attack. He then sat down and wrote a letter to Maraventano, flattering his courage and urging him to spare his men further hardship, and had it delivered under a white flag. Maraventano wrote back in a self-pitying vein, but assuring his opposite number that he would fight to the last bullet. Again Wingate wrote telling him that his courage and honour were known and it was not necessary to demonstrate it further at the expense of his men who had fought bravely and suffered greatly, and he had until three pm to answer.

Maraventano decided that he had no other course but to surrender. He would have known that the Abyssinian campaign was going badly for the Italians, but he had many options; he could have fought, he could have waited, he could have withdrawn along open lines of communication, he could have done all three and, to be sure, he could have broken out of the fort and annihilated Wingate's ragtag band, so why did he throw in the towel at that time? I will tell you why. The poor man was terrified. Against the evidence of Maraventano's own eyes, Wingate had, over time, put the fear of God into him.

This was an extraordinary gift that he had – I think one must call it a gift –which I once witnessed for myself in Palestine. Orde and I were at the home of the Weizmanns, he was convalescing from one of his injuries, I believe, and he was to return to his base of operations. I was packed and ready to accompany him, bright-eyed and bushy-tailed, and then he told me that I wasn't coming, and that I should return to our home in Jerusalem. But I was coming! Of course I was coming, I wouldn't hear otherwise, and then I made a terrible scene. I was a very difficult young thing at times, ungovernable, fearful moods and he was very patient usually, but on this occasion, I was standing in the middle of the drawing room, creating, growling, snarling, as the servants say, and he produced a revolver. He calmly put a shell into one of the chambers, twiddled it to the right place, presented it at me and said, 'if you don't behave yourself I shall shoot you'. I believed him, I was terrified. I instantly came to my senses and passed into a mood of sunny cooperation. At the time I was awfully pleased with him, I thought it was exactly the right thing to do, but now looking back, I wonder why I didn't look him coolly in the eye and say, 'Very well, shoot me if you must'. After all, we were in the home of the most important man in Jewry, standing on a very attractive and old Persian carpet, with priceless paintings and first edition books all around us, would he really have been so inconsiderate to his hosts? And I believe shooting your wife at short range is a criminal offense. And all because I wanted to follow him to his camp! And yet there I stood, my mouth suddenly gone quite dry, thinking, 'mother will be annoyed'. How did he do it?

Perhaps Signor Maraventano is now sitting in an old and very beautiful castle somewhere in Tuscany – I very much hope he is – sipping one of those small cups of coffee, asking himself the same question. Anyway, the effect of Wingate's precipitate delivery of the Emperor to his capital, was to make the victory over the Italians as much the Emperor's as it was that of Generals Platt and Cunningham, and this did not go down well in Cairo.

Wingate was duly summoned to GHQ and hauled across the carpet for having disobeyed orders. His temporary rank of Colonel was taken from him and he was reduced to Major. His proper request for pay, restitution and decorations for his soldiers was turned down, he was treated with disdain. At the higher level they were not even angry – bemused is perhaps the better word – that a junior officer had interfered with state business; powerful interests were involved. There was surely no precedent for such behaviour. It is one thing to disobey a command, and quite another to overrule policy. What infuriated was the fact they were prevented from acting against him because his connections with powerful people in London was known. At the lower level, it wasn't just a matter of sniffing the wind, his fellow officers shunned him because he wouldn't play the game; he might have been back at Charterhouse.

Major Wingate became belligerent. He wrote a very angry report of the campaign, an ill-advised report, critical of certain officers, at one point insulting, which further inflamed the general animosity towards him. After the war I was with Derek and Mary in their home, and he told me that he was shocked by some of the reports he heard from Orde's officers of the Ethiopian campaign. I think the problem was that he went into Abyssinia with a great rage for what had gone before, and he took it out on everyone he met, making only the smallest distinction between friend and foe.

I am going to say something now, say it I must. Most writers would put it at the end, a sort of postscript, but I'm going to plant this rather large assertion somewhere in the middle so that the reader may carry it in his mind as the story unfolds, and this is as good a place as any. What kind of man was Wingate? Here was a man who moved through his life with a burning, restless ambition to make his mark on the world. He believed himself to be without peer, he recognized no authority apart from God. About a year after we were married he failed to gain admission to Staff College. A mere captain, he decided do something about it. He knew that the CIGS at the time was in the Plain, observing maneuvers, it wasn't far from our house in Bulford, so he climbed the hill on which the great man stood, surrounded as he was by lieutenant-generals and ADCs, a good crowd. He insinuated himself into the group, stood directly in front of the CIGS – his name was Deverell – introduced himself, and asked him if he was aware that he (Wingate) had been passed over for the staff college of Camberly, and proceeded to inform Deverell of the reasons why he should not have been passed over, placing supporting documents in the great man's hand. Did you ever hear of such imbecilic impertinence? What had this insignificant matter to do with the Chief of the Imperial General Staff? That is not the extraordinary part to the story. What is incomprehensible is the fact that the CIGS didn't have him whipped on the spot. Deverell was almost tongue-tied, taken entirely off-balance by behaviour for which, again, there was no precedent.

Wingate was sure of himself to a superhuman degree. Was he insane, as many commentators have suggested? I would say not. Not that I am a judge in such matters, my own sanity may be called into question. His grip on reality was comprehensive, his mind ranged over great distances, he had an infinite grasp of detail, he connected things which were beyond the range of others, he might have been a match for Napoleon. One doesn't read about griping colleagues and enraged superiors in the records of Alexander of Macedonia because such trifles were erased by the brilliance of his achievement. Wingate was killed before he could amass a body of work which would have silenced the bleating of small men who stood in his shadow. How else is one to understand this extraordinary man?

As I was saying, the generals in Cairo were livid but without redress. Unfortunately Orde now came down with symptoms of malaria, which he neglected to attend to in a proper manner. He was administered medicine which had powerful side-effects and he experienced daytime delirium and intense Wingatian depression. He decided that there was nothing to live for, so he cut his own throat. There are a number of ways of committing suicide, some requiring more determination than others. The unsuccessful Roman general fell on his sword. That couldn't have been easy; how did he prevent the hilt from slipping along the ground? Or prevent himself from toppling sideways and the point entering the spleen or liver, which would have given him a slow death? He would have had to bury the hilt in the ground, spread his feet very wide apart, and throw himself forward with some force. Perhaps a judicious shove was the final service of the faithful armour-bearer. Well, the same goes for plunging a general-purpose knife into one's throat and certainly for this reason he failed. He was found by a stranger and rushed to hospital. Within hours all of Cairo knew of it. I don't doubt that the sound of corks popping could be heard in Cairo that night because now surely Wingate was for the madhouse, his career finished.

Chapter 9

Mother had become Orde's most devoted follower, she twittered in his presence but never, I should say, flirted, and wished only to bathe in his reflected glory, but more than anything she had to be introduced to all our new friends. Papa's attitude to him changed at about the same time but for different reasons and with different effect; it was when Orde got his first DSO. Such were the times, the country was changing. Under normal circumstances, let us say that a woman is walking down the street, she will look at the man she passes, modestly of course, his gait, the cut of his clothes, his eyes, his mouth or his hair, it is elementary mating behaviour. But now, it is all changed, her eyes go straight to badges and pips and ribbons and even a limp can be attractive because gallantry is the thing which is at a premium, a sort of savings account in the bank, that which confers protection and safety. Goodness, and when she spies at a distance the somber blue of the RN, preferably with a little braid on the cuff of the jacket, she becomes quite undone, you can't see her for pheromones. You see, a woman's most powerful urge is for security and she has an in-built barometer that tells her when danger is approaching – she will spot it long before the male of the species – and react accordingly. The barometers of the women of Britain in 1940 were falling, and telling their owners to send out mating signals to the men in uniform, which of course made a man want to put on a uniform.

What is the mechanism by which one day a man says, 'I will not go forth, this is not worth dying for', and the next day, the same man will say, 'I cannot live forever, let me at least die gallantly'? Winston Churchill was a large part of it; he came to power, it was as if he had turned a switch, courage spread across the land and Britain was redeemed.

At this time great balloons were floated high in the air all over London, held to the ground with steel cables to snag German bombers as they passed, and in that jittery, waiting atmosphere, one could pick up property in central London really for very little money. Papa bought me a flat in Mayfair, close to Shepherd's market, it had an entrance hallway, two small rooms and a kitchen with standing room for one, and every wall was a bookshelf except where there was a door or a window, it fitted me and my books like a glove. He put 300 pounds into my bank account, and set up a direct debit of a small amount of money every month, a sort of allowance, so that I wouldn't have to go out to work. He was throwing money around as if there was no tomorrow, which was exactly the point, and it wasn't for his feckless daughter, of course, it was for his son-in-law's armour-bearer, to enable her better to serve him, and provide him with a hearth while he was out there protecting us all from

Hitler. To this hearth, our little nest, the conquering hero was now to return

I hadn't seen Orde for 15 months and hadn't heard from him for over four. I had of course avidly followed his brilliant campaign, Tony Simonds sent me a marvelous account of Orde's work, as did Akavia, and then I learnt that he had suddenly been taken ill and rushed to hospital in Cairo. There followed a most remarkable procession of our dear Jewish friends who made the difficult journey from Jerusalem to be at his bedside, and who wrote me letter-reports on his recovery. I remember in particular a letter from Ben Gurion, so very out of character, assuring me of his good colour and high morale, and sending me his warmest wishes, I thought it strange that he of all people should have made this particular journey, but I took it for what it was. I wanted desperately to go to Orde, but I would have had to disguise myself as a soldier to get a berth on a ship, and no one could tell me when they would let him out of hospital – I pictured myself waving to him as our ships passed one another on the high seas. There was nothing for me to do but wait. After about two months I was notified that Orde had left Cairo, then that his ship had docked at the Clyde, and then I was asleep in bed early one morning and the phone rang and it was my husband calling from a phone box around the corner to tell me that he had arrived. This, now, was the first time I had heard his voice in 15 months, and it had changed. 'Why didn't he come directly to the apartment?' I remember thinking, 'was it to give me time to pass the crew of HMS Penelope out of the window?' I was awkward, I said, 'why don't you come up?' or some such thing, I should have been excited, and squealed on the phone like a normal woman.

I suddenly felt very, very anxious about seeing him, it had been so long, and he had gone so silent on me, I didn't know exactly who this man was anymore. I needed to fortify myself, take a deep breath. I was standing in the doorway to our flat in my dressing gown and slippers, watching him as he walked up the staircase in his faded uniform, with a large, well-used kitbag over his shoulder, he didn't look at all officer material. His steps were more deliberate than I remembered, and when he drew close enough, I saw something in his eyes, and then the large, fresh scar next to his adam's apple.

I don't know what happened next. I think I understood in that instant that the wound in his neck had been self-inflicted. I remember I felt a sudden stab of pain in my own neck, my body felt quite weak, I let out an involuntary scream, covered my face, and then I think I launched myself at him, threw myself on him in floods of tears, almost casting the two of us down the staircase he had just so laboriously ascended.

My affections for my husband altered during our years together, as is surely the case in every marriage. Whereas in the early days, while we were waiting to be married and after, what I feared was the intensity of my obsession with him, latterly there were times when I felt a positive dislike for him, which I had to push down. He drove himself so hard, he drove his colleagues hard, and on occasion he forgot himself when he was with me. It was only a shadow on the surface of something very solid, but the climate had been subject to change. The shock on the staircase had the effect of permitting me to enter that solid something; perhaps for the first time in my life I was experiencing a true empathy for another being, binding me to him more tightly. I understood – with awe – Orde's unique capacity for suffering and depth of feeling. Look at me, three-legged tiger, struggling to uncover my stunted feelings, and now read this, flowing freely from Peggy's pen to Derek in 1972:

'Many times he himself mistook the way, but his faith only once, I think, wavered... No man can have gone so far into the extremes of himself, and come out unharmed and victorious. Orde was a great man in every possible sense of the word.'

After a separation of nine years (an unspeakably cruel separation), and from a distance of two rapidly diverging lives, Peggy had perfectly understood what I had barely grasped. How could Peggy have known that Orde had come out of this nadir experience unharmed and victorious? Who knew this apart from me? No. It came down to this: Peggy had loved Orde more than I, understood him better than I. Is there no justice in this world?

We had three months together in London until he would be called away again, and throughout it all, he kept this delightful serenity. He was almost effulgent, he had a sort of glow about him, it was remarked upon by all our friends. I remember thinking, it was almost a prayer, 'if I had the knowledge that the attempt would not come off and I had the power to put him through this agonizing experience, knowing that his life would be spared, I should have put him through it, because it made such a difference to him'. And I see no reason to alter that belief of mine. As for Peggy, I feel an outpouring of love and chagrin to this towering, stoic, passionate English woman. I want to hold her and be held by her.

Orde's medical report was not good, as you can imagine, and he was on his way to being invalided out of the Army. It was clear to me that there was nothing wrong with him mentally or physically. Whatever had afflicted him had passed, and he was now ready to return to the fighting. He appeared before an army medical review board and was declared unfit for active duty, the War Office didn't want him back. Chaim was in London, extremely concerned, and willing to do everything in his power to rehabilitate Orde. Of course Chaim's influence even now was considerable, and he put this influence at our disposal. He called for Benzion Khounine to examine Orde thoroughly, and he concurred with my own view that Orde was as fit as a fiddle. Benzion went to see his old professor, Lord Horder, who had been the Royal Physician for many years, and was now a ministerial advisor to the Government. He explained Orde's predicament and persuaded him to examine Orde.

There followed three long examinations of Orde by Lord Horder, and they got on rather well. Horder then received visits from Chaim Weizmann, Leopold Amery, Lewis Namier, Patrick Gordon Walker and uncle Tom Cobley and all, who presented themselves at his consulting rooms to vouch for Orde's mental stability. I never met Lord Horder and therefore I don't know how he understood this feverish political activity surrounding his patient, for he wasn't a man to be pushed around. He then spoke to colleagues of his on the Medical Board, and was told that their decision had been final and not subject to appeal, so when Lord Horder submitted his own report on Orde to the War Office, he added a personal note that if Wingate was not re-designated 'fit for active duty', he would resign from his job at the ministry. Orde had this effect on certain people. Well, this finally did the trick, because Orde received his clean bill of health in short order. And all the while, just the other side of Trafalgar Square, that hypocrite Churchill was bellowing at Alan Brooke, 'where are my young generals?' His most promising young general was sitting in London under his very nose, Churchill had not only heard of him, he had met him, and remembered him, the name of Wingate was on people's lips. And let us recall this moment in history; the Japanese have just invaded Burma, the Germans are within sight of Moscow, and in GHQ Cairo, those cowardly British generals, so recently toasting my husband's demise, would soon be feverishly burning their papers and re-arranging their bank accounts as Rommel advanced on Egypt. Orde's activities on behalf of the Jewish Legion were behind the obfuscations of the Medical Board. The war was going badly for Britain and there was a desperate shortage of combat officers, yet keeping Wingate out of uniform and out of Palestine meant more in certain circles than winning the war. To hell with them.

Having jumped through that particular hoop, Orde now required a staff appointment. One of the Labourites we had befriended through Leopold Amery was Harold Laski who thought highly of Orde, and now weighed in on his behalf. Harold was irrepressible, one felt he had a finger in all God's pies, and he took himself to see Churchill, and told him to his face that if Wingate was not returned to active duty, he would raise the matter in the House of Commons. Chaim gained an interview with Churchill, and made a forlorn appeal, 'send Major Wingate to organize the Jews for the defense of Palestine against the German advance'. Letters on Orde's behalf were sent off to Generals Wavell, Ironside, Dill, Alan Brooke, and it felt as if the gods themselves were involved in a celestial battle over the fate of this one small man, for now Lord Moyne stepped into the fray and declared 'if Wingate is allowed back into Palestine, the entire Near East will go up on flames'. What utter nonsense! But Moyne was a powerful and wealthy anti-Zionist sitting in the Colonial Office, and it was known that he had Churchill's ear.

While these Olympian deliberations were going on, Orde and I were having the most wonderful time together, and I felt younger than I had ever felt, certainly younger than I had felt when I was young. He was technically supposed to report back after his convalescence, but he worried that if he did, they might succeed in shunting him off to a pool of officers and lose him in further red tape. So he decided to vanish, to dive beneath the surface. To avoid being seen, we steered clear of Piccadilly and the main thoroughfares, and took to the side streets, and if he saw anybody wearing red and gold tabs approaching, we immediately took cover, giggling like two schoolgirls. It was at this period of his life, too, that he indulged his respect for the navy, which he'd always strongly felt. He used to tell me when I first knew him that the navy in peacetime was the only efficient service, because it was the only service that had an acid test. He didn't seem to notice the air force at that time. The acid test was that they had to navigate their ships and make a landfall. Whereas the army in peacetime had nothing to do at all, no acid test. He always spoke of the navy with affection and respect, and he amused himself at this period by refusing to salute any military uniform, he'd only salute a naval one. Various astonished midshipmen with half an inch of gold braid used to get a terrific salute, and one day we were out walking in the West End and we saw old AP Herbert coming towards us. He was quite unmistakable, he had a schnozzle as long as your arm, and he was in the river police I believe, he did a very good work of war anyhow, gallant creature. He was wearing a scruffy navy blue outfit with a sort of yachting cap, and Orde drew himself up and saluted quite splendidly. AP Herbert, amazed, saluted too and passed on.

One night in January, Orde and I were in Hill Street, not having gone to bed but preparing for it, when we heard the usual air raid warning at about 11 o'clock, and the sound of the German bombers and their sinister engines overhead, then the whistle of their sticks of bombs. We heard a weeeee, then a very dull kind of thud very near but no explosion. We looked at each other, thought about it, took no notice, until a while later the head porter of our block of flats came to the door and said, 'there's an unexploded bomb sir, at the public house behind your bedroom window, and the police have asked us to evacuate the building, will you please prepare yourself to leave. All the occupants of this block of flats are going to the air raid shelter of the Dorchester.' So Orde said, 'well, very well, it will take some time' and closed the door. We looked at each other and we said, do we really want to spend the night at the Dorchester with strangers, or shall we remain here? It is very unlikely that the bomb which is lodged in the Red Lion will actually blow us to smithereens, these bombs were not of such a magnitude, and between us we decided to stay behind, we didn't want to be shifted by the bloody Germans.

Having once decided that we were going to stay, the next thing we had to do was to furnish ourselves with some reason because we knew perfectly well that we would be visited by the guardians of the people's welfare. And indeed we were; almost at once, an air raid warden, the chief air raid warden for the district, excellent man, solid decisions and hard-working, he came in and said, 'you are preparing to leave, are you not. We know it's a 500 lbs bomb and we think it will go off at any moment. The whole area is to be evacuated, may I ask you to leave at once?' Orde said, 'yes indeed, don't worry about us we shall be quite alright, and the air raid warden left, having many things on his mind. Finally came that representative of that body of men for whom I have the greatest respect of all, the police. A large British constable appeared in the doorway, and he said, 'sir, why have you not left, you know that everybody in this area is supposed to go to the Dorchester Hotel and take cover there, this bomb may explode at any moment, and Orde said to him, 'officer, you and I understand these things, I have secret papers here, I am in charge of them, I must remain by them, I cannot leave the building'. If the police officer had paused to consider, he might have asked him if the bulk of the papers was so great that only an elephant could carry it, or that he had to sit beside it all the time. But, sensible man, he accepted it, another member of a uniformed force and an officer at that, he accepted his word, and withdrew. And then we settled down to wait for the bomb to explode.

We made one or two concessions to it, we took our mattresses into the sitting room, laid them on the floor there, we opened all the doors and windows so that the blast would have free passage and not blow the walls in too much perhaps, and then we lay down peacefully on our mattresses and waited. At dawn, the bomb exploded. It entirely demolished the little public house, the Red Lion, reducing it to a pile of gravel and rubble and, to my great delight a free passage though which the sunlight came in the morning to my bedroom. Nobody was hurt of course, everybody had been evacuated by all the civilian services. We were in the sitting room on the other side, lying on our mattresses, when we heard the explosion, we got up and I looked out of the sitting room windows which had been repaired in makeshift manner after a previous blast. It was a lovely, soft clear morning, the sun had not quite risen, the sky was a hyacinth blue, total silence, there was only us in the whole of Mayfair, windless, clear, and as we looked out of the window, we saw the strangest phenomenon. Down from the blue heavens fluttered layer upon layer of paper, immaculate sheets of writing paper, the same size, the same shape, like snowflakes they fell and they came down slowly, slowly, without a sound and they filled the whole horizon, and down they fell past our window, and that was the only effect that the bomb had on us, I saw a sight which I shall never forget.

Orde was invited to go down and lecture at South Eastern command, somewhere in Kent. I think it was on the Abyssinian campaign, and the weather was freezing, it was

December or January, and they sent an open jeep or land rover for him. He lectured for a couple of hours, and he came back in the same car, and contracted the most appalling throat infection called streptococcus viridans. I believe it turns your throat green, hence the viridans, it also brings a stench of corruption, the whole flat stank. He was frightfully ill with a temperature up in the 104's, and Benzion, that devoted friend and doctor, stayed beside him a great part of the time, and brought him a throat specialist from Harley Street, a little man like a terrier who thankfully didn't mince his words at all. He took us out after examining Orde and said, this can be a fatal disease and there's nothing we can do for it. If the infection passes the natural barriers - glands or something – it will enter his bloodstream and he will die of septicemia. He then departed. Orde had been ill for some time, I don't remember how long, ten days, two weeks, something like that, I used to sleep on the floor beside his bed.

His sister Monica is convinced that she nursed him, but actually she was away, she was doing something else and she couldn't come, but Sybil Wingate left her important war work to relieve me for two days. Then we got in a night nurse for him, an excellent woman, an Australian I remember, she was slightly doolally, she saw blue flames around Orde's head; well I think she probably did see them and it was I who was lacking, because I couldn't. Anyway, on this particular night, the specialist said, the next 36 hours will determine whether he lives or dies. Benzion and I, leaving him with the night nurse, went and sat in the sitting room. and Benzion said nothing He just thought and thought, and presently at about eleven o'clock, he said, 'I've had an idea, it may not work but I'm going to try it, and then he mentioned the name of some new drug. I think it was cortisone perhaps, or a related substance because he told me that it was obtained from the cortices of dogs, from the great nerve that runs down your spinal column, or at the base of your brain. Anyhow, a potent source of various substances, I suppose. He said, 'I hope we shall be able to get it, we shall go out now'.

So we went out into the black and silent streets of wartime London, about half past eleven at night, and we started to tour around the big chemists, the really big ones in the doctors' area, Wimpole Street and Wigmore Street, they stay open all night, there for emergency cases. And you know it was eerie, it was something to remember. Everything was totally empty and deserted, no lights in the streets, no cars, nothing, no people. We went to one of these great emporiums where a little wicker gate admitted us to a sort of barricaded door and silent rooms smelling of cosmetics with shelves packed with this and that, and far-away in a corner, standing at a tall desk writing in a ledger, a little man in a white coat. Benzion showed his credentials and asked for the stuff, and two or three times we had the same experience, the man went into a great safe, a sort of strong room where they kept the valuable drugs, and he poked about and came out and said he hadn't got it. It was now about half past midnight and Benzion said, 'we'll go to a last place, we'll go to the wholesale warehouse at Parke-Davis', and this is where we went. I have no idea where it was, but they had it, it was in a stone bottle, not large but solid stone; not solid, obviously, but if felt as though it was. And I remember we got back into the car and drove like hell and got back to Hill Street, and he injected Orde with it, something like one o'clock in the morning, and then we sat down to wait.

At 8 o'clock the night nurse left and we went in to see him, and Benzion put his hand on his head and then he said, 'the fever is less'. Well, he turned the corner, turned it that morning, and he recovered smoothly without any check. He couldn't swallow for weeks. When he could swallow, I set him on oysters and claret, Shepherd's Market provided them. Fancy being able to get oysters, and being able to pay for them too! And papa's wine merchant round the corner in South Audley Street provided the claret – I had to pay for it of course – and by the time he got out of bed he was looking as sleek as a racehorse. He looked wonderful, very handsome too. Orde lived life at such a frighteningly intense pace that I came to regard these bouts of illness, terrible as they were, to be nature's way of protecting him from seizing up like a racing car engine. I could not but notice that with every reverse Orde seemed to come back stronger and steadier, the check did him good.

During the two days or so that Sybil came to relieve me, I moved in with the Weizmanns. I dragged myself across the way to the Dorchester where Vera had made up a bed in the sitting room. She took one look at me and wrote a prescription for a powder and sent someone off to get it – there were two Dr. Weizmanns – and bestowed upon me two very good nights' sleep. During the day I didn't stir from my corner, reading magazines, nibbling hotel delicacies, and sipping sherry while Chaim and Vera went about their business, again I felt entirely at home. People came and went, I knew that there was no progress with the Jewish Legion, the news coming out of Europe was unbearable, I could now observe the strain he was under, they were getting ready for a trip to New York. Over lunch Chaim grumbled about Churchill, he said, 'I know that he has a very soft spot for the Jews but does not lift a finger to help us. He says he cannot but I say he will not' and then he added cryptically, 'I intend to go over the Prime minister's head', which I took to be a reference to his upcoming trip. The following day Vera took me out to lunch and then to Selfridges which was packed, just another day in London during the Blitz – one felt so proud to be British – and then we arrived at Victoria Station where she had promised to see off a friend. We were standing together on the platform alongside a magnificent Pullman train. In those days chocolate brown and cream painted carriages were a feature of the more sumptuous services, and each of these splendid pieces of rolling stock was endowed with a name, the name of a woman. And these were painted very large on the side of each carriage. Now as Vera and I patrolled arm-in-arm, I turned my eyes to these carriages, looking at them admiringly, they were always so fresh and spic and span, and I saw two of them coupled together, and the name of one of them was Vera and the name of the other was Lorna.

Orde got his appointment but it was very far from the one he wanted. It had something to do with the Chinese in Burma, his rank was not given, all we were told was that Wavell was in charge and he had specifically asked for Wingate. I later discovered that Leopold Amery was behind it, he had cabled Wavell suggesting that he send for Orde. He was ordered to proceed to Delhi, but by sea! Harold Laski heard about it and went straight to Churchill, 'they are sending the best guerrilla fighter we have by sea!' A cable arrived to send him to India by air, first priority. Everything quickly came into sharp focus. The Wingates all came out of the woodwork to say their farewells, there was the usual panic, all the last minute things to attend to, papers to arrange, but this I take in my stride. What I do not take in my stride is saying goodbye, because I have never learnt how. I do not like station platform farewells – it's all people seem to do in the films of this period – not because I don't wish to be sad, or because I'm embarrassed to make a public display of my feelings, it is neither of these things. When one's husband or son goes off to fight in a great war, one has no idea how long it will be until one will see him again, or indeed if one will see him again, and this is indeed a time to pull out one's handkerchief. But it never occurred to me that Orde would not return. I knew not only that he was doing something he enjoyed, but that he was also performing a service for the country, and that at the same time he would probably be covering himself in glory. I called to him from the door to our flat as he went down the stairs, 'good hunting!' which I think is a very good thing to say to a warrior, but I don't think I would have shouted it on a station platform in London in the winter of 1942.

Chapter 10

I was now perfectly content to be on my own in war-torn London, my mind was at ease on a number of matters, I had a large number of friends of all kinds and both sexes, I had a char lady who came in occasionally and cleaned me up, and I ate all of my meals out. I decided to get a job, something interesting, and presently I found one, a cloak and dagger job. I was neither the cloak nor the dagger. I was a cipher clerk in SO2 which was the headquarters of SOE.

We worked in Marks and Spencer head office, which had kindly been donated to us by Simon Marks, and the whole place was partitioned, honeycombed with small offices in which men and women of varying value worked, or pretended to. Some of them were no doubt doing great things, others were simply spivs, because SO2, and indeed SOE, was a very mixed concern. Its achievements were very great in some fields, no praise is too high. The operators in the occupied countries, this was our principle work of course, they were the stay-behind men or the moonlight drop men who went in to organize resistance and sabotage in France, Norway, Holland and Belgium. They had outposts in Africa, and of course all British staging posts and listening posts, Hong Kong was perhaps the furthest away, Australia hardly came into it, she was not fighting any particular war in her part of the world. But we had one or two posts in benevolent neutral countries like Portugal, although none in malevolent neutral countries like Spain. Tangier, though, which was Spanish, provided a keyhole through which to peer and listen. Incidentally, SOE commanded a good deal of money, they provided it with a secret fund, I never knew how much, I should think it was considerable – of course in war money ceases to have any meaning, you simply have to make the stuff in the basement.

The job was quite interesting, I was one of the operators that had to deal with the moondrop men. I was trained in their special codes which were supposed to be unbreakable and had them locked and unlocked and re-unlocked on a kind of square paper, strange alterations to the texts and ins and outs of all kinds, quite a difficult job, one had to concentrate very closely. These men each had a certain period in the 24 hours when he came on the air on his own private wireless transmitter and he was picked up by the BBC special SOE sending-and-receiving station which was somewhere in England, I don't know where. Then this information would immediately be passed by the BBC to the SOE, in code of course. Each shift of cipher clerks had one person trained in this particular code, and I had to render it into clear, and sometimes the messages were very heartrending. I remember there was a particularly splendid operator, I think his codename was 'Overcloud Major' and he was working in Norway and one day I received the message,

'Gestapo surrounding the house, good luck, goodbye'. That was the end of Overcloud Major, we never heard from him again nor did we hear what became of him.

One day I went to the files, I used to arrive half an hour early some days to weed out the files that had accumulated during my period of rest, and I saw that there was a cable, of course in code and carefully decoded by one of my colleagues, a cable from one of our SOE people in Tangier, saying that the Spanish government would be very glad if the British government would make them a small present. This would help to keep them out of the war, otherwise they might possibly come in on Hitler's side, or pass him more information than they did already. And what do you think the small present was going to be? Well it was a cathedral costing two and a half million pounds. We built it for the Spaniards in Tangier. Just how much good this did our cause I have no idea, but I would say very little indeed. If they were going to keep out of the war because of a cathedral, I think one could have offered them something smaller, perhaps, it might have kept them out just as well. A parish church perhaps, anyway that was Tangier.

There were other amusing cables, Cairo was a great place, an immense number of people congregated in Cairo, people of the lowest caliber many of them, and SOE was no exception. Our people in Cairo were a thoroughly bad lot, corrupt and ineffective, like the Egyptians themselves, and on one occasion I found a cable, it was considered so important that it had been split in half which is what they do with such secret information; they send one half in one cable and in case the enemy tumbles to it they send the remaining half in another cable so they perhaps don't get it. This was a suggestion by some Egyptian lady, well, Levantine lady, married to an Egyptian diplomat and a former mistress of Pierre Laval, the satanic little fellow and collabourator running Vichy France at that time with poor silly old Petain, the gaga Marshal. Laval, black and beady like a blood-sucking spider, was apparently vulnerable to this person's charms, and it was suggested that she go to France on behalf of Britain and try to achieve some kind of God-knows-what with Laval. What was she supposed to get him to do I wonder, that was not specified. The nub of the matter was that she was going to be EXPENSIVE REPEAT EXPENSIVE: 10,000 pounds. Well, I'm sorry to say that the expenditure was authorized.

On the whole it gave me a very dusty outlook on human behaviour. If anything could have made me cynical, working in that office would have made me cynical. A cynic is somebody who suspects the motives of his fellow man, and it seemed to me that the motives of many men in that particular organization were base; they were mean and they were base.

Although it was interesting enough, we worked exceedingly hard, we had four shifts because the work was so concentrated. For two nights running in every eight we worked 12 hour shifts from 9pm to 9am. In the summer months, with all the windows closed as they had to be, summer and winter – in case some scrap of paper should float out and Hitler should pick it up and win the war on it – we had very little air to breathe. I fell a victim to anemia, and one day, walking home from a luncheon engagement, I lost my memory.

It was a beautiful clear day in summer, and to this day I don't know where I'd been, or with whom I'd had my luncheon, but I arrived at the corner of Grosvenor Square from North Audley Street, heading of course towards my flat, when suddenly I realized that I didn't know where I was going. I asked myself 'what is your name?' No idea. Searched in my bag and my pockets for some sort of clue but there was none. Grosvenor Square lay before me, bathed in sunshine, peaceful, secure, so I said to myself, 'I obviously started out on this journey knowing where I was going, so I must be on the right track. I will walk around Grosvenor Square and see if I can recover my memory, and if things get too bad, and time passes, and I still have no clue to my identity, I'll go to the police, because they are experienced in these sorts of things and they know the questions to ask you.

I turned left and I started to walk very slowly along the broad pavement of Grosvenor Square, and I asked myself all kinds of questions. Do you know what's happening in the world? Yes, there's a war, I knew all about the war. Your parents, can you remember them? No, I couldn't remember them. Are you married? I looked down at my wedding ring, Yes. To whom? Complete blank. Can you remember anything about history, what has gone before you? Yes, indeed, William the Conqueror, 1066 and all that. And so I went steadily, slowly forward. I knew all about what was happening outside my own life, and nothing of myself. Now as I progressed and went round one side of the square, then a second side, by the time I was on the third side, I began to feel alarmed I mean quite seriously alarmed. And so I did what I've always done, I began to talk to myself as if I was two people. It's alright, I said, your memory will come back, don't worry, it's only temporary, now, now Lorna, take it easy. Lorna! Lorna Wingate, 39 Hill Street, of course, and it all came flooding back again, so I went home, somewhat shaken. About five days later I'm rung up by some man in my flat. Now I knew who he was when we began the conversation and we talked to each other, half way through it I forgot who he was, I had no idea who was talking to me. I did my best to finish the conversation in some sort of hurry and to this day I don't know who it was. When I put down the telephone receiver, I called up Benzion Khounine and I told him what was wrong with me and he came round and told me that I'd got to stop this job, and go home for a long holiday. 'I shall write you a certificate', he said, 'to say that you're suffering from industrial anemia', what a wonderful disease I wonder if it still exists. I think I might have looked a little pitiful to Benzion, because he looked at me with a soulful expression, and said, 'Lorna, you are a green rose, and nature has decided to discontinue the experiment'. He could not have said anything truer, or more likely to lift my spirits. Anyway I went back to Scotland and quite soon got better

The war was a sort of holiday for diplomats, if they were too old to fight I imagine they went skiing and sailing in South America, because now all outstanding disputes in the world were being settled on the field of battle. The Jews, as we have seen, hadn't an army, and they weren't skiing and sailing in South America, they were in fact about to be butchered in Europe, and if the Nazis were the hammer, Great Britain and her allies were the anvil. We know now that the Nazis were still looking for a distant Island to which they might ship European Jewry until late 1941, but they hadn't the tonnage to do the job. Britain had the tonnage of course, but would not have made it available to the enemy even if that could mean saving the Jews because Britain had its own problems and the Jews were no concern of hers. Chaim finally, reluctantly, bitterly, accepted this to be the truth of the matter, therefore he went to America. If an historian wishes to know the moment in history in which the center of power in the world shifted from London to Washington, the date of Dr. Weizmann's arrival in New York is good as any. The tide hadn't yet turned militarily of course, Midway was still some months away, but they say that the Jews have a sixth sense about this type of thing and this is a good example of it.

A short while after my bout of amnesia there came a knock on my front door one evening and it was Victor Cazalet. People called on me all hours of the day and night, but I hadn't expected Victor and naturally I was curious. He was a firm Zionist and true friend of ours, a man of considerable influence. We sat down, I offered him a drink, we had a little gossip and I could see that he was impatient to talk about something, and then, with a coy smile, he told me what it was. He had received a note from Dr. Weizmann that morning. Chaim had sat in Washington this last week with the American President, and he had brought up Orde's name, and Mr. Roosevelt interrupted him and exclaimed, 'yes, Wingate, I have heard of him, he is an excellent soldier!' Well, I was astonished as you may well imagine. And proud! And then Victor reeled off more names that meant nothing to me, of important people in Washington who have agreed to bring pressure to bear on Mr. Churchill to have Orde brought back from India and posted to Jerusalem, to organize the defense of Palestine. I asked Victor if Orde was aware of these goings-on, and he said that if Orde didn't know by now, a message would be delivered to him in Assam in a few days, and then he added with emphasis that I should not refer to it in my correspondence; surely he didn't think that I was that foolish!

I kept this knowledge to myself, terrified of causing a foul-up in some way, and I remained in a high state of anticipation. This had become a pattern for me and for all lovers of Zion, and it once again ran true to form. Roosevelt spoke to General Dill and wrote to Churchill, and General Marshall, and Secretary Stimpson had become involved, but they could not move Churchill either to release Wingate from Burma, or to create a Jewish Division. Nothing doing, as the Americans say. Why was Churchill so obdurate on the subject of Palestine? He always claimed to be a Zionist, and I think indeed it might have been an enthusiasm of his at one time, but by 1942 he was completely focused on winning the war and saving the Empire, which was entirely proper, and he had put aside this particular enthusiasm, never to return.

Winston's attitude to the Jews at this stage is characterized by an action he now took. There was an unpublished poem written by Rudyard Kipling entitled 'The Burden of Jerusalem', and it was presented to Winston by a friend of his at the British Museum. Kipling wrote it at the end of his life, and his wife decided that it should not be published because of the controversy it might arouse. I imagine that the poem came to him as he perused the newspapers of the day, with weekly reports of Jewish misfortune. It's a beautiful poem but also cruel. Kipling saw the suffering of the Jew as his destiny, a thing between him and Him, nothing to be done about it, and sometime in October 1943, Churchill sent a copy of this unknown poem to his friend Franklin Roosevelt on the qt, a private communication from one great man to another. What was the meaning of this gesture? I think he was expressing his sorrow and personal discomfort about the fate of European Jewry, and felt that Roosevelt would understand the poem in exactly the way he had, and say, 'too bad for the poor Hymies, (I believe that is the American slang for Jews) but I guess they have it coming'. Churchill had washed his hands of the Jews, he knew of course what was going on in Europe and, as Chaim himself said, he wouldn't lift a finger to save them. In fact, because Palestine was now so central to Churchill's postwar vision for the recovery of British power, the smaller the number of Jews clamouring for entry into Palestine after the war, the better. In this sense Britain, holding her nose and turning her head away, provided the anvil to Hitler's hammer. In 1937 Orde had argued that the Jews of Palestine were essential to the Empire. In 1940 Churchill decided that the Jews of Palestine were inimical to the Empire. By

1945 Britain had won the war, but her empire had ceased to exist.

Orde was not being idle in India, he was making a nuisance of himself at GHQ in Delhi, making enemies and winning followers. He wrote to Michael Calvert, 'it is because I am what I am, objectionable to my critics though that is, that I win battles'. I thought that most succinct. Michael Calvert was running a school of jungle warfare when Orde arrived, and he became a believer right away. It was no small thing for this known and respected military thinker to defer to the new arrival, but he had the intelligence to see right away that he had much to learn from Orde, and he describes the process in the book he wrote, with humour and humility. Orde told me in one of his first letters that it would take a great deal of time to organize a campaign in this theater. The British Army in India, reeling from successive trouncings at the hands of the Japanese, was rotten with defeatism, apathy and confusion, but herein lay Orde's opportunity. Objectionable as he was, he was the only man in the place who was willing to attack the Japanese, and had a credible plan to do it. This was manna from heaven to Wavell, and because he had faith in Orde, he backed him to the hilt.

This was going to be a very long separation for me, seventeen months, constantly thinking about what was happening to him, plans and prospects, I had a lot of amusing things to do myself but naturally he was the central point of my thoughts. Many wives, army wives are not always interested in their husband's work, they find other interests in life and tend to go their own way, then merge at cocktail parties. Orde managed about one or two letters a month, he wrote them in a kind of military shorthand which I could decipher, and he did me the honour of going into great detail about what he was doing because he knew I understood these things and was interested in them, and I would duly write back, offering my own little commentary, 'surely you will have considered such and such', and then he would respond to my commentary in the most considerate and serious manner. These meant more to me than the most passionate love letter, I felt closer to him at this time than any time hitherto. I had for many years been buying second hand books on warfare, and not only were my bookshelves filled with some fairly weighty tomes, I had actually read them. He was at that time evolving his theories of jungle warfare and redefining the term 'lines of communication' which I found fascinating; how very useful I could have been to him there in the jungle; I would have been good for the men's morale, too, surely military regulations with regard to wives should not have applied to me! After a while he had to censor himself as his work advanced, he couldn't write about operational detail, obviously, so the letters became more commonplace, but one wanted to keep in touch.

Somewhere around about the summer, a thought came into my head. It occurred to me one day that Orde had no friends of his own generation and this was perfectly true. Derek was not exactly a friend at that time, he was an old acquaintance much valued – friendship perhaps could be used of their relationship – but they were not particularly close or so it seemed to me. I wondered what would happen if he should ever need, not a kindly clique of high-up civilians which he had already organized some years before, nor devoted young things with something of his own flame about them who were no doubt beginning to congregate about him, but solid people between thirty five and forty in the army, who he could discuss things with, or call on if he needed them.

This thought flitted in then flitted out, and a little while later, I suppose it must have been a couple of months or something of the sort, Derek suddenly turned up at my flat, quite uninvited and unexpected and asked me out to dinner. He didn't have Mary with him for once, so I thanked him very much and we went off together. As I said, never very happy together, never great friends, in fact I disliked him (slightly), and I think he disliked me slightly too and we sat on either side of the dinner table. I looked at him and I thought, 'Derek, well, I suppose there's always Derek'. And then I thought, 'Derek is not as fond of Orde as Orde is of Derek, and if Orde asked him to do something, it's quite on the cards that Derek would say no'. I wonder how one could attach Derek in some way. And I thought, well, he's accustomed to being governed by a strong-minded woman, and it's just possible that he would answer a female voice when he wouldn't answer a male one. I wonder how I can cast a line across his nose so that I can reel him in if he's wanted. Very cold-blooded, I know, but these were the thoughts, so I thought 'well, no harm done in trying, if it doesn't come off, in future times it won't matter all that much, I'll try it'. So I tried it. Poor Derek, I don't think he enjoyed himself much, he seemed terrified, and then he went back to where he came from.

One night, I think in the autumn of 1942, early autumn, there was a terrific air raid. It was my habit never to go to an air raid shelter, every block of flats had one. The Dorchester Hotel just across the way had a large air raid shelter where VIPs might have been able to go, passing the time doing their various things, some playing l'ecarte and some reading the Bible. I preferred to lie in bed, I used to listen to Top Music on the BBC late night program, and when it faded out it meant that the German bombers were approaching, and then I used to take up a book, I felt that the second floor of a block of flats was as safe as anything.

A Green Rose

Air raid shelters were not always perfectly safe. Bombs sometimes whizzed in at an angle and, leaving the main structure untouched, somehow lodged themselves in the basement and blew up the inhabitants. So I lay up in bed enjoying the comfort, reading Gibbon's Decline and Fall, I remember, at that time.

There I was, tucked up in bed, I used to await the night's happenings, and one night, there was as I say a really bad air raid. One used to hear not only the rather thrilling vroom, vroom, vroom of the bomber engines, but you'd hear the sticks of bombs falling and they always fell in threes of course, and they'd come down with their weeeee – bonk, and you had to see how close the latest bonk was to find out if the next one would get you, and this night the bonk was pretty close. It actually shore through the Rothchild house opposite my sitting room and plunged into the basement. It was a black night of course, no lights anywhere. I rushed through to find all my windows blown out, and the wall of the house bulging on that side. What was really agonizing was the sound. There was no sights to be seen at all but the night was full of sound. There was the sound of rushing water, it was like a torrent, it was like a river. It was a river, it was the water main that ran down Hill Street and served that whole area. The bomb forced an entry into the corner of the Rothschild house, and penetrated the water main, and the water was rising in the basement. And in the basement were twelve Free French girls making coffee for their comrades in the upper floors. They were drowning and nobody could get to them, and I heard their screams, and I heard the men trying to get to them. It was impossible, and they drowned. Afterwards the house was vacated, naturally, and for the rest of the war the Rothschild ballroom, all green and gold, hung open to the air opposite my sitting room windows. The whole of one side of the house was shorn away.

A similar thing happened in South Audley Street in the Egyptian Embassy, a good solid house. The Egyptian Ambassador was obviously like myself, he preferred to lie in bed waiting for death in comfort, but his employees preferred to descend to the basement when the air raid warnings came. Same story, the bomb left the ambassador intact on the second floor, killed everybody in the basement.

Some nights I went to dinner parties. They were organized by a woman I liked very much, many people jeered at her, Sybil Colefax, she was a lion-hunter but she was also a warm-hearted and decent woman. She couldn't help this compulsion and urge to ingather the great, I was not great, I was merely a makeweight who was sandwiched in among the men to amuse them. On this occasion, I remember, I was sitting after the dinner party when a person called Professor Joad, I don't know what he was professor of, philosophy perhaps, well-known as a verbalizer on the wireless, he came up to me, dirty little man with a grubby little beard, and he started to talk to me in a patronizing way. This was an occasion I remember, it was about the only time in my life, when I thought of a quick comeback. Afterwards when the whole thing's over you think of the comeback, but this time I had it. He said, 'and what are you reading at the moment? And I said, with perfect truth, 'well as a matter of fact I'm reading Gibbon's Decline and Fall of the Roman Empire'. He said, 'How mannered'. 'But not bad mannered' said I, quite loudly, and I stood up and walked away from him. If only one could always be so quick on the ball. Nasty little man, egg all down his waistcoat, a womanizer too. But not this woman.

I was once asked by a fatuous journalist how I felt about my looks. I think my looks were adequate, it's easier to get things done if you're pretty. I was not vain, any advantages I possessed of any kind whatever were by luck, not by accomplishment. But it always seemed to me that what one was given in the way of physical attributes should be put at the service not only of oneself but of one's friends. Why be so mean and niggardly if some dear delightful man showed signs of wanting to possess one for half an hour, or something of the kind, why not? He was a friend, it gave him pleasure, it gave me pleasure. Of course, it's a sign, I suppose, of a lack somewhere, that this particular gesture, which should really be a gesture of confirmation, something or other, love perhaps? A partnership of some kind? For me was not, it was merely a courtesy which I accorded the men who wanted it, and whom I really liked. A friend of mine, talking to me about Bertrand Russell and his affairs, said that she thought that people who are promiscuous were sometimes searching for love, something they'd been deprived of, perhaps in their childhood. Now, she was feeling generous towards me at that moment, and I think she was directing this to my address, and of course I would be honoured to be equated with Bertrand Russell, even below the belt. But the fact is I was not searching for love, I think I might have been a more complicated character if I had been. I think I might have been happier if I was searching for love, I might have found it somewhere, but I've always thought that love is something that has to be offered, and not sought. I was a pleasure-seeker in wartime London, I was not the only one, it was a strange and wonderful time to be young and alive, because one felt so very, very alive.

I remember I was taken to dinner at the Dorchester by a delightful man who was a great friend. We walked up the dark street between my flat and the hotel which was not a very great distance, passing as we did so the American Officers' Club which stood at the corner of South Audley Street and Hill Street. And after we'd had our dinner, we stepped out into the dark of the night, with a bombers' moon overhead, and intermittently the sound of bombers taking advantage of it, and we made our way back to my flat, my friend was kindly going to esquire me to my door. It was half dark, it was three quarters dark, and we walked in the road so that we didn't twist our ankles on the curbstones, we were both tipsy, and as we walked along my friend began to sing:

> *Through the night of doubt and sorrow*
> *Onward goes the pilgrim band*
> *Singing songs of xpectation*
> *Marching to the Promised Land.*

It so happened that this was my school hymn. As a trembling child of 13, I'd been put down to learn this hymn at St. Leonards, it had many verses and I knew the whole lot, and so I lifted my voice, which was no voice at all, but I was inspired at that moment by the time and the place, and I found myself singing, and weeping, and then laughing on my knees in the middle of the street. This memory is one of the most vivid of my entire life.

Chapter 11

More than a year passed and Orde's letters became lighter and lighter on content, he was unable to share his activities by mail, and then they were reduced further to the type of thing you put on a postcard, acknowledging my letters and reassuring me that he was still alive, and then there came a total news blackout. This could only mean that some kind of climax was approaching, I had jungle dreams and wild imaginings, and I waited. Then one day mother called me up in a state of some excitement and asked me if I had read the Times this morning. Well, the hairs on my back shot up, I dropped the phone before she could say another word, and rushed out to the newsagent, biting my lip and clenching my fists, and there it was, on the front page! He'd done it! He'd given the Japs a bloody nose as he told me he would! No other name was mentioned in the article, it was entirely about Orde. The correspondent was in no doubt that a British officer called Wingate was a genius and a hero and an enormous killer all rolled into one. The article was short on detail, which was infuriating, but as it should be. I was immediately inundated with phone calls, all our friends came to the flat in the hope that I would have more information which of course I did not, but I threw open the drinks cabinet and we all had a long and very noisy party. Then I received a cable from him, 'FEEL LIKE AN ILL-TEMPERED DOG WHEN EVERYONE STARTS PETTING HIM', and I pasted it on the front door.

A week later there was a program on the radio about him! My husband had become a celebrity, like a film actor, and I felt myself elevated in some way, I was pummeled with attention and I started to feel that I did not belong to myself, but that I was there to serve a general purpose. I think it was unfortunate that Orde was not with me at this time, he would have stood in the limelight and probably acted correctly, and I would have stood to the side and slightly behind him, smiling sweetly. The initial feeling of euphoria had flown entirely, I wondered how long this would be going on. I finally agreed to give an interview to a newspaper, and when I read it in print the following Sunday, I was so mortified that I packed my bags and fled in pure terror to Aberdeen.

There are those who like to look in a mirror, and there are those who do not, I'm sure a mental doctor could tell me why that is. Seeing myself in print was a thoroughly unnerving experience, and not to be repeated. I decided to go back to my old home. I took the precaution of not telling mother I was coming, I traveled incognito to Edinburgh, and camped at the house of an old friend of the family, Hilda Rogerson, and she sweetly agreed to drive me up to Aberdeen. When we arrived at Tilliefoure, she went in to see mother in the main house, and I walked directly to father's fishing lodge. I think I was rather flattering myself, but my reaction to the newspaper reporters was quite intense, there should be a word for it containing the suffix 'phobia'. Papa vacated the fishing lodge and returned to the main house, and I equipped myself with a large supply of books, and settled down very happily, a little girl again but now treated with less indifference by my parents.

'Chindit I', as it is known, was named by Orde 'Operation Loincloth', an obvious reference to Tarzan. This had been a grueling operation, many brave men had died, not through enemy action, but thirst, injuries, exhaustion and snake bites. It wasn't easy to quantify success and opinion was sharply divided. The most telling result was the enthusiasm of the survivors and their total belief in Wingate. Orde had set out to test a theory, and that was LRPG, which stands for Long Range Penetration Groups. He wanted to show that small groups of soldiers could operate far behind enemy lines, disrupting enemy operations, and have all their needs supplied by air. His opponents in Delhi contemptuously declared the operation a failure, they fully intended to hold Orde accountable for the suffering of his soldiers. He produced a report on the operation, and Delhi GHQ did its utmost to suppress it, but a copy found its way to 10, Downing Street.

'Loincloth' was indeed an act of bravado, but it was also a serious military experiment. Churchill read the report and instantly understood its significance. In spite of the Delhi professionals' view, word had got out, and Orde was now some kind of a national hero. His success meant that he would be staying in India in order to continue his work. I resolved to go out there to join him; I would book a passage using my maiden name and stay in the hotel nearest his base of operations, I hadn't decided whether or not I should ask his permission, there were arguments on both sides.

A Green Rose

One day, about a month or six weeks after my escape from Hill Street, I received a telephone call from Orde, saying that he'd just arrived at the flat, a thing that was quite unexpected by either of us, and asking me to board the night train from Aberdeen and meet him the next day in London. Imagine my joy! I had just time to catch the bus and get myself a third class sleeper on the seven thirty train, and I set off. I took with me clothes that I thought would be adequate for my short stay in London where I could always replenish them from my wardrobe, and when I was lying in my crowded little compartment, and I on a lower bunk, we came at last to Waverly Station, and to Edinburgh at about 11 o'clock at night, or rather later. The train seemed to be staying an unconscionable time, but of course it was war and nobody expected things to run to timetables, but after it had been there for twenty minutes, or twenty five minutes, in the distance I heard some heavy masculine boots clumping along the linoleum of the corridor, everything blacked out, of course. The boots behaved very oddly because every few seconds they stopped, there was a pause, and then they clumped on for two or three seconds then stopped again. And presently, sure enough, they came to our compartment, and the door was quietly slid aside, and a soldier in battle dress murmured, 'is Mrs. Wingate in this compartment?' I piped up from where I lay in my jersey and knickers, and he knelt on the floor to talk to me. There'd been a message he said from my husband, would I leave the train immediately.

I gathered my suitcase together amid the interested glances of the other women in the carriage, 'no bad news, I hope', said one, kindly, and I was decanted onto the platform and the train rushed away. I was taken to the Railway Travel Office, a nissen hut where of course everything was humming although it was now getting on for midnight, and some blank-faced people who were obviously intent on keeping their cool, took me into the inner office and said that 10, Downing Street was on the line. And when I lifted the receiver, sure enough there was Orde who'd just finished having dinner with the Churchills. He told me that they were passing through Edinburgh the following morning at eleven, and that I was to report to the station and present myself to the stationmaster at ten o'clock, and he would take charge of me until the train arrived, whereupon I would be allowed to join the train. 'Yes sir!' I barked, there was a pause and he giggled and then I giggled, and then tears were pouring down my cheeks, and this went on for a while, then I imagine he replaced the receiver because the line went dead. I pictured the Prime minister watching his young warrior giggling and I turned around and the entire room was staring at me. Well, I rang up Hilda, long-suffering woman – this was the middle of the night – and I went round to Murray Place, and she very kindly climbed out of bed and tucked me up in the spare bedroom, and the following morning I went back to the station and was met by the stationmaster.

This is where things began to go askew as they do in those dreams where, rather as in Alice Through the Looking Glass, if you want to go south you have to move northwards. The stationmaster was a superb figure because in those days they still wore their black silk hat, a pink rose in the button hole, a morning coat and striped trousers. He was a middle aged man, extremely Edinburgh to look at, very East Windy indeed, and he was obviously very angry, and very disapproving. He led me to a suburban platform, there was nobody about at all. Obviously security had been informed, there was not a single human being in sight or in sound anywhere, or any train. Sharp at eleven steamed in a long sleeper train with all its blinds pulled down. Orde appeared on the step wearing tropical uniform, and looking very pale, I turned to shake hands with the stationmaster

A Green Rose

who shook hands with the air of the greatest possible distaste, and I got on board. Orde and I went along to his little rumpled compartment, he was in extremely high spirits. He told me, rather frankly I thought, that he had made it quite plain to Churchill that he was prepared to leave a note for me when I got to London, and that I would wait for him until he returned from Quebec a month later, and Churchill said, quite typically, 'but that would be cruelty to animals'.

At one o'clock lunch was served and we were invited to sit with the Churchills at their foursome table. Now the whole of the general staff and the joint planners, the combined operations team under Mountbatten, about 250 cipher clerks, secretaries, ADCs and general dogsbodies were aboard this train, nobody else. The luncheon with Churchill was a very qualified success, he and I obviously disliked each other from the start. I say obviously, I mean we looked at each other with exactly the same expression in our eyes, no enthusiasm. He spent practically the whole of the luncheon telling me how much he detested Mrs. Roosevelt and Mme Chiang Kai shek, the wives of his two largest but not most powerful allies. He told me some scurrilous stories about Mme Chiang Kai shek, I don't think there were any scurrilous stories to be told about poor Mrs. Roosevelt. I admired both these women this side of idolatry. One was hideously ugly and very high-minded, from New England, and the other one – they were as different as chalk from cheese – beautiful and in the timeless tradition. Anyway, I sat rather gloomy and glum while I had to listen to what seemed to me to be an ill-advised sort of tirade. What I should have realized was that he was sending me a signal that he didn't like strong-minded women. Various people who were sitting at the little tables on the other side, occasionally glanced at us discretely. Averill Harriman for example who was Roosevelt's Ambassador-at-large, a very influential man and a man, I think, of integrity and intellect, accompanied as always by his daughter Kathleen, aged about 30, who was tall and dark and handsome as he was. But of course everything was very quiet and subdued, I remember that the roast beef was quite delicious, I hadn't tasted anything like it since the war began.

The train arrived at the dock, and on rather a grey day, we climbed into the tender, and set out across the calm grey sea to the enormous grey slab of a ship, the Queen Mary which was lying about a mile offshore. When we got to the Queen Mary, there was a sort of gaping gangway in her side, she was so large that it was not possible to enter her by means of a companionway, or a gangplank, you had to go in as if you were mounting a tank attack, and we walked up into that great gaping hole. At the top we found ourselves on a great platform, and we met this extraordinary figure. Extraordinary I mean, to see it in what was a great ship because although the Queen Mary was a depressing ship for anybody who loved the sea, she was more like a floating hotel, and not a very attractive hotel at that. Still, she was manned and designed by people who were concerned with sailing. But there was not much that was nautical about her that we could see, least of all this fellow at the top of the gangway. He too was wearing a morning coat and striped trousers, but no hat and no flower in his button hole. He looked quite as sour as the stationmaster, in fact his manners were worse because he was positively hostile. He took us up in a lift to show us our rooms, our state rooms, and in order to make conversation in what seemed to me an oddly chilly situation, I said, 'do you make this voyage often?' and he turned to me with fury in his eyes and said, 'I'm from the ministry of Transport', and we left it at that. After he'd opened the door of the charming suite of rooms that Orde and I were to occupy, he said to me, 'I hope you think this is good enough for you, it's the bridal suite', and he slammed the door. And that was that. Now Orde always said that if things begin well, they'll probably go on well, and vice versa.

The next six days were very busy ones for the people on that ship. They were isolated from telephones, though not I would have thought from carefully coded messages. We had an escort of two destroyers, but the poor little ships were practically invisible in a smother of foam because they had to bust themselves to keep up with us. The Queen Mary relied on her speed to avoid the U boats, and I think the destroyers were only a token, probably to pick us up if we were torpedoed. All the top men on board spent every day, and often all day in conference with one another.

That voyage was a very mixed experience for me. In the evening they circulated in each other's state rooms, giving small dinner parties, Churchill invited me to one, and our relations deteriorated still further. I believe he had no charm whatever, he totally lacked it. On the other hand of course, like some vast building, like Bleinheim Palace itself, superb. By no means elegant or graceful but massive, one had to admire while coming nowhere near love. Portal, I remember, asked me to a dinner party with Katherine Harriman, and he wouldn't even speak to me. Orde was not there. This must have been due to some unpleasantness in my nature, some lack of charm because Portal of course was Chief of Air Staff, and he would have no particular grudge against my husband. We ate our meals in the VIP dining room, which was a very pleasant oblong room with several tables down one side containing six people each, and eve-rybody sat at the same place every day. At our table was myself next to the wall, then Orde, then a very nice man called Guy Gibson, the bomber, the dambuster, a most delightful young man, modest without being humble, and on the other side, Ismay, Mountbatten and Portal. Two of the men who were opposite me never addressed two words to me at all. Ismay occasionally talked to me, and always with a kind and gentle expression because he was a dear man. Several of the generals were extremely resentful that Orde was allowed to have his comforts on board in the shape of a wife, they made no bones about it. One of them laid a complaint in fact. Portal, dreadful old ninny, turned to Guy one day while we were all sitting together and said, 'why should Wingate have his wife on board, why shouldn't you have your wife on board?' And Guy Gibson firmly replied, 'I see my wife every day, and Wingate hasn't seen his for 18 months'. On the day we were to disembark at Halifax, we were having our last meal on board, Portal was talking to Gibson who sat opposite him, and suddenly said, 'of course, I like your wife' with strict emphasis on the 'your', 'there's nothing wrong with her'. Then he paused and said, 'no, there's nothing wrong with *your* wife'. Well, I looked up and saw Ismay's eyes fixed upon me, kind and compassionate, but there was absolutely nothing one could do.

It was an extraordinary experience, it lasted for about a month, and what was curious about it for me was not the air of high tension, which everybody must have felt, but the very unusual position in which I found myself. Some of these very senior men exhibited highly deficient behaviour, and a great deal of it was caused by that old enemy, envy, which so many of the men who attended the conference from among the British delegation felt against Orde. I discovered then that technique of insult which one man in an official position can apply against another man, involving his tender parts and vulnerable places. For instance the treatment accorded to his wife.

I believe I had a reputation, in fact a double reputation. In the first place I was supposed to be a friend and possibly a confidant of many of the Jewish leaders. The people on the boat were well-informed, and given the way many felt about Orde, if there was only one of them who knew about our 'disgrace' in Palestine, he would have made it his business to pass it on to the others. It's a fair bet that most of that company disliked Jews anyway, so both we and the Jews were damned by association. Then there was the matter of my reputation as a fast woman, it all went back to that fool Harry Slesser at the Fildes'. One doesn't know how far this story spread, the Army is like a large boy's school, but it would surface from time to time in my career as an army wife. In Palestine, I had been invited to an official function at one of the big hotels, Orde was away doing something, and I, the chastest of wives, was sitting between two men, neither of whom would speak to me. The one on my left turned to me, major somebody, large moustache, and said, (I was then aged twenty perhaps), 'you're a man-eater, aren't you.' Well, I didn't even know what a man-eater was, I'd never heard the phrase before. I answered rather pathetically, 'surely I'm not as fierce as all that, am I?' and he turned his back on me. I looked across at the woman opposite and saw a gleam of sympathy in her eye, she knew perfectly well that I wasn't a man-eater.

On the Queen Mary since I was probably more appealing than most of the wives of these curmudgeons, I was easily cast as the boat's harlot. Indeed, I really had no job being there in the first place. Every single person on the boat was there to do a job. Guy Gibson, splendid man, he was not there to confer with the Chiefs of Staff, he was there to do a lecture tour of North America, showing the flag, and who better? What was I doing there? I was there to provide home comforts for a junior colleague preferred by the Prime minister. In fact I don't think anybody would have minced their words, they would have said, 'Churchill has provided him with his woman', and I don't think Orde would have caviled at this description. But was it such a good idea to take me along? I think the tone was set then, and my position was a difficult one. In the midst of this gathering of great men who were accustomed to going to these conferences in a body, together, suddenly I show up. I was a carbuncle.

There may have been another reason, and most interesting in its way, why all these men were so hostile to this pale and quiet young woman. I said that things started to go askew the moment I met the stationmaster at Waverly, and he took me to a suburban platform to meet the train that was carrying Churchill and his staff to Quebec. Now why, you might ask yourself, should a completely detached person such as the stationmaster at Edinburgh, why should he have felt anger and disapproval when he had to stand beside this young woman? I'll tell you why.

I am severely short-sighted, and have been all my adult life. When I lived in London during the war, I found the torches we were allowed to use, which always had to be masked by tissue paper, were quite useless to me, my eyes weren't good enough to see the curbstones by their feeble light, and I often had to go about in the dark in London. I had to go to my job which was shift work, 9pm to 9am, 3pm to 9pm, and so on, often in total darkness, no torch was going to stop me from breaking my leg. I found a stick was what I needed, all blind and half-sighted people find a stick more useful than any other aid. But what did I do, did I go and get myself a white stick? No that would have been embarrassing for the people round about me because I'm not blind. Did I get my self a modest something like an umbrella? That would have been alright. No. Ass that I was, I went off to Aspreys and bought myself a beautiful shagreen stick, in fact I bought two. One of them was pale brown with an ivory top, and the other was an exquisite sort of jade green, also topped with ivory. They were very sleek, smooth and unornamented but I suppose they were flashy. They were beautiful you see, I was never able to resist beauty.

I used to go about London with my sticks, and I found them a wonderful help. I tapped my way to my work, and to my pleasures, and they saved me from breaking my ankle over and over again. But I didn't use them during the day, naturally I could see where the holes were in the road. But when I went down to meet Orde, when I caught that train from Aberdeen at the beginning of August, and I was taken off it in the middle of the night, I had my stick with me because I thought I was going to be in London, and that I'd need it in the dark. If I'd had my wits about me, I'd have given it into the keeping of Hilda Rogerson, but then I might have had difficulty in picking it up again, so I carried it with me on board the Queen Mary, and it was too long to put into any suitcase, so I carried it in my hand when I met the stationmaster at Waverly.

This is an interesting point, all psycho boys of course will confirm me when I say this; the stick, like, I don't know what, the sword or the helmet or the charger are a symbol of male virility and command, women who carry sticks are loathed on sight by every man, well practically every man, who meets her. Like women who wear monocles, in fact more, because women who wear monocles may be fools and affected, but women who carry sticks carry the male symbol. I think rightly the men feel that they have taken upon themselves a presumption, they've taken on themselves something to which they are not entitled. This damned stick which I could not leave behind and could do nothing with other than carry it all the time, had an immediate effect on every single man who saw me with it in my hand, why didn't I throw it overboard?

Orde brought in two major bones and laid them at Churchill's feet during the Quadrant conference. Firstly he impressed the Americans who were friendly but skeptical that the British were really going to fight in the Far East. He had a persuasive eloquence when he wanted, you know, smooth and forceful, and he was just the man for the Americans, he liked them. He addressed them at a vital conference of the American naval chiefs, the air force chiefs and the army chiefs in which he outlined his plans for the conquest of Burma, and at the end of it, as Derek says in his book, they agreed to come in with all the help they could offer, air force help mostly. This was a big bone that he brought back to Churchill.

There was another bone, smaller in size. There were only two Chinese at the Quebec conference. One was TV Sung, Chiang Kai shek's brother-in-law, and the other was his valet. We only saw his valet in the corridors of power, but TV Sung who was extremely aloof and by no means friendly – Chiang Kai shek hadn't got much use for the western powers – TV Sung had been instructed to come along to say that Chiang Kai shek would not cooperate, and that no help could be expected from the Chinese. Orde changed all that. He and Sung had some kind of talk together, he came back and told me where I sat in our bedroom, reading, and he said, 'Sung is a nice man, I like him. He was not very friendly to begin with but we had an excellent contact, and at the end of our talk he told me that he was going to recommend Chiang to cooperate as fully as possible. Well, we all know that 'fully' doesn't mean to them what it means to us. It was another bone that Orde could bring back to his shield and defender. Yes, I think he worked his passage alright.

I never saw such a collection of ailing grandees as there was at the Quadrant conference. Churchill was famous for wearing out his secretaries and his chiefs of staff, and these men worked terribly hard, many of them worked for 18 hours a day. Churchill had learned long ago how to run his machine, as you know, he read the newspapers in his bed in the morning, then he did some business from his couch, then he got up, he knew how to manage himself.

But they, poor things, who had to get up at seven or eight in the morning, and get through a day that didn't include a rest in bed after lunch, were summoned by him to work or carouse until 3am, were completely flaked-out and began to look very pale around midnight, old men with white faces and red noses and black-ringed eyes. They passed infections to each other at various times too, I got a dreadful sore throat and can say that I was infected by the chiefs of staff. I was attended by a quite horrid old man called Lord Moran, Churchill's private physician, should have been spelt with two 'o's instead of one. Afterwards he wrote a scandalous book, he wanted to make money and obtain kudos, in which he described his patient Churchill's symptoms and how his illnesses and various weaknesses progressed. Dreadful. Well, this awful old man, in his book, had a few words to say about Orde, he said, 'I met Wingate and to me he seemed hardly sane'.

There were some people at the conference who were not jealous of Orde and were not disapproving of me. One of them was General Dill. Another was the Foreign Office contingent which suddenly appeared. It was small but it was high powered. Sir Alexander Cadogan who was the head of the foreign office, a man who had been seconded to the Office of Economic Warfare, but he was later on in fact our Ambassador to the United Nations, and also to Paris, and some delightful younger person who was no doubt very much on his way up. We had one or two meals with these two men and I found the atmosphere very pleasant. But on the whole there was no fraternizing, not only between myself and other people there, but not much fraternizing by Orde. At that time the wildest rumours were current, and being relayed to India where I'm told the panic was extreme. The story was that he was going to be designated Supreme of South East Asia, and he very nearly was. There was another that he was going to supersede Auchinleck, a thing that Churchill would have been very glad to see him do.

We arrived in Canada within a cloak of secrecy, the entire docking area was empty of people, and we boarded the train that was to take us to Quebec. We had to put in about 36 hours of very slow travel through these tedious little conifers which clothe so much of Canada. It was late summer, there was no colour except a beautiful blue sky and an occasional charming little lake, pine trees, logging roads twisting away with red earth here and there. Orde and I were cooped up with the joint planners, and some high-ups from the Admiralty, and one or two people from the War Office. We had a sort of drawing room to ourselves, Churchill had gone on with some different form of transport, an airplane perhaps, and we had to put in several hours of conversation, fairly successfully. At Quebec we were assigned a suite fairly high-up at the Frontenac Hotel, and Orde of course was immediately sucked in to the round of conferences, and very important they were. He worked hard, he concentrated all his waking hours in marshalling his ideas and pushing them across to the Americans and to the British; no trouble with the Americans, great trouble with his own people, as always, and I spent a good deal of time walking about Quebec myself. I enjoyed Quebec because although the Quebecois are total curmudgeons, they hated the British because Wolfe defeated Montcalm, they hated the Americans because they are a powerful neighbour with different aspirations to their own, but curiously enough they hated the Free French too, and stoned a contingent of Free French sailors when they marched down the street. This was because Quebec was founded before the revolution and still, in certain places, flew the Fleur de Lys. What a people! But I loved their old town and I spent hours wandering about the back streets.

When the conference came to an end the Churchills and Orde, the chiefs of staff, Mountbatten and two or three other of the top hierarchy, not only the titular tops but also the tops in the think tanks and so on, they set off for Washington where they were going to have conferences at the Pentagon. Anybody who didn't fancy much traveling back in a bomber – Orde did and the Foreign Office boys did – we all headed for the Queen Mary, and it was a very different set-up now. On the voyage out there was no one on board except the very large crew, and 250 or so people accompanying Churchill. On the voyage back there were still 200 people from that original contingent including myself, but there were also 16,000 troops, mostly Canadian.

When we arrived on board, a perfectly delightful woman called Joan Bright who was head of the cabinet secretariat, had the job of seeing that the VIPs or quasi-VIPs like myself got the right sort of accommodation. She came to me and asked me whether I would like to share a cabin with Kathleen Harriman which would have the advantage of having a porthole giving light and air of the outer cabin, or would I prefer an inner cabin which I could have to myself but which would be lit perpetually by electric light, and serviced by the air conditioning. I had no doubt that Joan Bright had already asked Kathleen whether she would be prepared to share a cabin with me, and she must have said yes which I take very kindly of her. Well, I had no trouble in making up my mind about that; I liked Kathleen Harriman but I didn't want to embarrass her by spending all my time in her cabin and mine, and making her feel that she possibly had to try to talk to me. I didn't want to embarrass Joan Bright by sometimes leaving the cabin so that Kathleen Harriman could enjoy it in peace, and sitting quite alone, and possibly become the target of one or two remarks by passing generals, so poor Joan Bright would be asking herself what she could do to make my life more cheerful; far better to have a room to myself, and stay there, and that's what I did.

I never saw any of the social life that went on in the ship but I should think it was both cheerful and civilized. I avoided the saloons, not one of which I ever saw, I didn't want to sit in an armchair for hours and hours every day, passed and re-passed by people no longer under the same pressure of work. A nice lot as indeed they had been on the way out, but having pink gins, and having conversations from which I would necessarily have been excluded. I could possibly have joined the cipher clerks who were all Wrens, and the Wrens was much the best service anyway, and they were all top Wrens who'd been creamed off, so they were not only intelligent and well-schooled, but they were often exceedingly pretty. They were mostly of my age, but in their company I should have felt like an old lady.

I went for my meals to the same dining room as we used on the way out, but this time I took to myself a little table for two, which stood with others of the same kind in a line of stalls down one wall intended, I suppose, as a snug tete a tete area. As before, everybody stuck to their own seats, some of the men had meals in their own quarters and invited their friends to eat with them but there was a big round table which held about eight people, quite close to me, at which Kathleen Harriman and Joan Bright and Head and several others used to eat their lunches day by day. When we'd been out about three days, Head stopped at my table one day – he and I incidentally had taken a long drive one day in a one horse shay in Quebec. We had not liked each other very much but we'd got on alright and I was grateful to him for taking me on this outing, though I dare say he did it as much out of curiosity as out of kindness. But when he stopped and said, 'will you have lunch with me tomorrow', his was a familiar face and I was pleased. I said, 'thank you very much, I should like to'. However the next

A Green Rose

morning there was a knock on my cabin door, and a grinning ADC said, 'Mr. Head won't be able to have lunch with you today', he turned and walked away. Nor did Head ever speak to me again, certainly not to apologize. This, I suppose, was a simple method of taking me down a peg or two. It didn't afflict my mind very much because – I'm telling the truth when I tell you that my mind was occupied with very different things. However I was rather depressed when I tried to make my way back to my cabin one day, I never could find my cabin, I could find my way to the dining room because it was signposted, but in this unpleasing ship you had to take lifts to various levels, and then walk in different directions. The old-fashioned idea of a great broad staircase which led you more or less directly to the decks to which you were directing your steps was quite out. You had to walk first north and take a lift and then get up somewhere or down somewhere and walk south, and I used to dread trying to find my cabin.

I usually attached myself to some small group of people who were making their way in my direction, and on this occasion it was Joan Bright, Kathleen Harriman, and a tall, well preserved man of about 50 who was a general in charge of all the transport at the War Office. What a desperate job, I can't think of anything worse. So much worry and so little glory attached to it. If things go right, people take your work for granted, and if things go wrong you are put over a barrel. Anyway, he was not bad-looking, and I asked if I might walk with them. When we got to the first lot of lifts which were side by side, we pressed the button and nothing happened. Pressed it again, still no lift, I said something impatient and the man said to me, 'why don't you try that one'. So I walked over to the second lift and pressed the button. And then I heard him snigger, and Joan Bright came over and took my arm gently and kindly and glancing down with my bat's eye, I saw a placard saying 'out of order'. Joan Bright and Kathleen Harriman didn't raise a smile, we climbed into the lift which by this time had arrived, and as we ascended the man said, 'the trouble with you is you have no sense of humour'. Well, I never breathed a word about anything, I just stood in perfect silence from the moment Joan had led me to the lift until I got out, and the other two women stood in perfect silence too. But I'd never seen this man before, I never saw him again except perhaps in the distance when I didn't recognize him. Why did he do a thing like that?

There was one quite funny incident, it is very typical of how life is lived, and of human nature. I was sitting one dinner time at my table, as usual reading a book. Nobody ever interrupted me, as I say and I was very glad that this was so, and I was not particularly pleased when a shadow loomed up and I saw an extremely good-looking naval captain wearing his becoming blue uniform, fair and with that indefinable air of success which attends some people. He said, 'do you mind if I have my dinner with you?' and as he said this, he dropped his life jacket on the floor and without waiting for my reply he slid into his chair. Well I was annoyed, my book was exciting, I had to close it and say, 'not at all', and spend the next forty minutes talking to this perfect stranger, and I had a strong suspicion he was there because of all the gossip there had been aboard the ship – naturally there was nothing for them to do on ship except to gossip, you can imagine the sort of things they were saying, and he, obviously a noted charmer, had said, 'oh, leave her to me, I'll find out if there's anything there', and he started.

This was an object lesson to me, his technique was all wrong and this was so surprising in a man of his attainments and experience. His name incidentally was Anthony Buzzard, so he told me, he died many years ago, with all the honours, a full admiral I think, and his technique was that most primitive one which people who have not been properly trained employ when they are embarrassed at having to talk to the person with whom they're sitting. He began by asking all sorts of questions about myself and I answered them civilly but uninformatively, I asked him no questions about himself at all, I wasn't interested. Of course if he had any sense, seeing that I was not an easy proposition, he would have picked up my book and said, 'ah, I see you're reading Agatha Christie, do you like her? I prefer Dorothy Sayers myself, I wonder if you've ever read that extraordinary book of hers called 'Five Red Herrings' which all hinges on the train timetables of an obscure part of south west Scotland, and then we would have been away. I would have responded quite normally to some sort of sensible approach of that kind, flexible approach.

Towards the end of dinner which was a pretty brisk one because conversation was not flowing free, we got on with our eating instead, he soured up and his expression changed and so did his manner. In the end, he asked me the crowning question to which I was unable to give the right answer, 'do you like winter sports' he said gloomily. Now I didn't know it until I read his obituary but he was a member of the skiing team of the Royal Navy and so my reply couldn't have been worse, I said, 'no, to tell the truth I detest them, I'm very bad and I don't like the places where they happen. I don't like ice and snow'. Dead silence. Well, we got up to leave and he said to me, 'what would you like to do now?' and I said, 'I should like to go back to my room and read a book', so I said, 'I'd be awfully grateful if you would show me the way back because I always get lost, so he took me to the door of my cabin and this time he said, and his expression was quite unambiguous, 'is there anything more I can do for you?' 'Yes' I said, 'I wonder if you would arrange for somebody to bring me some more books, good night', and about ten minutes later a dear little Wren in her

Donald Duck hat with a large smile came round with a pile of books which I plunged into at once. I was quite comfortable in my room, the only trouble was the tannoy system which of course penetrated every place in the ship, it had to because we had dropped our destroyers, they didn't accompany us on the homeward journey. Instead the ship made a steady 32 knots the whole way across the Atlantic, jinking of course according to plan. It took six days going at that speed, she relied on her speed to save her, and if she hadn't been saved, imagine the haul that the Germans would have made. 16,000 troops! The accommodation even of that enormous ship couldn't run to a bed for every man and so they were divided into three contingents, red, green and blue, and two lots were always under cover, and one lot was always sleeping on the decks. It was early September, quite warm, pleasant weather luckily, they shifted over every two days, they ate in shifts, they lived in shifts, all dictated by the Tannoy which never ceased from troubling all through the 24 hours. At nighttime there would be an announcement about every twenty minutes or half an hour, during the daytime about every ten minutes. I was rather touched and amused by Kathleen Harriman's reaction to all this. At the very beginning when we were just finding our quarters she said to Joan Bright and to me with an expression of real stupor, she said, 'do you know that there are *colonels* sleeping on the deck! I feel *bad*' she said, 'about having a bed when there are *colonels* sleeping on the deck.' I thought, 'well, you are a nice young woman, we in Britain take our military ranks so much for granted that no colonel is going to mind sleeping on the deck because he's a colonel. He's going to mind if he's got arthritis in his hip or something of that sort'. But I liked her attitude.

They made the crossing without mishap thanks to marvelous organization, one was very proud of the British, the way that ship was run, my goodness. We were taken up to the bridge on a sort of organized tour and met the commodoure of the Cunard fleet, who was in command. He had a couple of other captains under him doing various jobs but the worry that that man and his officers must have been subjected to doesn't bare thinking about. He was a big man with bushy black eyebrows and a wonderfully steady manner. We were also taken down below to the kitchens which of course were quite superb, and there the head chef told me that that morning he had broken 32,000 eggs for breakfast.

Chapter 12

Orde flew back in a bomber from Washington where he had been seeing the President, together with Churchill, and landed in London two or three days before I did. I came down from the Clyde by the night train, and found him pottering in the flat in a dressing gown, very cheerful, quite steady. His sister Monica was looking after him, 'how are you getting along?' said I. 'Not at all well', said he, 'I simply cannot get my staff together, and I've got a very short time in which to do it'. He said, 'of course the first person I thought of was Herb'. Otway Herbert was a contemporary of Orde's on Salisbury Plain, a gunner, been through the Staff College, I was chummy with his wife Muriel at Bulford but we saw very little of him because he was working so hard to get into the staff college. '...so I thought of him right away' said Orde, ' and I went around to the War Office and asked him to join me as my

GSO1. He thanked me very much for asking and said he was completely tied up with the staff planning for D Day. In fact he said, he was GSO1 to a poor general whose name I think was Bridges who was so terrified of the responsibility that had been thrust upon him that he was drunk all the time, and Herb had to do two men's work if not more, so he was out'. Now Orde, although he was as steady as a rock, and he was when things were tense, obviously feeling that time was running out, he was rather worried, so he said, 'nobody who's got good staff officers is going to release them, I can't get anything except the riff raff'.

Every good commander-in-chief has to have a chief of staff, and every good chief of staff would hope for a good commander. Now when you get these two rare birds flighting together, then you get great victories. Napoleon and Berthier, Montgomery and Coon. Mongomery I would venture to say, of course in a hushed voice, was not a really great commander, but he was good enough, I think he was very fortunate in his chief of staff. Now a really good Chief of Staff can make his way without serving a good commander. But even a good commander can't make his way without a good Chief of Staff. So, I said, 'well, there's always Derek, isn't there.' He was not enthusiastic, he was, after all, a very knowledgeable man, and he knew that Derek didn't have the brain power; he hadn't been to the staff college any more than Orde had, but Orde could make up with genius what he lacked in academic theory (logistics or whatever they call it nowadays). He didn't really feel that Derek was going to be the man, however he sent for Derek who came at once, bringing Mary with him, and they came round to the flat, and the two men went to the sitting room while I sat in the bedroom.

After about 15 minutes, Orde came out, again looking perfectly steady but rather glum and he said, 'Derek won't come'. 'Why not?' I said. 'He's frightened' said Orde, 'he's quite frank about it, he says the job is far beyond him and he doesn't want to take it, he's refused point blank,' So I said to Orde, 'I'll try'. Now most men would have said, 'do you really think you can achieve what I can't?' But he was never like that, he was always ready to let anybody have a go. So I went into the sitting room, closed the door firmly – fortunately Mary had gone off shopping somewhere – there stood Derek by the window, looking dazed, and well he might, I went up to him and said, 'what's all this?' He replied, 'I'm terrified, I can't possibly go, the job is far too large for me' So I said, 'this is nonsense, Orde needs you, he's got to fight his own people in Delhi before he can get at the Japs, if you don't go he won't have anyone who is loyal to him, on whom he can rely. And apart from that, it will be your gateway to preferment, it's exactly the sort of thing you should be doing, let's call him in now and tell him you're going'. I spoke in firm, commanding tones, reminding myself that Derek is governed by a strong-minded woman, and he said, 'alright, I'll go'. 'And no more bones about it!' I added. Derek agreed, he was marvelous. And from that moment on he was absolutely first class, he never wavered. He rushed out, he had far more friends and acquaintances of his own generation than Orde, he gathered together an excellent band, it may have been varied in quality, but a splendid team, and some of his choices were absolutely first class. Derek behaved so well, and he never looked back, and because he was a hollow man he was capable of holding the fire, the interior fire of another mind, and Orde simply poured his spirit and ideas into Derek and he became a vessel, and a very excellent one too, devoted, loyal and efficient.

By the time Orde was engaged in gathering together forces to command in the war, he accepted people for what they were, and this made him much easier to live with, he judged less harshly, it had not always been thus. Orde had been a rather dogmatic young man, a tendency at times to be lofty and superior and self-involved, and quite intolerant of people who didn't aspire to the things to which he aspired. I think that when he jilted Peggy, he experienced such a fall from grace – he realized that he was a sinner like the rest of us – and he came to accept himself as such. Just as he lifted me with his Wingatian character, something of me may have rubbed off on him, and by the time he got to the point of taking part in great affairs, he was far beyond the simplistic notion that you had to make your whole life, so to speak, a prayer to God.

Many roads thou hast fashioned
All of them lead to the light

He was taking people in a far gayer, more liberal frame of mind, he was taking them for what they had to offer, and valuing them for what they were, and not demanding that they be a part of a greater whole. He would never have got on with his motley allies; his staff in his final campaign was composed of every sort and kind of man. Most of them were very well-behaved and respectable, one or two of them were not, and he dismissed the scallywags. Orde was very good indeed at assessing the older generation military mind, he was excellent at choosing the young, but he used to go astray sometimes when dealing with his own age group.

He found a character called Romily, he was a sort of military barrow boy, the sort who, when he sits down beside a woman, says, 'haven't we met before?' Well, he was one of a stream of people coming to Hill Street to interview, and having had to entertain him for half an hour, I knew a little more about dear Romily than I did when we sat down, so I suggested to Orde gingerly, 'do you really think you should take this man with you, don't you think he will bring the staff into disrepute? Because he's so obviously a spiv.' And

Orde said very gaily and sweetly, 'I'm taking him because he's a spiv, a super spiv, he can get anything, and I'm going to be short of a great deal of equipment and Romily will be able to procure WT sets, Transport, he can even get me a submarine if I want one', said Orde confidently. Well, I felt very dubious, especially when I heard he was taking with him his girl in the guise of his secretary, and that she wore an orange velvet coat and skirt. They all climbed into the airplane together, and no doubt all climbed out at Delhi airfield, where they were met by the high-ups and, in due course first the lady, then Romily, had to be passed-out onto the streets. But Orde did like Romily.

Once Orde had been gazetted a major-general, he had to rush off to find a tailor – time was so short – and have his uniform made, with its lovely scarlet and gold lace and the baton and sword crossed on his shoulders. It took three or four days from start to finish, and then we rang up Harold Laski and asked him to come round for a drink. Harold was a Jew as well as being a prominent left-winger in Parliament, and he had really gone out of his way to help Orde in his difficulties, as I have mentioned, and as he entered the apartment, I had Orde take up a position in his brand new uniform in the center of the living room, and Harold came in, and saw him standing there in all his glory, and do you know what he did? He burst into tears. He went up to Orde and patted him, then he sat down on the sofa and wept. Well, that's the sort of effect this man had on his friends. It was a great sight. But of course there was more to it than that. This was indeed a time of trial for the Jews, assailed from every side, and in all this darkness and misery, there was one beacon of light, one champion who had stuck his neck out for the Jews, had suffered considerably on their behalf, and yet had risen out of the fire and now stood resplendent before him. If Orde had been seated on a white charger, on a marble plinth, the effect could not have been more potent.

I had complete faith in Orde, he could do no wrong, I knew I should always be safe with him, and do great things at his side. He was now certain to make lieutenant general during the war, and field marshal after, and I didn't think I would like that very well. I started to worry about being the wife of a field marshal, and to baulk at the idea of it, I was being petulant before the act. Just before he parted I gave Orde a lecture on ADCs; I have always had a thing about them. In our army they are looked upon as a low form of life, there hangs about them the smell of the catamites of Alexander the Great. Has anybody ever seen a really hideous ADC? Grace and good humour seems to be the principle characteristic of the breed. And the ability, of course, to get on with the commanding officer's wife. So I told Orde 'If I ever find myself in a position of authority with you, where you had one or more ADCs, I should require you to choose them on the basis of their efficiency and their soldierly qualities as well as their social ones, because I will not allow any ADC of yours to be degraded to the role of poodle-taker, and setter-out of place cards at the dinner table. If we have to give receptions at which people circulate and need to be introduced to each other, we shall employ something other than your ADC for these social traffic duties. No soldier, however young, should ever be subjected to the indignity of becoming a social secretary'. These were, more or less, my parting words to him. Indeed, Orde chose an excellent ADC for his coming campaign, his name should not be forgotten; Captain George Borrow. After he'd been killed with Orde, I wrote to his parents to say how sorry I was and I got back such a nice letter from his father in which he said 'George was so proud to be ADC to your husband, he worked like a black to keep the General going'. I knew just what he meant. The family was connected by blood to George Borrow of Romany

Rye and Lavengro, and must have had gifts which are not very common among military families. I don't think George Borrow should be forgotten.

Orde was received in Delhi with sullen resentment. He had made well-publicized remarks about the Indian Army that had upset a lot of people, Churchill had threatened to put him in charge of the entire Indian Army, and there was the small matter of the radio program broadcast from Delhi by the BBC after Operation Loincloth, to which I have already referred. The program-makers didn't have a lot to go on as far as the campaign itself was concerned, so the narrator confined himself to a sort of biography of the man. And he wasn't going to talk about his training days, or his trip into the Libyan desert, the listening public would have turned off their radios, so he talked about his political ideas.

It was very accurate and up-to-date because they had sent someone to Delhi to interview him, and so the narrator talked about General Wingate's loathing of racial discrimination, his discoveries in Palestine, his support for independence in Abyssinia, and self-determination in general, and his views on justice and world government. He said that it was the role of the British Empire to set nations down the path to self-government etc. Well! It got by the military censors because it contained no military secrets, but surely it was far worse from Delhi's point of view, and I can imagine the reaction at GHQ India. It was a call for secession! They started referring to Orde as 'Robin Hood'. I have no doubt that this ill-advised broadcast set the scene for the second campaign. Orde had to fight tooth and claw to get Delhi to provide him with the things he'd been promised at Quadrant, and since his dictum was, 'if you have something unpleasant to say, say it unpleasantly', I would say he was fairly hated by the time he'd finished with them. One senior India Army officer in particular took Wingate's depredations very personally, and would never forgive him. His name was General Woodburn Kirby, and we shall meet him in a later chapter.

Every one of Orde's campaigns was a novelty. I think I would be right in saying that Monty's approach to a battle was to steadily build up his forces with absolute professionalism, then move cautiously against an enemy he outnumbers, preferably by a factor of 3:1. Orde's approach was to closely study the enemy's dispositions, closely study the enemy's terrain, discover his weaknesses, forge a weapon uniquely suited to the task, and take the enemy by surprise, the numerical odds always heavily in the enemy's favour. The contrast could not be more pronounced, it was the difference between a highly competent house painter and an artist of landscapes, the difference measured in the quantity of paint expended. I don't know whether Orde's unique economy was born of circumstance; a lacking in men and materiel, or a Calvinist aversion to waste, it was probably both. I think it is a mistake to characterize Wingate just as a commander of irregular forces. He worked with the materials at hand, and had not yet been entrusted with an Army Corps; he was the youngest general in the British Army. David felled Goliath with a pebble to his exposed supraorbital ridge, then went on to command armies. Likewise Orde would have commanded armies had he lived, and even with great formations he would, I am sure, have continued to innovate, surprise and overwhelm, and with a modest butcher's bill.

I had a channel that could get mail to Orde at the front within two weeks, I wrote to him to advise him that he was about to become a father. We had talked about children for the first time during his last stay in London, and this was something he very much wanted. I had by now had two abortions, I had a woman in London, a refugee from Czechoslovakia who took care of me, and she was extremely good, I recommended her to everyone I knew who was in need of her services, and we all swore by her. Finally, at the age of 27, I was ready for motherhood. The war had changed me. The great danger that threatened England, then the passing of the danger, had imbued me with a very great love of England, and an urge for renewal. I suddenly wanted not one child but many children, I wanted to have my husband back, and to have a house, and to fill that house with little Ordes. He wrote back to tell me how happy he was, and how much he loved me, and then gave me a long list of instructions about what I must and must not do, and what I must eat, and he ended by telling me that although the outlook for our friends was gloomy we should not despair because Jerusalem was never far from his thoughts, and that we should soon return to our friends in Eretz Israel.

Operation Thursday, or Chindit II as the historians like to call it, was his largest and most complex undertaking so far, the preparation and planning immense and, as I said, Wingate encountered fierce and constant opposition from Delhi from day one, every obstacle was thrown in his way. The plan itself was mutating in a dizzying manner as events unfolded, which they were doing consistently in 1943-4. Initially the plan called for marching four brigades into the heart of the Japanese defensive arena in Burma, as part of an allied ground offensive planned for the Spring of 1944.

The Americans loved Wingate for his thoroughly (un-British) gung-ho, 'can-do' attitude, and they wanted to be a part of his show, such had been the impression he's made on them at Quadrant. They were already providing 'Thursday' with an American air arm, they now wanted to throw more aircraft at him, and said, 'why wear out your Brigades with a two week jungle march, we can fly them in, in two hours, with gliders'

Piling innovation onto innovation, Wingate instantly reconfigured his formations, and retrained his brigades for fly-in, runway-building, and the use of light artillery and other equipment not previously deployable, and presented a new plan.

Then Churchill and Roosevelt, for reasons of grand strategy, cancelled the ground offensive from India and China into Burma (400,000 men), which rendered Operation Thursday (15,000 men) irrelevant. Slim, Mountbatten, Wavell and all the generals shrugged their shoulders, this type of disappointment was something that came with the job; Churchill had the bigger picture, Churchill called the shots, the generals did as they were told.

Meanwhile the enemy was preparing his own offensive from Burma into India, intending to dislodge and destroy the British land army in their last outpost in the Far East, and the British forces prepared to meet this threat by digging in. [A small footnote: The enemy commander, General Mutaguchi, stated after the war, that his offensive into India would not have been attempted if he hadn't seen Wingate's Operation Loincloth with his own eyes; one of Japan's most senior and respected generals was a student of my husband.]

Wingate would not shrug his shoulders. He could not be budged in his resolve to meet and defeat the enemy, this was his reason for being, cancellation was not an option for him, he would not be denied his battle. He abruptly reconfigured his small force to meet the new situation, and announced his determination to attack the enemy, on schedule, with or without the general ground offensive, alone if necessary. The British raised their eyebrows and muttered, but the Americans said, 'we love this guy'.

Wingate did what he'd done in Palestine, and in Abyssinia and even in Sidcup, and what he would have done in the event of a successful invasion of Britain in 1941. He executed a sort of military pirouette; he rotated the thing and turned it upside down with perfect poise, he turned lead into gold. Like the great captain that he was, he said, 'Let the Japanese attack. I will choke off their supply lines, and their offensive into India will bring ruin upon them'. He carried Mountbatten, then Slim, and finally Churchill.

By the time the operation was primed and ready to go, it had become entirely and unreservedly a one-man show; all responsibility had come to rest on his shoulders, and all the generals and air marshals and Wingate's loyal officers and men stood and held their breath, you could hear the proverbial pin drop. I should mention in passing that Orde contracted typhoid in the middle of this tempest, and was confined to a hospital bed (with Agnes McGeary in attendance) for an entire month.

It was a most daring attack deep into enemy territory, and I would say that it went off almost exactly according to plan to an uncharacteristic degree. During the next 19 days his forces consolidated and went out to meet an enemy taken by surprise. Mutaguchi was thrown by Wingate's thrust, and his plans were disrupted. And closer to home, the excitement of Operation Thursday was felt in Delhi and further afield, and Wingate's critics and opponents melted into the mist. On the 20th day a Dakota transport plane carrying Wingate crashed, and he was killed along with his excellent ADC and ten others. Without Wingate, Operation Thursday fell apart, it could not have been otherwise, end of story.

Part II

I remember being mesmerized by the images on television of Jacqueline Kennedy cradling the head of her dying husband, her clothing covered in gore. I remained rooted to the spot in my living room for three days waiting for a sighting of this most famous widow in the throngs that descended upon Washington. I never felt closer to another woman as I did at that time. Did I carry myself with such decorum? Of course, she went on to marry that most fascinating man Aristotle Onassis, a good friend, as I recall, of Winston Churchill. I would have my pick of such men. Orde had been my life. I carped and grumbled like any wife worth her salt, but Orde was my life. One of my complaints was that I wasn't allowed to go with him into battle. Well, not only would I now be allowed to go into battle, I would have the field entirely to myself. The battle I would have to fight was for his reputation and good name. Now I come to the part of my story which is the reason for the telling of it.

Chapter 13

I was in Aberdeen in my seventh month with Orde's child when I received the news of his death. I suppose I was shocked, stunned is a better word, like a cow which has been struck a blow on the head prior to slaughter. Mother of course was in floods of tears, then papa came up to the house to comfort her, and slowly I recovered my wits and behaved as Orde would have behaved in this situation; I went to my room and wrote a report. I took a piece of paper and drawing a line vertically down the page, on the left side at the top I wrote 'accident' and underlined it. On the right side at the top, I wrote 'sabotage' and underlined that. Then I proceeded to list, and when the column on the right reached the bottom of the page, I started a new page without a vertical column, and I wrote and wrote until I fell asleep. I had two great distractions at that time. The physical presence of Orde inside my body, and the volume of attention I was accorded by many kind and generous people. Sack loads of letters and telegrams from the great and the mighty and from people I'd never met, addressed to Lorna Wingate, Aberdeen, or Lorna Wingate, Scotland and, in one case, Lorna Wingate with no address whatever.

At a time when there was no shortage of widows, I became the most famous widow in Britain. I was the young, photogenic widow of the young brilliant general; not many generals are killed on active service, particularly those on the winning side. The letters arrived in small Post Office bags and were delivered by our excellent postmaster in person, and then there were the obituaries, personal testimonials, a very good one from Slim, Orde's commanding officer for Chindit II. I was inundated with requests for newspaper interviews but I now knew better so I politely declined. What was going on inside Lorna? Was she grieving? What is grief? I do know that I was bitterly angry with Orde. I could picture him brushing Derek aside and stepping onto the doomed aircraft, leaving himself open, by dint of his arrogance and infernal impatience, to the most bumbling assassin, suddenly Inspector Clouseau comes to mind. His next appointment was far too important for him to observe a modicum of caution and self-discipline, and wait for his assigned pilot. Perhaps the fool thought he was safe because he was an instrument of God's will, was he not. If he had allowed me to be there at his side, I would have told him not to board, and I would have made him listen to me. I should have been there, my place was with him, even in death, now I was left to live on alone, to carry the burden of his reputation, and all it implied, on my narrow shoulders.

I tried to think clearly. I knew I had to conduct myself with extreme caution, that Orde's enemies would close in on all those connected to him, my experience at Quebec had been instructive. I sent a cable to Derek - he and I had no code arranged, so I had to send it in clear

– I said, COLLECT ALL ORDE'S PAPERS PUT THEM IN A BANK THEY WILL BE NEEDED – he would know of course that I meant the military papers, not his private letters and things. Naturally it would be read before it got to him, I think I worded it correctly. There was no response, I hadn't expected there to be. Two weeks passed, I was somewhat sour and withdrawn, I couldn't stand to be around mother who had assumed the role of chief mourner, and I couldn't look at a newspaper, I didn't want to know about British victories which did not include General Wingate. One tea time, a guest, a dear old friend of the family, mentioned in passing that command of the Chindits had passed to Lentaigne. I suddenly sat up and demanded that he repeat what he said, and the poor man looked terrified. I proceeded to lose control of myself in front of a roomful of people, behaving, I suppose, as I should have behaved when I was informed of the death of my husband. Orde regretted having taken Lentaigne in the first place, he had no understanding of LRP, a typical Indian Army type, Orde intended to replace him. What nightmarish thing had happened to allow this disastrous outcome? And what did it mean for Orde's men, and for Calvert, and for Derek? *Derek!* Orde had designated him to command, he gave him an explicit instruction, he said, 'if I'm killed, you take command of the force because nobody else is capable of doing it, and if for some reason you cannot, then you must give it to Calvert'.

I already suspected what lay behind this, I sent Derek a second cable, 'WHY LENTAIGNE? YOUR ANSWER BY RETURN'. I was now fluctuating between rage and depression, and mother, understanding me so well, and showing excellent good sense, had me consigned to a nursing home in Aberdeen. It was presented to me as a precaution, my pregnancy was to come to term in six weeks. Now I scoured the newspapers for information about my Chindits and I became more and more certain that the cause of this abysmal decision had been Derek's moral cowardice. But why, if he was in a state of terror and disarray, did he not give the command to Calvert? The answer was provided by Derek himself. While in the nursing home I received a series of very long, detailed and emotional letters, they were very good and interesting letters as a matter of fact, almost tearful, very affectionate but he wanted somebody to lean on. In these letters he told me the story of how, remembering clearly Orde's instructions, he had been frozen in terror at the prospect of having to assume Orde's mantle, so that when Slim had called him and said, 'Who should take command, how about Lentaigne?', the relief was so great that he could only muster, 'yes, general', knowing full-well that the position was his to assign. He had lost his nerve and disobeyed his dead commander. He not only refused his responsibilities just at the moment when his obedience was so greatly needed, he passed the command to a hopeless choice, this man Lentaigne, he couldn't have chosen anybody worse.

I verified all this with Agnes McGeary when she came back and she of course was at the heart of the matter from the start. Agnes McGeary was a matron in the Queen Alexandra's Royal Army Nursing Corps at the 16th casualty clearing station in Assam, and was responsible for Chindit casualties in both campaigns. The Chindits adored Matron McGeary and honoured her, she was called out by Derek to care for Orde when he was in hospital with typhus, and she came to stay with me on a number of occasions in Scotland. After the war I said to her 'I have a feeling that Derek went to pieces after Orde's death, did he not?' and she said, 'oh yes, completely'. She shared my opinion of him and so was quite ready to talk freely to me, and added, 'but of course we were all unnerved by the General's death, there were so many rumours circulating that one could become paralyzed, and one needed to think only of the campaign, but Derek ceased to function.'

Derek's letters also contained a day-to-day account of his difficulties, and his difficulties of course were enormous, as I fully understood. Derek's frank admission of failure, couched as it was in the most intimate and trusting terms, acted as a balm to my nerves and went a long way to dissipating my anger. Two months or so went by, I was trying to learn how to become a mother, I received news that Derek was coming home. As a matter of fact he'd absented himself without leave, in the manner of Orde. Then I got a telephone call from him, saying that he was at his father-in-law's house in Lancashire, and that he had *all* the papers. You can imagine my joy, because there are two things that I've more or less lived my life for: One was that my Jewish friends should triumph in Palestine, and the other was that Orde's reputation as a commander should be established. I'd been through the burden and heat of the day very close to him, had seen his suffering, his agonies of frustration when he got no support from his own people for these so obviously excellent ideas that he had developed over the years. It was a huge relief that Derek had at last extracted them from the files because, had they been left there, the odds were that the enemies who had tried to suppress his first Chindit campaign report would have descended on these files and suppressed relevant information about the second (the reader can never know how implacably venomous a jealous soldier in the operational can be).

Derek said that he was bringing them up to me for safekeeping, and sure enough, he arrived a few days later with Mary, his very strong-minded wife, in Aberdeen, and he was carrying two suitcases. They were crammed with files, every one invaluable, all the training files, the plans for the future, everything was there, private letters from Mountbatten, Churchill's signals, the lot.

I had made up my mind that I would take Derek to one side to discuss another matter that was weighing heavily on me. Mother was in the kitchen with Mary, and I found Derek in the library. 'Was there anything unusual about his death?' I asked, rather vaguely, in the manner of clearing one's throat, and I watched him closely. He didn't reply for a moment, and he had his back to me, as I recall, and then he turned to me and said, 'Prior to it, it was entirely unexpected, nothing seemed more unlikely than that the General might be killed, he was the safest, most cosseted man in India, he had a loyal bodyguard of 10,000 not including the Americans. After it, we realized that no one was actually watching him, we were all too busy doing our jobs. The idea that it had come from our side was anathema, if such a thing was thought possible we would have all packed up and gone home. So there was no discussion on the subject at Chindit HQ, one was far too busy, nevertheless it was there, the thought that it might have come from our side, and it was deeply shocking.'

No meaningful investigation of the crash was ever undertaken because no one clamoured for one, indeed the mere whisper that a British general had been assassinated by his own side would have brought down such a deluge of shame and fury on the whisperer, that no one dared, not even Calvert. It wasn't the time, and there was no profit to anyone in pursuing this line of inquiry. In due course Orde's remains would be shipped off to America to be laid to rest in Arlington Cemetery, without the family even being notified, there is no finer example of the expression 'swept under the carpet' than this final indignity. It might be said that his success was his death warrant for it was not intended that he should succeed on such a scale. Orde was brought in to win points at Quadrant, and then to shake up

Delhi, but Winston was playing a vast game of chess, and there was no part for Orde in the endgame. I'm not suggesting that Churchill ordered Orde's elimination, he was genuinely fond of him, but Churchill had many lieutenants who strove to anticipate their master's wishes. Lord Moyne was such a man, and he was well-known to the Jews.

For my part, the fact that he died seemed all quite proper, it's part of the pattern, I've never missed him for that reason, extraordinary though it may seem to say so. Such people come and go, one mustn't hold onto them. I never felt like holding onto him and it stood me in good stead. If you don't cling, you don't get torn apart when that which has grown through your branches is suddenly wrenched away. I idly wondered if one day an anonymous, or semi-anonymous note might pass through my letterbox from a man, perhaps a dying man wishing to unburden himself of an act, a crime weighing on his conscience. But if I had the smallest desire to avenge Orde's death, what sweeter revenge could there be than the coming into being of Israel?

Derek and Mary wouldn't stay in the house with us, they did not of course find themselves in a very happy relationship with my mother whom they disliked, or with me whom, I realize now, they had never liked either. They told me that they intended to leave the following morning, in fact they arrived in the late afternoon of one day and left on the morning of the next. I was rather saddened because I'd hoped they'd stay for a while, and we could have had long talks together, however I had the files. But as Derek was leaving to go to his hotel that night, he said, 'by the way, I must take the files away with me tomorrow morning because I'm going to start writing the account of the campaign'. I was horrified, of course, but I felt that it was vital that he should, so I said to Derek, 'very well'. 'I must return quite soon' he went on, 'because I'm absent without leave, but I shall stay in London for a fortnight and during that time I shall make a synopsis of the campaign, and as soon as I'm at liberty I shall write a book about it. When I leave again for Burma I shall send the files back to you by a sure hand.' So, he left with Mary, and mother and I sat down at the dining room table and we spread out all the files. She was very helpful, took a paper and pencil, and throughout the night I went through the files, I scanned through as many as I could, it was an immense task, I only jotted down those that were of vital importance, in order of precedence, and what they were about, roughly – I didn't read them.

At about half past seven or eight the next morning, I finished the task, and at about nine or thereabouts, Derek reappeared with Mary, rather sulky by now, and gathered up the two suitcases. I said to him, 'Derek, don't take away anything from the files because I've been through the lot and noted them all down'. 'Impossible!' said he, you can't have done such a thing'. 'Oh, yes', I said, 'one can do anything if one really wants to very much and I spent the night doing it, so good luck to you in your writing, and send them back to me when you finish your task. Go to Rachel Wingate if you want someone to help you because she's perfectly secure', and then I bade them goodbye with as much affection and cordiality as I could.

I received a letter from Derek after a few days in which he said that he'd been in touch with Rachel and that she would bring me back the files herself. Then I had another letter from him saying that he'd gone back to his father-in-law's house, and was shooting partridges – those wretched partridges that keep cropping up, dear little birds, but I now associated them with stress – then my heart began to sink. Came the time when he was due to leave the country and Rachel got in touch with me saying that she'd come up by the night train, bringing the suitcases with her. She arrived early in the morning, when I opened the door for her I found that she had no suitcases. Then of course my heart descended completely, to the ground. She handed me a letter from Derek, she herself was rather upset and had nothing to say, the letter said, 'I have put the files in the care of a third party where neither you nor I can get at them, and it's no good you trying to contact me because when you get this letter I shall be in an airplane on my way back to Burma'.

I became totally unmanned and burst into floods of tears, I foresaw terrible prospects ahead, Derek idle and distraught, unable to get on with the writing of the book, the files God-knows-where. His reason, so Rachel told me – a most unflattering one - was that he was afraid I'd try to write the book myself, or get somebody else to. Now my mother, the night we were listing the files, had said to me, 'this man is not going to give these papers back to you, Lorna, you mustn't let him have them', and I had replied, 'impossible that Derek could be so mean. He must have them because he has the book to write and the book is more important than anything else, so even if he doesn't give them back to me, he must still have them'. 'I think you are very foolish', said my mama, who probably knew more about human nature than I did at that time, 'but you must do as you think best'; I did as I thought right, of course he had to have the files.

Two years elapsed and I had heard nothing from Derek. Orde's papers had by now become an obsession, I attached far too much importance to them, I behaved as if I had found and lost the Holy Grail, whereas in fact the papers were of minor importance in terms of Orde's legacy. After a number of years, once I had regained perspective on the matter, I surrendered them to Derek without a murmur, and never saw them again. For the present, however, I think I was prepared to kill for them.

Jonathan and I went to stay with the Wingates in Godalming, Rachel was keeping the house going, but it was emptying out of people, one by one, and I think she wanted our company. She had invited us down for three months, and it was a pretext for the siblings to ingather and adore the infant, they were all wonderfully besotted with Jonathan because he was a very real connection to something that they all missed dreadfully. Having Jonathan under their roof raised their spirits greatly – not my idea of a holiday of course – but they were as tender with me as they knew how. Naturally Rachel and I discussed these papers and she told me that she knew where they were. They were in fact with Mary's father in Lancashire in his house there at Formby – Mary was a Miss Formby before she married. So I told Rachel that I was going to try to get them back, and I went off to London. I knew of course that Derek would never give them to me if I asked him. He was not in the country he was in India at the time, but Mary was actually at home in Formby. I went off to London and I got in touch with a delightful young man, a friend of mine, a Jew from the East End of London, from Stepney, called Moggy Margulias, very good-looking, very upright, very intelligent – we were just good friends y'know. Now Moggy was in touch with a large number of interesting people, I told him the story and I asked him to find me two skilled safe-breakers, preferably Jewish, who were discrete and responsible. Then I said that I was going off to a firm of lawyers, the best I can find in the City, 'I shall arrange for the defense of these two men should they be caught burgling Mary's parents' house. And I would of course take the blame myself, and if it's any help to them, Moggy, tell them that they will be well rewarded'. Moggy said, 'leave it to me', I went off to a firm called Van Dyke and Oppenheim, the most wonderful Dickensian set-up you ever saw, exactly like those drawings by Cruikshank, early Victorian rooms full of shadows, massive furniture, and the most wonderful little gnome, Mr. Oppenheim who was the senior partner, sitting in his great office all lined with beautiful books. I told him the tale, and asked him if he would undertake our defense, should these men fall into the hands of the police. He looked at me for a while and then he said, 'we shall be honoured. If they are caught, I shall arrange that they shall have the best defense available'. Then he said, 'we, of course, will make no charge'. How very Jewish, I thought to myself; a people who are both practical and romantic, a delightful combination.

    I went back again to Godalming feeling much comforted, for I'd been very unhappy for a long time, worrying about these things, and I thought I'd better tell the poor Wingates because they never knew what I was going to do next, and if I was going to be had up in the Old Bailey or in the papers, I thought they'd better have prior information. I told Rachel who was always far the most sympathetic, and she said – she didn't move a muscle, excellent woman – she said, 'have you thought of asking Mary for them, I know that she's in London at the moment'. 'No', said I, 'I'll do it tomorrow'. So I got in touch with Mary and she asked me to lunch at her club in Upper Brook Street. And I in turn asked her for the papers. Do you know, I was stunned with amazement because she said, 'of course, if you want the papers, Lorna, you shall have them'. I'm going back to Formby tomorrow', said she. 'Can I come with you?' says I. 'Yes'. So I did, and they were duly unearthed from an ancient tin uniform case, I put them into the suitcases that I had prepared for them and I went back again to London.

    The Moggy operation was quickly unmounted, thank heaven, and as I sat in the compartment, looking at the suitcases on the rack on the opposite side, I wondered whether I was suffering from hallucinations, I could hardly believe it. But then within a short space of time my euphoria changed to panic-strickenness lest Mary should want them back again. I knew quite well that Derek would of course have a fit when he heard that Mary had given them to me, and he would probably go straight to Rachel, and I suspected that Rachel would just hand them over to him when my back was turned. I imagined that they were all in it together. In this quite paranoiac state I went off sooner than later to Aberdeen with my little boy and the two large suitcases not forgetting my own suitcases with our clothes and toys, arriving at Tilliefoure a day later, exultant and exhausted. I hid the papers, and then went to bed without rising for a number of days, sunk in deep funk, I must have been in a very bad way.

Mary, poor soul, wrote me a letter, a desperately anxious letter, because Derek was furious with her,. When she told him the news he immediately sent her telegrams and letters telling her that she was to get them back at once, and then he wrote me a letter. Now, I had a secretary at that time, in fact it's fantastic to think that I had a secretary for about two years, and I had no money, so how did I pay her? I don't know, perhaps my father paid her, but she was an excellent woman and she put all of these papers in order for me, together with all my own papers. I used to dictate letters to her to all my friends all over the world, very dangerous thing to do because I got floods of correspondence back again, and only when she parted from me was I able to dam this fearful flow. By not writing back of course to anybody at all. Now, Derek, as I say, wrote me this letter demanding the papers back and I dictated – if I'd been on my own I'd probably never have replied – but I sent him back a letter, which must have annoyed the poor man terribly because it was smug, it was very courteous. He had spoken of his agony of mind at the fact that these papers were now in my possession, and I told him that it was time the agony was shifted to him, and that I was going to keep them. I added that if he wanted them for his book that he should have the use of them whenever he called on me, but that he'd have to use them in some place where I was too. I'd never give them to him to take away.

The Wingates were usually loyal and decent about my surfacings, but I cannot imagine what they thought of my conduct at this time. I was extremely unsteady and cornered, I can see it now, but I could also see it at the time. I was driven by a feeling that I was letting Orde and the Wingates down, and the more I tried to put things right, I seemed to be letting them down further, it was like flailing about in treacle. What were they saying about me? I was burning to know. To my face they were kindness itself, but surely they were in despair. Colonel and Mrs. Wingate had both passed on, but I remained, now more than ever, 'Little kitten', and ' lost little lamb'. Were they in contact with Peggy?

I think that I have been jealous of Peggy all my life. She was Orde's fiancée for six years, and I was his wife for nine. Did I add to his greatness or did I subtract from it? How would it have been if Reginald Buckland hadn't been on the boat, and if I hadn't taken this man from Peggy but he had married her as fortune appeared to decree? I come back to this again and again. In his book, Derek writes that Orde needed, 'somebody alien to himself' – that's a very cruel word to use – 'who is aggressive and uncompromising'. He says somewhere else that Orde and I used to have fierce arguments, and Peggy elaborates too in her letter to him on the fact that he and she were so blissfully happy but he couldn't marry her because he had to steel himself to become, to fight his partner to become a Stalin, a man of steel for the world he was going to inhabit, a quite different world. Is Peggy saying that I was hard and unyielding?

Many years later, I was invited to tea by a girl who had been at St. Leonard's with me, not in my house but about the same age. She'd come temporarily to live with her aunt, and I went round. Now this was a dear girl, very sentimental, who'd had a sort of crush upon me, and her aunt had told me that she'd cherished this affection for what, twenty,

twenty five years or something, and was now overjoyed at the thought of seeing me again. We sat down to tea and she was, I noticed, very silent, she looked at me with her sad pansy-brown eyes, and said, 'I would never have recognized you, Lorna, there is nothing left of you but your eyebrows... when I saw you at school you were so gentle, you seemed so far away, I thought you would never cope with life, I've never seen anyone so changed'. I was saddened by this because she so obviously thought I'd changed for the worse. Was this the seventeen year old who'd forced on a strong-minded man an image of aggression?

When Orde was killed, I received, as I said, the most touching letters from Jews everywhere. My friend Robert Henriques told me that there was a lost-messiah quality to the grieving and yearning among the Jews, a special prayer had been composed for Orde and was used in synagogues across the world, in Palestine flags flew at half-mast. I and all the dear Wingates believed that Orde's reputation would only grow, and that he would sit in the pantheon of great Englishmen alongside Nelson and Byron; was Orde not a composite of these two men? And in that moment of universal grief, leaders and experts, that is to say the politicians and the generals who knew of which they spoke, attested to Orde's greatness. Generals Slim, Wavell, Old, Gifford, Scones, to name but a few gave lofty tribute to their fallen colleague. Not given to hyperbole, these dry, calculating, jealous professionals who agreed on nothing by day, now were as one in calling Wingate 'brilliant', a 'genius', the 'greatest of his generation', the 'greatest of the century'! I had read and heard the tributes from Germany, Russia; from Japan, too, in due course the tributes would arrive. This was all well and good, but while the Te Deums were being sung, and the world was praising him to the heavens, his work in Burma was crashing to the ground, no less than that damned, doomed Dakota.

Derek had had his epic fail, I have recorded my fury and bitter disappointment with the man, he knew better than I what had been lost. Of course, if Lentaigne had had a shred of decency he should have turned the job down. He had no understanding of LRPG, and no desire to learn, he now rode the Chindits into the ground. Derek wrote in his letters to me of the horrors of Lentaigne's command. Would it be unreasonable to suggest that Lentaigne willfully undermined the Chindits, egged-on by his chums in Delhi, in order to discredit a concept to which they had been so vehemently opposed? Derek wrote that Lentaigne had formed a strong dislike of Wingate and considered himself to be the better man. Well, after the better man had finished with the Chindits, he returned to the fold in Delhi where he was promoted and duly honoured, but he never showed his face at a Chindit Old Comrades reunion, and he didn't live to a great age.

Chapter 14

I shall now tell you about Michael Calvert, the finest and the bravest soldier Orde had ever known, and about our meeting at the first ingathering of Chindits after the war. Jonathan was about four years old, I recall, and I had left him at Godalming where he was happiest. The inauguration of the Chindits Old Comrades Association took place in Liverpool, and the first meeting we had – it was a two day event – was held in a hall that had once been a theatre, with a stage and curtains, a little dusty. I was seated in the front row before a stage, between Wavell and Mountbatten on one side, and Slim and Scones on the other, there were a number of other generals there at the front, it was a very good turn-out. I had accepted an invitation to be a Patron of this association, and I had been told that I, as Patron and widow, should be the last to speak. I was not unduly nervous, I'd done this kind of thing once or twice before by now, they had assigned 900 tickets for this event, it was a full house, and so I sat and waited my turn, probably wondering how long it would be until I could curl up in my hotel bed and continue with my book. I had never met a Chindit grouping in the flesh, and although I was touched to be asked to serve as Patron, I wasn't entirely certain in my own mind what the purpose of such an association was.

Mountbatten was first up, spoke very nicely as I recall, and he was given a good round of applause, laughter at all the right places, the men were quite restrained, not quite sure of Mountbatten, one felt. After him came Slim, and then Wavell followed Slim, and he spoke beautifully, almost poetically as usual, and was given much the warmest reception because he had always been a loved general and had done a great deal of work to bring the Chindit association into being, and finally it was my turn. I was dressed in a tight-fitting black woolen two-piece with a little sequin hat, I had all the military badges on my lapels, and I was wearing my highest heels, and of course no make-up apart from my usual crimson lipstick, I wanted to look presentable to these dear men. I mounted the stage slowly and myopically and made my way to the lectern. Before I had traveled half the distance, the men were on their feet; an ovation and I was yet to utter a single word! I carried a large black bag in my left hand, and when I got to the lectern, which stood several inches too high for me – I imagine it had been set for Mountbatten – I positioned myself beside it awkwardly, waiting for the audience to allow me to speak, and while I paused, a most unexpected emotion gripped me and I felt tears coursing down my cheeks. I felt I should do something with my hands, wave, or gesture for silence, or wipe my cheeks, but I couldn't move. And what is worse I seemed to be provoking them with my appalling vulnerability, I might have been terrified, for the men were now stamping their shoes or boots on the floor and making the stage beneath my feet vibrate.

I had of course prepared a speech of about four minutes duration, but Wavell was quite impossible to follow, and I was afraid that I would embarrass myself and not be able to complete my sentences because of the strong emotion which, as I said, I was experiencing. Now, I had in my bag Orde's battered Wolseley helmet; it had been salvaged from the wreckage and sent to me in Aberdeen, and I had never known what to do with the damned thing so I decided to donate it to the Chindits. I imagined that I would wait to the end of my speech, cross the stage, and present it to the chairman of the committee. But I saw that the men were not going to allow me to speak so, for want of a better idea, I reached down into the bag, pulled out the hat and held it girlishly aloft high over my right shoulder. There was a sudden silence in the room, a sort of collective gasp, as if I had broken an ancient military taboo, I looked to the faces of the generals, but of course everything was a soft blur. This had been most ill-advised, I didn't know what had possessed me, at that moment I wanted to die, sinking into the floor would not have been sufficient. Then after what seemed like a long time, a man stood up, I detected some movement in the central aisle, and shouted – barked like a good RSM – with a thick Liverpudlian accent, 'Three cheers for the beautiful and the brave Mrs. Wingate!' The roar that followed was immense, it was like three hard punches to my solar plexus, I had to fight to keep my arm aloft and not to collapse in a heap. And then they cheered me wildly and without restraint, this had ceased to be a reception and had become something else, the generals had become invisible not only to me, hierarchy had fallen by the wayside. The men were giving voice to the loss of someone they and I had loved deeply, and there was anger in it. I placed the hat on the lectern, turned and crossed the stage, concentrating

A Green Rose

on getting down the steps without falling on my face, and returned to my seat. This, I think, gives the reader a taste of what it meant, to serve Orde Wingate.

The following day saw the laying-up of the Chindit banners in Liverpool Cathedral, Anglican Cathedral, a glorious building by the way, full of light and soaring windows. Next was a cocktail party for all the guests and the city notables, and I was standing there, talking to some people when I noticed a man purposefully pushing his way towards me. This was Michael Calvert, he had the appearance of a scholar, nervous around the eyes and carelessly dressed, not at all as I had imagined, and I should not have wanted to talk to the man if I hadn't known who and what he was. He seemed ill at ease in this setting, and we didn't slip into conversation despite my best efforts, but he wanted to meet me again, in the near future, and said that he would call me. Strange man, I thought.

I met Michael in London about a month later, he invited me to his club, and he emerged from his shell. It was most rewarding, but there was no closeness. He told me of some of his post-war experiences, for example he became governor of Bergen in Norway together with a Russian ally and a German who had been governor throughout the war. In our frugal British way we sent a brigadier to govern Bergen, you don't have to pay him as much as a general and you can always demote the poor fellow when you've finished with him, but the Russian and the German were both Lieutenant generals, and according to Michael they all got on extremely well together, and had a happy time. In fact, the German was supposed to hand the place over to the other two but they really ran the place in tandem, and when the German and the Russian heard that Michael had been one of Wingate's boys, they were delighted, and the German said, 'we followed Wingate's career with the greatest interest from start to finish'. Well, that might have been politeness, but the Russian said, 'ah we went one better, as soon as the second Chindit campaign came on the air, we revised our whole training program, and made over a great part of it to Wingate's ideas, so of course, Michael was bucked. He was currently on Montgomery's planning staff, and it had been whispered in his ear that he was being groomed for CIGS. I was of course delighted, wonderful to think that Calvert, Orde's best boy, should become CIGS one day. He'd been to staff college, was supposed to have a massive intellect, you know, and of course quite unexceptionable in every other way.

I noticed as we were talking that he had a rather strange, slightly distracted look. He told me that he had been shown the minutes of a meeting of the Army Council, in which they had discussed the future line to be taken about Wingate and the Chindits. It was felt that Wingate was a bad example for young commanders to follow, damaging to discipline and morale, and 'they don't want any more Wingates in the army'. 'Well', I said 'They can put their minds at rest because there won't be any more Wingates in the army for the simple reason that there aren't any left, those men are just being childish.' He said, 'no, it's quite straight-forward, Lorna, they are telling me that I have a bright future in the army but I must distance myself from the Wingate influence.' I told him that I was very sorry to hear it, and because I didn't attach a great deal of importance to this exchange, the conversation moved along. And then he said, out of the blue, 'I'm thinking of leaving the army and going to East Africa, I've been offered the job as manager of a brick-making concern.' I was appalled, 'Michael, you can't possibly do that', said I, 'you've been all through the vicissitudes, and think of your training, your future, you are a soldier born!' 'Well, the money's better', said he. 'Money?', snorted I. 'You mustn't think of that', then I thought, 'it's no good just saying these things, the man seems to be in trouble of some kind, mental perturbation sort of thing', so I said, 'would you consider taking on the command of the Jewish army, if I could get it for you?' A wonderful thought had sprung into my mind, Michael as head of the Jews, invincible of course. So he said, without looking at me, 'er yes, I should be interested'. Really he was interested in knowing whether I could bring home the bacon, that was all.

It just so happened that I had dined the previous night with some old friends high-up in the Haganah, who were in London on an arms mission, and I imagined that they could be found at their hotel which they were using as a sort of HQ. So away I went in a high state of excitement, called them on the phone, and this proposition was put to my friends, and back came the answer, 'we should be glad to offer the appointment of chief of staff to Brigadier Calvert, he can't actually command because he's not a Jew'. Of course they had Yigael Yadin, wonderful man, and quite capable of beating several armies single-handed I should think, with his intellect anyway, but with Michael, with all the staff he could put together – and after all his father had been an archeologist, what a combination! So, like a dog with two tails, I ran back to Michael and I told him that the appointment was his. He was still sitting having tea at this eternal little round table with a far-away look and said, 'If I were to be embroiled in near eastern politics, I think I should prefer to fight for the Transjordanians'. Well, fair enough, nobody is compelled to want to fight for the Jews, so I said, 'yes, indeed, they are delightful people but do you think they really need you, Michael, they are already officered, they have John Glubb.' He thought about it for a moment, and then he looked at me grimly, and said, 'the Jews bring a man bad luck, look what happened to the General.' There was a fairly long silence in which we both made each our own mental calculation about whether to pursue this particular subject, and then I perked up and said, 'well, I hope you won't go and fight for them Michael, I don't want you to come up against my friends'. Then I had another thought. 'Would you be interested in a kind of holding job? Military attaché somewhere, it's a dignified appointment, it keeps you in the eyes of your superiors, you can learn something about another country and also the ways of diplomacy'. 'Yes' said he, without enthusiasm, 'I should be interested'.

This time I went off to one of Orde's admirers called Adrian Carton de Wiart, and I told him the tale. He knew all about Michael Calvert of course, admired him immensely, greatly distressed that the man might be leaving the army, so he said, 'well, I'll try, I'll go to my friends at the War Office and see if they'll release him, and then we'll try to get him into Chunking', which was Chiang Kai shek's capital, somewhere or other in China. Chiang Kai shek was still in command of China, or thought he was, and of course he was a great friend of Carton's. Carton was the sort of man, 'no sooner said than done', and off he went. He called me up after a few days and said, 'it's alright, the War Office will release Michael Calvert, and Chiang Kai shek said he'd be delighted to have him there as Britain's military attaché'. But this time I said, 'Adrian, tell him yourself, if you will. I don't think he likes to be beholden to women'.

About four days later, Carton asked me to dinner. Well, it was always a joy to have a meal in his house because he had the most wonderful cook, the food was delectable, and that night there was some soup I remember, a wonderful buttery colour, rather thick, and when I was about three quarters of my way through my plate, Adrian said, 'I saw Michael Calvert two days ago'. 'What did he say?' said I. 'He refused the job'. 'Oh dear, what a pity', said I. 'Yes, I think he left for Germany yesterday'. I felt smitten, I felt second sight coming, fairly naturally sometimes, one doesn't have to seek it, a dreadful revelation seemed to flood upon one, and on this occasion I was absolutely sure that Michael was going into some kind of disaster. I said nothing more, presently I looked up and I saw Adrian's bright dark eye fixed upon me, he only had one eye, a man of great perspicacity and experience. If men realized how attractive they are when they wear a black patch, more of them would put one on and take it off when they wanted to see something. And he said, 'would you like a second helping of soup?' And I said, 'yes please'. That was our commentary on Michael, and I never saw him again. Now, a little while later, about a year or so, there was a discrete paragraph in the paper about Michael, that he'd been cashiered for buggery in Germany. Dreadful, dreadful. And when Agnes McGeary came to stay with me for a second time in Edinburgh – she was as great an admirer of him as I was – and I asked her what had happened, she said 'he had been drinking and he lost his sense of direction and the most unfortunate thing happened'.

Another year passed and I moved from Edinburgh, and there was another Burma reunion at which Slim, now governor-general of Australia, turned up, with his very nice wife. By this time I had heard that he'd started to go sour on Wingate and the Chindits, but he was totally civil to me without being cordial, and we had a long talk; nasty face the man had. One of the things he said to me was, 'do you know anything about Michael Calvert?', and I said nothing, so he said, 'he's in Australia, I tried to get in touch with him but he wouldn't have anything to do with me', and I thought, 'well done Michael'. But of course it was a great pity because whatever he'd done in Australia, I'm sure it was not what he should have been doing, it was not up his street or worthy of his talents.

When the war ended things like heroism became just so much meaningless guff. A man with a wooden leg had no place, for he belonged to another age. A man would put his hard-earned ribbons and medals in a box never to be opened unless by curious grandchildren, these are the careless ways of the world; I myself sold one of Orde's medals for 25 guineas ten years after he died. But I never lost my taste for gallant men, and Adrian Carton de Wiart was such a man. He had performed acts of outrageous courage in the First War, he was a known figure in Europe, we were extremely fond of each other, and I was never handled so intelligently by a man. Everything we did together was for me a pleasure and a revelation, and I learnt important lessons. After the First War he retired to a vast estate between Russia and Poland, owned by some friends of his called the Orazivilles, and they donated to him a slice of forest country intersected by streams, and when he went to a dinner party he crossed the streams by boat. He lived in a shooting lodge, he told me, a log cabin of surpassing sumptuousness containing beautiful belongings, for Carton was a great connoisseur, and he was very much respected in Poland, in fact when the war was over they wanted to make him their king, but he very sensibly declined. One never knew exactly what he did in life, he had homes in Warsaw, London and Paris, and much of his time he spent in shooting and, although he had only one arm and one eye, he was a good shot and he used to shoot wild foul among the Prepet Marshes.

One day when he was away in London, some thieves broke into his hunting lodge and took a number of valuable items, and they also took his favourite shooting jacket for good measure, which as you can imagine had been specially made for him. When he came back he was greatly incensed, and he told the police in Warsaw that they must catch these people. After an interval of time his factor took him out into the woods that surrounded the lodge and there lying on the grass were three bodies, the police had done their work, the thieves had been killed and behold, one of them was wearing the shooting jacket. Carton was furious. The jacket was torn with bullets and covered with blood which meant that he couldn't wear it; he didn't notice the man inside the jacket. Carton was fairly robust about some things, and yet he could cry about others. When we attended the opera or the theatre, he would weep – boohoo – at the slightest provocation, even a book could get him going, and the sight of it made me cry, which I resisted doing but felt better for. The upper part of his body was very badly scarred and his bones were broken, he must have been in constant pain but would take nothing for it.

I think that the criterion, the touchstone of what you should weep for is other people's miseries, you must never weep for your own. You should show emotions at all times proper. Men should embrace each other, fathers should hold their sons in their arms and kiss them, this dreadful business of shaking hands should be abolished immediately. One should cry whenever the occasion demands it, but the occasion should never be your own sorrows. There are certain moments in life which demand tears. I used to go to the Edinburgh Tattoo with my son, Jonathan, and there is a great moment when all those thousands of people in their scraping of feet around about the castle forecourt circle, and the castle outlined against the stars, black, the lights all out, with the boom from the Argyle battery, and then, far away, the sound of the pipes, the lights go up, and over the drawbridge come the pipers and drums. Now this was a moment when I never failed to weep but it was because this was true poetry, they were beautiful men, life-enhancers, and they were recruited for death. And these are the contrasts which one must recognize, they make life what it is, they make it worth living, after all, all life ends in death, thank God; can you imagine anything more dreadful than to live forever?

Live forever, never, never!

But it's when youth meets death. Youth and strength and beauty, that's when you find it begets poetry, and that's why one weeps when one sees these splendid men, beautifully dressed, all ready to deal out death and receive it. The French who have a great language – I wish I knew it better – have evolved over the centuries various formula for expressing their understanding of the glory of an honourable death, death on the field of battle. Now the English who have a language I think even more splendid than the French, and who have not died less honourably or less often, are tongue-tied when it comes to expressing their feelings about these things. Possibly our feelings are inchoate, more and more muddled as the century progresses; 'make love not war'? Make love *and* war! I would say. I'm thinking now of the response when the roll is called and the dead don't answer. 'Mort sur le champs d'honneur'. Splendid. What have we to offer? When Nigel Wingate was a colonel in the gunners in Italy during the war, the news came through of his brother's death, and the French general commanding French troops in that area was a man called de Lattre de Tassigny, one of the old school, a chevalier, and he came to Nigel and said, 'Colonel, I felicitate you on your brother's glorious death'. I don't understand why people don't accept this. It increases the intensity of one's living to accept this kind of thing, and yet, you know, there are people to whom this way of thought is quite alien.

A Green Rose

During the war when I was going to these semi-political luncheon and dinner parties, I met a particularly nice woman called Lady Anderson. She was the wife of the Home Secretary in those days, a man called Sir John Anderson, bloody-minded sort of man, memorable for the small, cheap shelter that bore his name, which was issued to all householders who asked for one at the beginning of the conflict. They were meant to be dug into the bottom of your garden, they consisted really of a minute corrugated Nissen hut capable of holding about six people at a pinch, and you were meant to do all the work yourself by covering the corrugated iron with earth so that in the end you were, so to speak, responsible for your own safety, or lack of it. He was a great slab-faced fellow intent only on his own advancement, I would say, a Scot of the worst kind, but he had married, as her second husband, his first wife, a quite unusually intelligent and delightful woman. She had first been married to a young hopeful in the Foreign Office called Wigram, I think his name was Clive. He'd been stricken with polio, and his career had been ruined, but not his married life because he and his wife adored each other, and until his early death she remained his constant companion, and I imagine she was happy to be a companion to such a man with no more prospect than companionship.

She was a lot older than me and she had this fellow-feeling because she saw in me a young woman who was fighting to maintain her husband's career; not to advance it, that was his job, but to maintain a buoyancy, by organizing civilian cadres of friends and well-wishers, and she used to ask me to come and see her. Because I was a well-known fanatic, a Zionist, her husband thought me a totally unsuitable companion for her, and so she was only able to ask me to her house when he was not there. This amused me, it was unspoken of course but we perfectly understood each other.

One day I was sitting in front of her fire when in walked a very tall and handsome man with white hair and black eyebrows, and a small moustache, I think, and this was the Duke of Alba who was the Spanish Ambassador in London at that time. Dukes of Alba, they've been in the forefront of Spanish history for I don't know how long. It was the 17th century Duke of Alba, the oppressive governor of the Netherlands, Low Countries, that had been conquered by Spain who, on being asked by somebody why he never went to church he replied, 'I leave all that sort of thing to my wife'. Well, this sinewy spare figure in its well-cut dark suit came into the room and immediately bowed over our hands and made one of these absurd compliments which one takes as simply the small change of life lived at that level. 'Ah, my dear Ava, in your drawing room one can always find the prettiest women in London'. Well, we all smiled, gratefully in my case, and settled down. Now the point of the story is this. The Spanish of course were neutral, but they were not benevolent neutrals like the Portuguese as I think I've said somewhere else, they were *mal*evolent neutrals but of course Alba was far above all this kind of stuff, I mean wars come and wars go but families go on forever, and presently Ava Anderson said, 'you know, Guitane (or Louis or something), I can't get any oranges'. 'Oh', he said, 'no trouble at all, I shall have a case delivered tomorrow morning' 'Ha!' I thought to myself, 'thank God for those gifts and graces that rise above the hurly burly of war. Thank God for privilege, thank God for the international set, thank God for anything that doesn't become so egg-bound that there are no longer oranges passing to and fro across the frontiers of Europe.

After I retired to Aberdeenshire, Ava Anderson wrote me a letter, 'come and stay with me for as long as you like, Lorna, I should like you to live in my house and make it your own, I want you to do things and meet people again', and I was deeply grateful to her but by that time I had already laid down my responsibilities as Orde's wife. My position as his widow was very different, I didn't have to battle any longer to keep the cohorts together, and I didn't want to return to this attractive life of charming people. I had learnt a good deal about the actual people as well as the way the wheels of power went round, and I conceived an affection and a respect for many of them. They were not only hard-working but they had high standards of personal behaviour, and they were very intelligent, so many of them, it was a great pleasure to know them and to talk to them, but I didn't want to go back into that world. It was a special world which would have had to be lived in fully, I mean, it's not a place you can dip a toe in and vanish once more. Like all such worlds which are composed of social entities, you've got to carry on a steady purposeful contact, and this was not at all what I wanted, I wanted quite a different sort of life, and so I never saw Ava Anderson, or Viscountess Waverly as she became known when he achieved ennoblement.

I was at this time receiving a great many propositions, some decent and some indecent, I was wined and dined a good deal without, I think, being too indiscrete. This was a continuation of the pleasure-seeking period in my life, but I found I was constantly being pulled away from Jonathan, and having been pulled away I would be pulled back again by the thought that it wasn't right not to be with one's child all the time, but I was not in any way a natural mother, how could I have been?

One of the propositions I received came from the Liberal party. It is hard to say what my politics were, I thought I was a feudal communist. I was not at home in modernity, I was repelled by fashionable ideas in politics, I secretly longed for the romance and danger in feudalism, a world I had discovered in books as a child. But for the practical side of life I liked communism, this I had discovered in the kvutzot farms in Palestine, and it was no less a thing of beauty. Since the two things were antithetical, I placed myself outside the political debates of the day, aside from Zionism. There was a woman in Scotland called Louise Glencoates who lived over in Paisley where her husband's cotton reel factories were. She was an alarming woman, one could only describe her as hard, hard as the nether millstone, efficient, and very kind to me, and she persuaded me to go about speaking for the Liberals in Scotland. Her husband Robert was a dear, he was an acute alcoholic and had to be attended all the time because he tumbled down stairs, I think he took to drink to keep himself afloat, Louise was enough to drag any man down from his pedestal of esteem. I used to go and stay with them sometimes, and I liked them both.

Incredible though it is, I remember making three speeches at least in Edinburgh for a man called John Junor who later became the editor of the Sunday Express. He was editor and later ran a smear campaign against Wingate, needless to say this was after I had made the speeches for him and not before. He didn't get in. I heard him on the wireless the other day, cold bad man with a cold bad voice, but usually the Liberal candidates were dears.

A general election was coming up soon after the war, and one day, living in mother's house in Aberdeen – she had gone off to Palestine to avoid the Scottish winter – I received a communication from the Liberal Association of Hackney East in the City of London. Hackney East was a notable constituency both working and middle class with a very large Jewish population and that was no doubt the reason they got in touch with me, and it was the seat of the leader of the Liberal party, Sir Percy Harris, who'd been its leader for years. Now Sir Percy Harris had of course been furnished with a safe seat because they always are, they must be, and he intended to retire at this approaching election, his place as leader was taken I think by Joe Grimmond, what was to become of his seat? They decided to offer it to me, and a member of the association waited on me in Aberdeen, and asked me if I would accept the seat and would I go down to be interviewed in London by the constituency association. Well, I said I would.

Leaving Jonathan in charge of dear Gra – they used to be called governesses but now they call them something else – I went off to Hackney East and on a nasty, cold winter's evening I was collected by their chairman, a wonderful man called Leonard Blaustein, tall and sandy, early middle age, walrus moustache, wonderful sense of humour. He took me out to meet the members of the association in a very small, cold and dirty public hall where, on hard kitchen chairs, about 15 men and women were sitting behind a long table, naked electric light bulb illuminating the dust on everything. I should have been rather depressed by all this but I don't know why, the whole thing became a rollicking beano from the very beginning, from the word go, it went like a bomb. They didn't ask me any questions about my background or my politics or anything I can remember, all we did was laugh and talk to each other the whole time about completely irrelevant things, and the keynote of this was a sort of hilarity.

Presently the meeting, or the interview if you could call it that, came to an end, and Leonard – I was calling him Leonard by now and he called me Lorna immediately – and I, with several other people, piled into a car and started to tour round Hackney East, visiting the houses of faithful supporters. They were cocks of their own walk, these people, because it was a Liberal stronghold so everybody was in the highest spirits, and everywhere we had buns and coffee, and the laughter grew louder and louder. Finally the evening came to an end, one of the happiest I've ever spent, and

I went back to Scotland, prudently asking for two or three days to make up my mind, because it was not a case of them making up their minds about me, it was quite inside out, I had to make up my mind about them, whether I would take the seat or not. My dear friend Robert Henriques once told me 'you're a talisman, Lorna, your name is written on the ring of every Jewish finger in England, and it opens all the doors'. I indeed knew that I was loved by the Jews, and it was a very good feeling.

When I got home, I looked at my darling boy and thought to myself, 'I'm mad, I must have been under the worst form of mental aberration during the last 48 hours, I'm going into Parliament, I won't be able to get out of it, I'm going to sit there for four or five years, on a backbench, this little boy will be looked after by a nanny, I'll see him at breakfast time, I won't even be there to put him to bed if there's a division in the house, what illusion of usefulness have I been labouring under? So I rang up dear Leonard Blaustein and I told him that I couldn't take the seat, and I told him why, and because so many members of his association, like himself, were Jews, they perfectly understood because as you know the Jewish people put their children first, unlike the British, God help us.

Chapter 15

After Quadrant when Orde was in London for a short stay, we talked about what we would do after the war. He thought he might go into Parliament in order to give himself something to do, and to agitate for a Jewish state in Palestine. He also considered resigning his commission and going to Palestine to train and lead a Jewish army, both options would have been open to him. By 1948, Churchill would have been resigned to the creation of Israel, he had quite a different perspective on things now that the war was over and he was out of power. Nevertheless, he would have summoned Orde and said, 'my boy, I understand the generous impulses of a soldier's heart, you feel you must go forth to do battle for what you consider to be right, but think again, there are other paths that a man of honour may tread', etc. etc., and of course

A Green Rose

all those paths would have led to the green benches at the back.

Orde would not have accepted Churchill's fatherly advice, he would have gone out to fight for the Jews and we would have had a wonderful time. At that period the Zionists were very much persona non grata in Britain, and their success was written down with malice and ignorance by all the people who were qualified to write about it. So from being national hero, Orde would have become public enemy number one, because nobody is so much loathed as an ex-love. We would probably have had to stay in Israel for quite a long time, we would have wanted to, no doubt. He would not have taken out Israeli citizenship because he was very proud of being British. I think that at the time of Suez, anything might have happened, that would have been a turning point if he'd been there. What thrills and spills! But of course the moment of reentry would have been, I think, the Six Day War.

The people who have done the most to rehabilitate Orde's name are the Jews themselves, with their victories. Once the Six Day War had been fought and won and all the lone voices in Britain, in the staff college, in the War Office, among the serving soldiers, most of them of junior rank who had been crying in the wilderness that there was a different way of looking at war, Wingate was the man to follow, they would have grouped themselves together, as they did, and their outcry would have been enough to turn public opinion. He would have come back to this country because he loved England – he knew nothing of Scotland. Orde wanted to retire to Dorset, buy a little manor house and write books on philosophy, rather like old Derek. And what a very nice way to end one's days. But it would have taken time before he could come back and be welcomed. Who knows, Jonathan might have been a soldier in the Israeli army, instead of in the British Army!

Having turned down Ava Anderson, and the Liberal party, I now accepted a special assignment from my friends in Palestine, a commitment of three months only. At that time the Jews were in desperate need of weaponry of all kinds, they were putting themselves on a war footing, and they had to buy their arms on the open market and of course the open marketeers were stinging them for every pound they could. Mother stood in for me with little Jonathan, and I made my way first to Canada on a Danish cargo ship. It was soon after the end of the war and transport was very hard to come by, my ostensible reason – I had to give the government a reason for going abroad at all – was to attend a conference of gentile well-wishers of the Jews to be held in Washington. It was a delightful occasion, all sorts of interesting people from South America, they were honeys, the heroes of the occasion. The President of Chile was there, I remember, they all spoke up in favour of the Jews, it was really rather inspiring. Well, we passed our resolutions and we made a lot of friends in Washington.

I made my way to New York and I settled down in a suite in the Waldorf Astoria, a sumptuous place indeed. My mission: to extract from the kind-hearted millionaires of New York, and later of Canada, as much money as possible to be spent on Spitfires, heavy machine guns and other useful hardware. I had a handler in New York, himself a millionaire called Howard, a great Zionist, a man of about sixty five, I would say, and very knowledgeable about other millionaires. Howard took great pains to find out exactly what their financial status was before I approached them because I needed to know how much I could 'touch' them for, and I would go into each meeting fully briefed. He had made his fortune from gaming machines, and he looked like he had stepped out of a George Raft film. He told me that he was my pimp – a new word for me – and after he gave me the meaning, I asked him, perfectly seriously, if I was expected to sleep with donors, and he said, with great agitation 'Jesus, Mrs. W! None of those sons of bitches gets to handle the merchandize, it would be very bad for business.' He told me, 'you've got three things goin' for you: Your name, the fact that you are not personally Jewish, and the fact that you are a dead ringer for Vivienne Leigh, you even sound like her'. This happened to be true.

Howard took me to a friend of his who was a publicist in order to get my name and photograph in certain magazines and newspapers, then he had business cards made for me, and finally he took me shopping to Macy's for warm underwear, boots and a good heavy coat, it was November and the weather was freezing cold. What a wonderful way to see America! I arrived at the beginning of November, and I didn't go away again until the middle of January. I didn't take to New York. Many people say that they find it invigourating, I found it a soulless city, but at the same time I had to admit that it had a character of its own.

I was introduced to various well-intentioned millionaires, and one day a millionaire whose private fortune was 5 million pounds – I'm putting it all in pounds because that's what I understand – who had been vouched for by a lesser fish as possessing this sum, told me that there was a man whose private fortune was 25 million pounds, he was an engineer and he built underground railways and vast dams, he was a construction engineer and I think he landed a contract for building all the subways under Delhi. Howard went to work and discovered that he was a rather sinister figure who kept his private concerns very quiet, he had a number of congressmen in his pocket, and Howard concluded that I wasn't to approach this man. 'Is he a Jew?' I asked. 'Sure,' said Howard. 'In that case I will see him' said I.

I sent a note to his secretary, his name was Alfred, he responded in person, and it was arranged that he would come to my hotel to collect me, and take me out for dinner. On the evening appointed, when I'd just finished dressing, and was about to powder my face and smear on some lipstick, there came a knock on the door, the man was rather early. I opened the door and there stood a squareish, stocky person about 45 years old, very bright blue eyes with a pale, intelligent face, so I invited him to come in and sit down and asked him if he would mind if I went on with my dressing, and I turned my back on him and started to put on some lipstick. I talked to him while I was doing this, and after he'd been sitting on the sofa for about 10 minutes, and I was nearly finished, I heard him say, 'will you marry me?' Well, I took no notice, I thought that if he was drunk he'd be ashamed of himself the next morning, though he showed no sign of being drunk. If he was trying it on as a gambit or a joke, he should be ashamed of himself again, and would probably be only too glad if I overlooked it, so I went on with my conversation. After two or three minutes, he said, 'I don't think you heard me, I asked you if you'd marry me', I said, 'I think perhaps we'd better talk about it later on, and we went off to our dinner.

He made an appointment to see me again a day or two later, and he took me to an extraordinary place of the sort you can only find in New York, a restaurant where the floor was made of black glass, and everything was upholstered in white leather, very few people there and no wonder, it was so fantastically expensive. As we sat, surrounded by obsequious waiters, he said, 'if you consent to be engaged to me, I have a Rembrandt in my house here in New York, I'll have it taken out of its frame and rolled up for you to take back to Scotland as an engagement present'. I said, 'how good of you, Alfred' – we were now on Christian name terms, and no wonder – 'but I never accept expensive presents from people, if you would like to give me a bunch of flowers or a box of chocolates I should be delighted, but not a Rembrandt. So he said rather pathetically, 'the Philadelphia Art Gallery wants it, it's a nice Rembrandt, are you sure you won't take it home with you?' I said, 'of course I would love to possess a Rembrandt but not under these conditions, you must keep it yourself, Alfred. So we left it, he was not at all importunate, he dropped the subject and we went on talking about other things.

A day or two later we were out again, this time I begged him to take me to a place where the seats were upholstered in shabby leather, and the food tasted of something, and the price was one tenth of the place with the black glass floor, so he took me to a nice snug Italian spot downtown where everything was so much more homely and happy. Then when we were in the full flood of our conversation because he was a highly intelligent man, he'd never been married, he was a bachelor, he said, 'I know you don't like New York very much, I'm building a skyscraper and I'm reserving the 30th floor for myself. Now if you consent to marry me, you needn't live in New York all the year round, you can have a house in London, and a house in Scotland if you'd like one, and a house in Paris, and I have my eye on a castle in Rhodes, I think you'd like a castle in Rhodes, wouldn't you?' Clever fellow, of course I would have liked a castle in Rhodes'. So I said, 'with so many residences, Alfred, where would we live?' That was the end of that talk. A few days later we had another meeting – I was getting no money out of him all this time, I was getting rather worried – he said, 'think of all I could do for your boy. If you'd marry me, he'd have the whole world at his feet'. Well, my answer to that was an easy one, I said, 'but his father, Alfred, had nothing but his pay, and he didn't do too badly, did he?' I didn't think he ought to have the whole world at his feet, and Alfred was a man of sense, and he agreed, so we said no more about that.

The next time we went out together, and still no sign of any cash coming forwards for the armaments, he said, 'I think you are quite right when you say that we don't know each other', which was one of my ways of politely stooging him off, of course. He said, 'I'll tell you what, I'll take a house in Aberdeenshire, near your father's house, and I'll stay there for six months and we can get to know each other'. 'God' I thought, 'imagine this man coming to Aberdeenshire and sitting at my father's gates, my father's reaction! 'Don't do that, Alfred' said I, 'what will become of your business?' 'Oh, I'll have that well-organized, I'll get on an airplane from time to time and see how it's getting along', but nothing more was said about that. A few days later – intelligent man, you know – he produced his final trump card, and what a card it was too. He said, 'I'll tell you what, Lorna, you don't need to say that you'll marry me, if you will just consent to an engagement, I will get a destroyer – no trouble at all, I know where I can find a large destroyer at any moment – and I'll fill it with heavy armaments and airplane parts, I'll load it to the gunnels with everything that the Jews need, and staff it with technicians, and send it out there immediately. Now, what do you say to that?' Well, you know, for a few moments there I wavered, and I thought, 'no, you cannot serve the causes that you believe in by behaving badly, I would be deceiving this man if I were to marry him in order to get a destroyer full of heavy armaments for my friends. My friends would have to fight in the power of their own righteousness, and I said, 'no, can't be done'. Then he got into a dreadful state, he refused to see me ever again and refused what's more to give me any money, either, so that was that:

I saw three ships come sailing, come sailing o'er the sea,
And oh! But they were laden with pretty things for me

A Green Rose

One of the most delightful men I met in New York, well anywhere, was a successful scientist, quite young, a splendid intellect – I've always liked brains better than brass – and he and I were unofficially engaged, we went about together – you know one always imagines that these people are more interested in the love lives of microbes or rats. I was attracted by his wit and his intelligence, and because he and I were both Europeans, he was Italian and spoke English perfectly but with the Italian accent and intonation which is so attractive, so we came from different parts of the jungle, and when we were together we used to poke fun at the Americans. I like Americans, they're nice people, however they do sometimes seem rather alien; I remember spending an hour and a half with a man called Bernard Baruch who was an elder statesman in America, and greatly valued by successive presidents, when I left him I felt dreadful, I felt I was his grandmother, the man was about 70 but his outlook on life was so joujou.

One does tend to get rather patronizing when one goes over to America, and my friend and I, my boyfriend and I used to tell each other funny stories about the Americans. One day I said, 'David, have you noticed the extraordinary thing that happens when you have one of those great functions that you and I have to attend – he held an important position in a university so he did have to go to some of these functions – have you noticed this strange habit they have when they are giving a function at, say, the Waldorf Astoria, and the ballroom is furnished for the meal, great tables laden with flowers, silver, drapery, then in the middle of the day, they draw the curtains which they call drapes, and turn on the chandeliers, and everything takes place by electric lights, the ladies come in in sequin dresses and feather hats, and every woman has a hideous mauve orchid about the size of a tarantula pinned to her left collarbone. Apparently it's almost like a medal, everybody has one. It doesn't matter how pretty their clothes are, how lovely their toilette, it's ruined by these appalling flowers that they all wear'. And he said, 'yes, indeed I have noticed'.

A few days later there was to be another grand party, this time not luncheon but dinner at the Waldorf Astoria – the usual, top table at which he and I had to sit, I had to make a speech incidentally, he was no speaker so he was going to be quite quiet, but his various Nobel Prize winning friends were going to be there. I knew exactly what would happen, I'd be ushered in by the toastmaster, the chandeliers would be turned down, a spotlight would illuminate a soprano in a white dress standing on a rostrum with Old Glory unfurled behind her, and at a given signal she'd burst into the Star Spangled Banner, everyone would stand to attention, the lights would go up, and the meal would start. Well now, he was going to escort me downstairs to the dinner, and punctually came his knock on the door. When I opened it he stood there, I had my prettiest dress on, he proffered me a small brown square paper parcel. 'Oh, David how lovely', said I, 'is this for me?' 'Yes', said he. 'May I open it now?' 'Yes', said he. So I took off the wrapper and there was a cellophane box, and lying on its bed of cotton wool, one of these unspeakable orchids, pale mauve, absolutely hideous, exactly what I'd told him I hated most.

Swift thoughts flitted through my head, so I said, 'how lovely, David, how kind of you to think of giving me such a lovely present, I shall wear it', and I pinned it to my left collarbone. Now it was very clever of him, he'd put me in a spot. If I'd said to him. 'how can you David? you know that I told you that I detested this kind of flower' and I'd thrown it down on the dressing table in a pet, he'd be able to tell himself that I'd behaved badly. Bad manners. But if I accept it and pin it to my corsage with a stiff upper lip, then he knew that I'd have to stand up and make my speech feeling defiled wearing something I'd already said I found hideous. Why did he do it? I think he was telling me something, and I thought it disrespectful and hurtful, so I made up my mind to withdraw, and I tactfully did, and went back to Scotland, and then I got a flood of telegrams – jolly embarrassing. He knew that they had to go through the village post office, and the village post office was a clearing house for information in the whole area and they'd known me since I was a tot in a pram:

And I will love thee still my dear
Till all the seas run dry

I raised a great deal of money, something around 800,000 or 1,000,000 pounds for my Jewish friends, but I didn't do the work and I wasn't entitled to the credit, I was nothing but the cherry on the cake, I happened to be the person who made the speeches. The money when it rolled in, rolled in to my address but it was not I who deserve the thanks of those who were going to receive it. Part of it of course was a very easy wicket to bat on, it was in the days when the Jewish State, the embryonic state was struggling for its life, Moses in the bulrushes. I toured all the way across America and Canada, and after the third or fourth time of being introduced as 'Lady Wingate' I stopped correcting them, why spoil their image? Whenever I was introduced to a young Jewish man, I always told him in a most straightforward manner that his place was in Palestine where he was desperately needed, there would be time enough for his career after the fighting was over. I met one of these boys later in Palestine, and he told me that he was there because of me, and fortunately he survived the experience. I also raised money for the resettlement of children on the land in Israel when for twelve years I was chairman of the British

Committee for Youth Aliah. I did raise a lot of money by going about the country, mostly this country but sometimes foreign countries in cold, uncomfortable weather, and making speeches sometimes to small gatherings, sometimes to large ones; not a task I enjoyed. Even the kindly folk whose hands I shook and whose money I took were not enough to reconcile me to what I did, to help me to feel pleasure in what I was doing, I did it because I had nothing else to offer, and somebody had to do this rather dirty job – no, 'dirty' is not the word; this onerous and trying job.

I remember once they laid on Sir Keith Joseph, who was a most respectable character, to come and see me in London, he was the head of Bovis in those days, he was not in politics, and they hoped that he would make a handsome donation, but I, tactless fool, told the truth once too often. He said to me – he was a very presentable young man – he said, 'don't you find it very trying having to ask your friends for money?', and I said, 'I never ask my friends for money'. He left without making me an offering.

When the great battle for Palestine finally arrived, and was running into its eighth or ninth month, and the reports were pretty grim, I settled Jonathan with mother and presented myself in Tel Aviv as a volunteer. Ben Gurion was notified and I was taken to his office. I hadn't seen him since the night of the Blitz on Primrose Hill, and this was the first time I'd seen him in Palestine, and the impression I had was of a different man. In London he gave the appearance of a poorly dressed refugee, very much at a loss, but in Tel Aviv he looked every inch prime minister and commander in chief. I asked him what I could do to help, and he said that I should go about the country to encourage the troops where I found them, and he assigned me a giant called Sergeant Avraham who was charged never to leave my side and protect me from harm, and for two months I suppose I entertained the troops, or they entertained me.

A Green Rose

I came to know the commander of the Port of Tel Aviv. He was a Russian Jew, a delightful man, quite as Russian as he was Jewish, and in my opinion anyway, the most attractive of all the Jewish leaders were the Russian Jews. I don't know what it is, they are very Russian, of course the German Jews are very German and I suppose the English Jews are very English. Think about poor old Robert Henriques, who could be more English than he? But somehow my heart warms towards the Russian Jews, and this man was a professional sailor, he'd been in the Russian fleet, he was captain of the Port of Tel Aviv at a time – my goodness, he had so much to worry about, he had to defend the place with nothing but two machine guns. Now Tel Aviv was a lighter port which means that it had no proper harbor like Haifa, and every cargo ship had to lie off and wait for the lighters to come out, as they did from the Port of Jaffa next door, and bring in the cargos. It was of course a port of entry for armaments for the Jewish forces.

One evening this dear kind man said to me, 'we have an arms ship coming in tonight, an Italian ship, it's under an Italian captain with an Italian crew, and it's carrying heavy machine guns and various light armament, would you like to come out and watch the unloading?' Of course I said yes. So sometime after midnight in the black darkness, because we were always expecting Egyptian air raids, and a blackout had to be observed, and the occasional plane was seen overhead. The Egyptians thank goodness were pusillanimous and ineffectual as they have been throughout their history, for the last - what - 2000 years. More, perhaps. When they were under the Turks of course they were somewhat better, but when left to themselves, without the stiffening of foreign steel, they immediately succumb to inertia, ineptitude, so nobody was very frightened of Egyptian air raids. So after midnight we went out in one of the harbor launches, and there standing off was the Italian cargo steamer, blacked out of course, she was unloading into the lighter by lantern light, practically no light at all, and this man and I climbed onto one of the lighters and we stood there under the bulk of the ship, sensing rather than seeing the descent of the great wooden packing cases of machine guns and mortars, and rifles which were being lowered by derrick, encased in chains of course onto the deck of the lighter. We were standing up in the forepart of the lighter which was a great big solid construction and we could hear the voices of the men unloading and we could see the occasional gleam of lamplight, but that was all. Quite suddenly my friend gave me a violent push and I staggered back and down between him and me crashed an enormous crate of mortars, it had slipped its chain, it crashed on the deck of the lighter and the boat shook and shuddered, I was amazed because I felt the wind of it as it passed me. 'Are you alright?' said I to him. 'Yes', said he. 'How did you know it was coming?' said I. 'I don't know' said he. 'Something told me'.

We went aboard the Italian ship and we had a delightful evening with the Italian captain who was a sort of pirate, wonderful man with a face all stubbled over with an unshaven black beard, gay, kind. I remember vodka was his tipple, and I downed glass after glass of vodka, tiny little glasses and you're supposed to drink the stuff neat, and we sat down and talked about politics and life and religion, all sorts of things you're not supposed to discuss, and presently we climbed back into our launch as the ship had been unloaded by then. He was a sort of freelancer man, I don't know whether he owned his ship or whether he was merely pirating her for the money for the time being but he was a regular gun-runner for the Jews – I was told that the Italians were very helpful. 'I'm a professed Catholic' he told me, 'and I believe that the Jews are the people of God, the hand of God is upon them and they must win this war' I felt he was a man and a brother. So this was one of the happy evenings of my life.

I was called upon by Yaakov Dori, another gallant Russian, we had been friends in Haifa, and Orde had had a high opinion of his abilities, and he had been charged with organizing the army. He told me that young men walked up off the beach and were handed a weapon, there wasn't time to train them, if they survived their first 48 hours of combat, it meant that they were trained. I realized that what he might have learnt if he had gone to Camberley would have been of no use to him in his situation. He told me with feeling that they missed Orde so badly that it was forbidden to mention his name.

In Palestine at that time I came across what I believe to be a true miracle. I believe in miracles but this is the only one in my life where I was almost actually present. There was fighting of course throughout Palestine against the five Arab armies, rather a raggle taggle lot, apart from the Transjordanians, officered by British officers, well-equipped with British tanks and heavy armament, and the Jews had great trouble in holding them. Now the Jews were holding the line of the Jordan, indeed Transjordania was exactly what the word implies it was the country across the Jordan, and there was a Jewish village called Gesher, which is just a Hebrew word for bridge. And this settlement, very small and modest, a hamlet really, had been built beside a stone bridge which spanned the river Jordan. It was not a very old settlement, and not at all a wealthy one, it only had one small street a few yard long and it boasted two stone houses, one on each side of the street, everything else was built of wood. Now at that time I was going to and fro throughout the country, visiting the various outposts of the fighting, I and sergeant Avraham (he later became major-general Avraham) came to Gesher to see how they were getting on because they'd been having a bad time with the Transjordanians across the water. We arrived I suppose at about half past eight in the morning, the place was very quiet and we were met by the Mukhtar which is an Arab word meaning head man which was used by the Jews too to denote the head of their various settlements and villages, he was always known as the mukhtar. This was a youngish man I suppose about thirty five, exhausted by weeks of fighting and sleeplessness. He was perfectly steady, the place appeared to be semi-derelict, the shells had fallen amongst the wooden houses, one of the stone houses had had its roof blown off and on the earthen track between the two most substantial buildings in what could possibly be called the village street, stood a burnt-out lorry, down on its rims, completely blackened, metal seared and twisted.

The mukhtar took us to his little eerie, his lookout post that commanded the opposing bank of the Jordan and there we looked across the bridge which gave the place its name, Gesher, but there on the other side I saw the enemy in his emplacements and artillery pieces. So we said to him, 'tell us what happened', and he said, 'well, last night we had a most extraordinary occurrence,' he said, ' we wanted to evacuate the women and children, but we couldn't do it because the shelling was continuous, and of course the Transjordanians commanded the only road back into the hinterland, so we made up our minds that we would try to get them away last night. We put them into one of the stone buildings as being a safer place than any of the others in the village, and then when darkness fell, a lorry came up with ammunition, and of course all supplies had to be delivered under cover of dark, they were running short of food, ammunition was their great problem, and this very large lorry was something they had been long looking for.

This lorry crept up and parked on the village street in between the two stone buildings in one of which the children were sheltering and there was a strong wind blowing at the time, and just at that moment a shell came over from beyond the Jordan, and it crashed onto the engine of the lorry and the fuel tank, the whole thing burst into flames. Now the body of the lorry was piled, packed high with crates of explosive: hand grenades, bullets, and the men knew that if the flames once got back onto the crates, not only the lorry but the buildings on either side of it would go up, and the women and children with them. So they began to work, they didn't think of themselves, all they thought of was getting the explosive off the lorry, and he told us this in a very matter of fact way, and he said, 'of course we worked like hell but it looked as though it was a losing game, the wind was blowing the fire back, you see, so strongly. They were beginning to lick over the wooden boxes, and then he said, 'do you know what happened? The wind changed. Instead of blowing from north to south, it blew from south to north. We got the stuff off, and just as we got the last crate off, the wind changed again, and it blew from north to south, and the lorry was consumed.'

There's a parallel to that in history, Joan of Arc and Ginois, the bastard of Orleans, standing at the river looking across to Orleans, praying for a wind to carry their ships across, the wind changed, they looked up and saw the banners straining on their poles, then turn and blow in the other direction. It was considered a miracle by Joan, so I don't know why we shouldn't consider it a miracle at Gesher. And as though that was not enough, when the dawn broke and they looked across the river, all the Transjordanian tanks had gone and they never came back.

I was taken to meet the commander of the Jewish immigration, and he was responsible for the acquisition and the sailing of the refugee ships such as the 'Exodus'. Most of them were thoroughly unseaworthy because they had to buy the cheapest, and the ships were often beached and blown-up, and he said to me, 'we are going to call our latest ship the 'Orde Wingate'. Do you approve of that?' I said, 'indeed I do'. From the mainland of southern Europe they organized the ships that brought in the carefully selected, mostly young, and laid yet another foundation stone for the Jewish state. This was mounted by young men and women of great brilliance, wonderful ingenuity, and then the commander said to me, 'we've got another ship, and we're thinking of calling that the Lord Byron' Another freedom fighter, you see. I said, 'oh no, don't call it that, you have a marvelous man of your own to call it after, Yehuda Halevy, who lived in the 12th Century and was a great poet who sang of Zion and who never saw Zion. So they did, and I'm glad to say that Yehuda Halevy's name at any rate reached the shores of the Promised Land. They were great days of course, full of people doing sometimes splendid things, sometimes silly ones I suppose, but everyone was larger than life, and rather better I suppose.

Many of the commanders in this war had been Wingate's boys in the SNS, and if I arrived at a certain place with my great, burly bodyguard they would come and find me and drag me back to their encampments to feast me and introduced me to the soldiers. I asked them about their positions and that of the enemy, and they would pull out their maps and would explain everything to me in perfect trust. The act of being in a group of soldiers, hemmed in, going over a map and talking the language of soldiers did for me what shopping at Harvey Nichols might do for another woman; the aroma of cordite was my Chanel No.5. I felt that I could lose myself in this place, and didn't ever want to leave. Of course I knew I was a freak of nature, and knew how far I could go with this boyish fantasy, so I would take a deep breath and announce, 'I have to leave you brave men now, so who will drive me back to my room?' If the men had protested and clamoured for me to stay, if they had taken me captive, and tied me to a tent pole, I should have acquiesced, and put on a uniform, and gone out to battle with them.

One learns things, one picks them up by the wayside, knowledge blows into you almost like waste paper and you're not expecting it. Ben Gurion was still going to and fro in the midst of the fighting because bullets were still whistling overhead, he invited me to go with him one day to inspect the troops who had conquered Jaffa, and had taken over the whole port area and had annexed it to Tel Aviv so that Jaffa and Tel Aviv became one from then onwards. Now they'd had a pretty hard fight, Jaffa was an Arab port, it had been strongly fortified, and its fall had been bloody. The Jews were lacking all heavy armament and they had to make up with courage and ingenuity what they lacked in firepower. Now the Irgun who were the Fascist Jews, if you can use such a contradiction in terms, they had thrown themselves into the fray on the side of the Palmach, that's the assault troops of the Jewish Agency. They had fought like lions but of course their political opinions were anathema to David Ben Gurion, because Menachem Begin and his boys were very right wing according to his way of thinking.

In the kindness and generosity of his heart he allowed me to see this for myself, and we sat in the back of the car on this very hot day, and I remember being greatly impressed by the upholstery they'd arranged for the seats. It was obviously a vehicle that had been designed for a hot country, and they had a kind of wicker work upholstery, not the plush stuff which is supposed to keep our bottoms warm in freezing weather, but something for poor sweating inhabitants of hot countries. As we leaned back in this rather sumptuous vehicle, we progressed through Tel Aviv, and finally he and I came to the shattered buildings of Jaffa and there David reviewed his stalwarts, the regiments of this and that, talked to their commanders and so on. Now when we were on our way back, he said to me, 'there's a detachment of the Irgun who have been fighting alongside our boys and they are going to be somewhere around here', he said, 'I don't propose to stop and speak to them'. I was appalled. How could I, without being presumptuous, suggest to him that it didn't matter what a man's political convictions were if he'd offered his life in the service of a common cause, you have to stop and review him. So I said, 'David forgive me, but when we do reach them I suppose they will be lined up on the road like everybody else...'. 'I suppose so', he said. I said, 'remember that they died too. Stop the car, and get out and review them because they're your children, you know. You may think they're erring children, but they're still yours, and one must never disown one's children.' So on the border of Tel Aviv and Jaffa presently we came alongside a lot of shattered masonry, there stood a body of men, immaculate – of course the right wing always are - boots polished, buttons gleaming, berets on the side of their heads, and grim looks, my God! The expressions on their faces, they didn't know what he was going to do, you see, and he was, after all, the chief of the new Jewish state. He stopped the car, he got out and he did review them, but he didn't do it with any warmth. I wished he had. If he had just embraced their commander and said, 'my dear boy, I'm proud of you', who knows, it might have been easier for him later on when it came to the talking shop.

I saw now that Ben Gurion was a very great man, a massive presence like Churchill, but capable of human warmth, and with me he was all gentleness and consideration. We never referred to conversations we had had when Orde was alive, but I had a call to my hotel one day, shortly before my departure and a woman secretary said that the Prime minister wished to speak to me, and Ben Gurion came to the telephone and said that he was sending a car for me because there was an important happening, and he wanted me to be present. I reminded him that there was a shortage of cars and petrol, and that he shouldn't put himself to the trouble, but he insisted and insisted again in the sweetest and most complimentary manner, and so I put down my book, and put on my best outfit because I imagined there would be photographers, for this was to be the opening of the Knesset.

I was taken off in a car driven by a young girl to Tel Aviv and we came to a place with a great throng of people in a state of excitement, and I was led into a building, with such a cacophony of shouting and movement which often characterized official Jewish gatherings of this type. I was taken out onto a balcony where there were a number of people I recognized, some I hadn't seen for many years, who kindly beckoned me to stand with them, and in front of us was a sea of smiling faces and flags, the new flag of Israel. This was February 15, 1949.

One final vignette from Palestine, which I think will amuse the reader. I was resting in Tel Aviv for a couple of days between engagements, as it were, and I was rung up in my hotel by a young woman who asked for an appointment, and the next day she came round. She was a very personable, rather impressive girl, about the same age as myself, about 29, something like that, 27, 28, she was dark, handsome with a bold, flashing black eye, and she told me that she was going to write a book, and she'd had the presence of mind to make out a synopsis, and if I gave my approval she intended to write forthwith. I sat down and read this synopsis which was well set out, she spoke excellent English

I may say, although she was not from any English-speaking country, and as I read with growing amazement and dismay, I realized that what she intended to do was to write a semi-fictional fantasy about Orde and me. The story was concerned with a hero who came to a land not his own to liberate its people, and in fact followed Orde's career quite closely, the only thing was she made him fight his battles in Palestine, and die in that country, and then came the climax, which was going to be the final scene of the book; his peerless wife who had accompanied him throughout his vicissitudes, went up into the mountains of Galilee, came face to face with her husband's second-in-command or GSO1, I suppose we'd call him, and the two of them sealed a pact in the sunrise that they would now go forward together commanding the army of liberation. Well, what on earth was I to say? I didn't want to be the subject of this book, I didn't want someone trying to read my mind, and who knew if it would be any good? She was a very strong-minded young woman and I didn't want to alienate her by showing distaste, I thought she might go away and write the book there and then if I did, so after furious mental activity, I said, 'you and I... – this is most interesting of course, such an interesting idea – but you and I both want the same thing, I think, we want the young men and women who are joining the army now to look on Wingate as their pattern, and if you suggest that I had anything to do with his greatness as a soldier you will split his image and the young men and women will become confused, so I do ask you, lay this theme aside'. Well, the girl had excellent manners, we got on very well, and she went away and I never heard any more about her or the book. I hope I managed to direct her energies elsewhere, and that particular piece of nonsense was killed at birth. But imagine some stuff like this circulating in Israel with myself as a modern Deborah holding hands with her Barak. I think I'm probably more like Yael with her tent peg – what an iron hand that woman must have had as she drove the tent peg through Cisera's temple! There may be people who find their eye of the hurricane, their point of peace in another such as Orde, fortunate they. I do not. I think I find my epicenter in the contemplation of nature, and that's something best done alone. Marvell wrote a beautiful epitaph, it was on a girl as a matter of fact but it would do just as well for Orde:

> *Enough, and leave the rest to fame*
> *Tis to commend him but to name*
> *Nor can the truest wit or friend*
> *Without detracting him commend*
> *That his soul was on heaven so bent*
> *No minute but it came and went*
> *And ready his last debt to pay*
> *He summed his own life up every day*
> *Tis true, but all too weakly said*
> *Twas more significant, he's dead.*

Chapter 16

During the war, when I was living at Hill Street, my telephone was tapped. The Near East had been, so to speak, put into cold storage, the war was on and the Jews were desperately trying to fight for the British and being frustrated in their efforts, the Arabs were just hanging around on the outskirts waiting to see who'd win, nevertheless the Foreign Office was concerned to know what the Jews were up to, and they thought they might learn something from me. I don't think they believed me to be a person of importance but they thought that I might be a lead-in to others who were. A girl who was in my house at school – no great friend – came to see me in Aberdeen when Jonathan was about three or four, she came without invitation and quite unexpectedly, and she told me that during the war she'd worked at the Foreign Office, and she said, 'you know, you had a dossier there, Lorna'.

I didn't ask her what was in it, I thought it might have been embarrassing for her, but I wasn't surprised. I don't think I came under a 'purple warning' or whatever they tab them as, you know, I think I was pretty low down on the list of interesting people but they probably had a brief documentation of my antecedents and they certainly listened to my telephone conversations, and did so for some years after the war, and opened some letters too. It was the Foreign Office that did it, not MI5, I was not supposed to be a spy, what I was supposed to be was a contact with interesting people who were likely to cause trouble in the Near East. Now it's true of course that most people who deal with these documents – and don't make any mistake, there are thousands and thousands of dossiers in the Foreign Office and Special Branch and MI departments, and rightly so – we pay these people to do a certain job, for heaven's sake let them do it even if they do it on us. It's true that most of these people who handle these documents are discrete, I don't mean secure, that's something quite different, concerned with their own careers and future, but discrete about the material they see. However they do let drop a word here and there, particularly on the unimportant people like myself, and a picture emerges at the end. In my case, an unacceptable picture because remember I was not backing the Arabs as many a personable female has done before me, and got away with it, but I was backing the Jews.

The Emperor of Ethiopia was always after me to go out there, and I never wanted to go, I had a feeling that something would go wrong if I did. At last when Jonathan was six and I must have been 33, he asked us both to go in order to open the General Wingate Secondary Modern School in Addis Ababa, it was going to be the beginning of a university college which would take young boys from 13 to 19, I felt that I could no longer say no, I'd already refused three other suggestions that I should go out to Ethiopia. Jonathan had an infection of the throat which had lodged in one of his ears, and I knew that if I took him up in an airplane, although he was quite better, that he might well suffer a recurrence of pain in his ear. When we arrive in Ethiopia he might become quite ill, and I couldn't face the prospect of taking him to a country like Ethiopia in a parlous physical condition, so I left him behind in suitable care. I set off for Ethiopia with some misgivings; misgiving about leaving my son, and a general feeling of unease about what awaited me in Addis Ababa – call it a premonition.

I traveled by way of Tel Aviv and Nairobi because as my name was Wingate and I didn't want to go through Cairo. I didn't think the Egyptians would be very unkind to me but I thought they might take me off the plane, and keep me for three or four days, and make themselves troublesome, so I went via Israel and this took rather longer. I tried to get the Israelis to show a little interest in Ethiopia, I asked them if they had a message for the Emperor. Wouldn't they be interested for example in starting up a cattle enterprise because, you know, in Ethiopia they have great territories but very little technique, and I thought that as Israel was notably lacking in protein, they were having difficulty in finding meat for their citizens, why should Ethiopia not prove to be a partner of Israel? It seemed so suitable. I was horrified to learn that because Ethiopia had a Muslim population as well as a Christian one, it had abstained from voting for Israel in the United Nations when her de facto and de jure status came into question. Believe it or not, the Israelis, beloved idiots that they were, they were not going to have anything to do with the Ethiopians. 'We have no file', said Moshe Shertok, 'we are not concerned with the Ethiopians'. 'Come, come', said I, 'you must be concerned with the Ethiopians, they can give you what you need and you can give them what they need, technique. You need the basic commodities of life, food for instance, they've got the spaces, and also the goodwill if you will only exploit it, if you will only encourage it'. Well, you can't force common sense on people and Moshe behaved like a child and an ass in this instance.

I left Israel and went on to Nairobi which was the next leg of my journey. There I was met by kind friends, and after a day or two I flew north in a very comfortable little airplane passing Mt. Kenya on the way, splendid mountain shaped like a true mountain should in the shape of a horn like the Matterhorn. I was surprised as we passed this splendid peak rising from a great jungle of green, eternal snow on its summit, I was surprised that there were no shadows anywhere. The aircraft seemed full of light, you know the usual thing in an airplane is that sunlight comes in from one side or the other, but in this aircraft one seemed to be contained in a capsule of light, and then of course I realized that we were on the equator and it was noon, the sun was plumb overhead, and there were no shadows.

The Emperor had been very wise and cautious. His air force was run by the Americans, his educational system was run by the British, the Italians built his roads and maintained a good deal of his public works –they are very good at that, you know – only the Russians in their great faceless embassy surrounded by high fences like a deer forest, silent and apparently deserted with no sign of human life, only they were not permitted to undertake any responsibility in his state. It was said, I don't know with how much proof, that from the Russian embassy in Addis Ababa, the Russians were penetrating the whole of Africa. When I arrived at Addis Ababa the airport was rather shabby, it was run by the Ethiopians, and I was carried off to an enchanting palace, a sort of Petit Trianon in French style with a lovely garden all set with roses and lilies and seether trees and lawns, I had lion pits at the bottom of my garden but there were no lions in them, there was a little stream running down a green valley, and climbing plants overhead, it was an enchanted place. I was given a bodyguard of six Ethiopian soldiers and a corporal, on the first day of my visit they accompanied me wherever I went.

On the second day of my visit, I summoned my major domo, because my palace was fully staffed with chef and housemaids and major domo who spoke English, and I said, 'I want you to bring the corporal to me', and the corporal came and I said, 'now translate carefully; tell the corporal to go back to his commanding officer, and to thank his commanding officer for the courtesy he has accorded me in providing this bodyguard, that in a country so civilized and well-run as Ethiopia, it's quite unnecessary for a woman to be accompanied by a bodyguard because no citizen of Ethiopia would offer a discourtesy to a woman by herself. So away they went, the bodyguard vanished and I was able to get about by myself after that.

They gave me a lovely motor car, a Rolls Royce with a chauffeur, but the thing that really gave me most delight was the fact that it was all electric, in those days, it was not so common to have motor cars where you pressed buttons and cocktail cabinets opened up in front of you, and windows went up and down. I made my chauffeur drive me all over the place, not really so that I could see the countryside but so that I could press the buttons.

I had great fun in my flowery garden and my little pink and gold palace. On the first day of my arrival my major domo came to me, tall thin dark man with head of fuzzy hair, and he asked me if I should like to eat French or eat Ethiopian. Well, naturally I said that I should like to eat Ethiopian. This meant that the food was unutterably bad. The Ethiopians eat their meat raw, or almost raw, but they have been told that this is not acceptable to Europeans, so the poor dears toasted all my meat to the consistency of shoe leather, thinking this would please me. All the vegetables came out of a tin, and after a while I began to dread my mealtimes, and then I remembered that Orde had said that on his Ethiopian campaign, he had been sustained – and probably kept in good health – by drinking the native brew which was called tedge. I think it is brewed from grain, millet perhaps, and the tedge that he drank was the rough country stuff with the grain still in it, a sediment at the bottom, he told me it was delicious. He also told me it was exceedingly potent.

After three or four days of eating Ethiopian, I wondered how I could do something to make my mealtimes more palatable, so I asked my major domo if it will be possible to taste the wine of the country which my husband had told me was so excellent, could I perhaps have a bottle of tedge. Immediately there appeared from the Emperor's cellar a case of tedge, the very best Imperial tedge no less, and thereafter a bottle appeared every day on my luncheon table, tall bottle like a hock bottle. The tedge that I drank had no sediment in it, it was a wonderful moonlight green, I drank two bottles a day, a bottle with each meal, and it had no effect on me whatever except that it made me feel even better and happier than before but it was totally nonintoxicating as far as I was concerned, however it served to give some meaning to my meals.

When I'd been in Addis Ababa for two or three days, the wife of the first secretary of the British Embassy called upon me, a courtesy call, she was a delightful young woman only a year or two older than myself, perhaps the same age. She was rather cold. She asked me why I had never been to Ethiopia before, I can't remember what answer I gave her. She grew more friendly, and she asked me to come and have lunch with her husband and herself, and a day or two later I went along to the British Embassy, which was a delightful place, so very different from the Russian next door, rather like a nice English country house with one or two smaller houses in the grounds, a Sudanese sentry at the gate. The First Secretary's house was modern and small and unpretentious, and her charming husband was there to greet me, youngish man, there were little prams with babies disposed about, they had a few people to lunch who were connected to the General Wingate School, and when we were all assembled, the door opened and the most important person came in as such people do, last of all. He was a man, this was the ambassador. He walked in, and I fell in love with him. He was about 15 years older than myself, I suppose, not very tall, or very broad or very imposing, just the man I loved, and that was all there was to it.

What a catastrophe! I was appalled, I could do nothing about it, like an avalanche or an earthquake. We had an interesting lunch, he was way up at one end of the table at his hostess's right, I was way down the other end on my host's right, and we looked at one another from time to time, but that was all. But I was devastated and it had a profound effect on my later life. I was knocked off course, you see. It was just as if I'd been on an interstellar spaceship, and I'd been hit by a meteor. I was still powered but I didn't know what my direction was anymore.

Presently I went to the General Wingate Secondary School, I performed my function, I opened it, and this man and I were left alone to have tea together, surrounded by hundreds of people but we were permitted to talk together for an hour or two, and I can't remember a single word that we said to each other. And then he gave a dinner for me at the embassy, and we sat next to each other as before – my mind's a blank, I only remember my anguish, I don't remember anything that he said, indeed my mind was distraught – and after I said goodbye to him at that dinner party, I knew that I would never see him again. I had the feeling that this was going to be not a joy of life as it might have been, but it was going to be a tragedy, if you can call something so inconclusive a tragedy, that had no beginning, no middle and no end, all it had was consequences.

I'd been about 10 days in Ethiopia, I'd been about a little, I'd been to one or two official functions under the Emperor's wing, he was kindness and graciousness itself, delightful man, treated me as a princess, brought me in with the Royal Family to do all the things that they did during their liberation day, and so forth. He was a grand seigneur, the Emperor, he always did the right thing in the right way, but I was in torment and I thought that the only thing to do was flee, apparently the Ethiopians were rather annoyed, they expected me to stay for two months but I only stayed for two weeks, I wanted to get back anyway, and so I booked my passage back on the airline to Nairobi, and all was punctilio, and the First Secretary saw me off, and I climbed into the aircraft.

A most interesting physical phenomenon took place, I was the subject of something I will always remember with interest. I was in great agony of mind as I left Addis Ababa, and it was as usual a gorgeous day with the sky a warm, bright blue, the sun pouring down on everything, springtime in that part of the world. But as I got into the airplane I saw – not to my astonishment, I was past feeling anything like astonishment by then – everything was brilliantly clear but it was all in black and white, the seats in the airplane were white, bone white, and all the lines of the aircraft were outlined, clear and white, but outside the windows everything was black. They put me in the back seat, there was nobody else in the plane except myself, they put VIPs there so that when the crash comes you stand some chance of survival, and there I sat for the whole journey, and at some time or other I was joined by the co-pilot, delightful young man who probably thought that I needed amusing because

I remember he was sitting beside me, and I was tormented by his presence, I had to talk to him, you see, I remember hearing myself talk to him, he laughed and seemed quite happy so I must have seemed normal in appearance. I had no idea what was going on about me, and all the time everything that was bright in nature was black. The whole sky was like outer space, any object in it was illuminated but the whole background was like black velvet.

Presently we passed Mt. Kenya once more, on our right side rather than our left, and there it stood and every detail was clear to my eye, but it stood out against a black sky against a black earth. Some poet somehow has used a phrase, I don't know who or where,

'Rob the sky of light'.

This is a literal description of what happened to me on that journey. When I got out at Nairobi my friends were there to meet me, they looked at me strangely, perhaps I did have something odd about my appearance at the time, they looked anxious, they took me by the hand, took me to their house, of course, and there everything came back into colour again, I saw the garden and the bright flowers, and the blackness passed away, and after three or four days I returned to Israel and from Israel I returned to Edinburgh, and there I crawled into my hole to recover.

I'd gone back to my childhood, I wanted only to hear his voice and see him, and this was denied. The thirties are a carnal decade, one is at the height of one's powers then, one's physical powers, one is full of ebullience, and yet although I was 33, I loved him as a child would love. It's not that the wound doesn't heal, it does, but one is only part of one's natural creation, there's a loss that is never to be made up. He's dead now, perhaps he never knew that I loved him, I think it quite likely although I can't help thinking too that

A Green Rose

I must have shown it, I think I was as naïve as a schoolgirl, that anybody could have seen, probably by looking at me, these things can't be concealed. He was very sweet to me. I wish I could remember a single thing he said to me, but I can't. He was a recluse, like I am. I know nothing about him, only that he was the man I wanted. I know now that I was in a very weakened state, I was literally crushed. Perhaps this goes some way towards explaining why I now went on to make the two greatest mistakes of my life, one hard on the heels of the other. I've never forgotten him, and in a sense I've never got over it.

Chapter 17

The British Legion is an excellent organization run along military lines, doing important work and staffed by many hundreds of dedicated volunteers. They asked me to be honorary president of the British Legion. This would be an ideal position for an older woman, wife of a mandarin, or of a retired general perhaps, who is glad of the social contact that goes with the job and doesn't need to earn a living. It is also a useful letterhead to have when writing to creditors, headmasters, bank managers, and when writing letters of complaint of all description. Of course I wrote back, 'what a great honour' etc, and accepted the position, so now I chaired meetings, made speeches and went to Horse Guards Parade every year to watch the turnout, and there was always a large number of Jewish women at these events.

A Green Rose

At the time I held this position, German re-armament was in the news. The British government, and the French, agreed that Germany should be allowed to have a very modest army, a token force, and, like the previous time, it caused a great deal of discussion. I think really the French and the British and the Americans engineered the whole thing because they were afraid that the Russians were going to encroach into Europe, and they wanted the Germans to do their share of anti-communist, they wanted them to build the dyke against the communist flood. And so it was agreed between the three western allies that Germany should be allowed to rearm in a very modest way, I mean the whole thing was extraordinary, it was quite harmless, but it was seen as a beginning. And many people in England were greatly upset. 'What?', they said, 'the raw material for another German army and a Third World War? The Germans are totally undependable, we must keep them disarmed for a whole lifetime'.

That was not my view at all. How do you treat your enemies when you have conquered them? I think that the British have always chosen the wrong path. They have subjected their enemies to a period of probation during which they were second class citizens. At the same time because of our incurable British romanticism we assert that we owe them something. They were defeated, they are lying on the ground, we have got to pick them up. We picked the Germans up, the Americans helped us to do it, after both World Wars. But at the same time we left them far too long as second class European citizens. Now there are only two ways to treat your conquered enemies. One is to exterminate them, and this is quite a practical proposition – or was in days of old when numbers were so much smaller. And I myself, if I were a conqueror, I would consider it, I would give it first priority. I'd have no qualms about the unborn child, I would extirpate my enemies and then I'd have no more trouble from them. But of course, I'm only half civilized. In fact it is impractical to extirpate whole nations nowadays, Hitler tried it with the Jews, he had every modern convenience but he didn't succeed; not only have they reached their former numbers but they are far more potent than ever they were for the past 2000 years. That's perhaps an answer to the question, 'should one extirpate?' But the other solution seems to me to be the only one that offers itself. One must treat one's enemy as an equal, a partner if you like, not as a friend but as an equal, and one must do it from the very start. Let there be no period of probation – just a waste of time – begin as you intend to go on. Set him at your right hand, treat him as an equal, let there be no talk of thee and me, only we.

Naturally, the British Legion had an interest in this thing, and they asked me to come to London to join a demonstration at one of the big halls there, Caxton Hall or something, there was going to be a great meeting, MPs, cabinet ministers mostly, I may say, Labour, and people whose beliefs were on the left, were all going to gather together to make a demonstration against the rearming of Germany. And I thought about it for a while and I sent them back a letter in which I said I could not come and make a speech because I believed that Germany should be given everything that we ourselves possessed. She was a great nation, we should never have subjected her to any humiliation, and therefore I was in favour of her rearming, and I had to decline their invitation. Poor dears, they wrote back and asked me to resign, and I did, of course. I thanked them for their courtesy in allowing me to be their honourary president for so long, told them that I perfectly understood their feelings.

I became a Catholic at about this time. People asked me why I converted to Catholicism, my mother in particular wanted to know, and I don't think I had the answer. In those post-war years, a lot of thoughtful people were going back to religion, I wouldn't say it was the fashionable thing to do, but it was in the air. I think it was part of my trying to decide what to do with the rest of my life; without Orde and his enormous anchor in Godalming, at times I wondered who or what I was. I think that I had spent too long with Jews not to feel the value and comfort of belonging to a belief system. I liked certain Catholic writers, and I made the acquaintance of some Marist Brothers who ran a school in Edinburgh, and they were such delightful men, and had, one felt, superb intellects which they didn't use to make a name for themselves, they were teachers, you see, and dedicated teachers and, of course, chaste in their brown habits; what self-control these men developed over their lives, greatly to be admired in my opinion. I was interested to know how they went about things, and they answered all my questions, some of them fairly personal, and they had questions of their own, and they valued me, and we became very good friends. Then one day I was invited to a christening in a Catholic church, and I found that I liked the liturgy and the whole visual and olfactory effect, and above all I enjoyed the Latin because I understood every word. So I went up to the priest at the end of the service and told him I wanted to become a Papist! I never became a particularly good Catholic, my most recent confession was made about twenty years ago, but I have remained a Catholic to the bitter end.

I considered the possibility of becoming a Jew, I was very close to marrying one, it was my Italian scientist in New York of whom I was so very fond, but something prevented me; it wasn't any one thing, but a collection of things, and I think that one of them was that I felt that to be a Jew one had to be born to it, it wasn't something one could easily become. Not impossible, of course, many gentiles convert to Judaism and thrive, but I didn't feel that it would work for me, possibly because of my stubbornness, or some other reason. If I had found Orde and his family a little stifling at times, I might have been roasted by the warmth of a Jewish family, they never leave each other alone, I noticed that no sooner has a Jew left the presence of another Jew, they start calling one another on the telephone, this would not have suited.

Now quite ironically, for more than half my life I was taken for a Jew, and I shall give you an example of what I mean by 'taken for a Jew'. When I became a farmer in East Lothian (my next incarnation; read on), I was by now in my early 40's, I was despised by the local farmers, it wasn't because I was a woman, and it wasn't because of my stick, it was because there was a rumour that I was a Jew, I discovered this for myself from a neighbouring farmer. I'd go somewhere to order grain, and sometimes I'd get a good response, and sometimes I wouldn't, it depended on who knew it (or thought he knew it) and who didn't. There were a great number of Jews in post-war Britain who renounced their faith, and changed their names. I say a great number, of course one doesn't know the number, these things can't be known. But I had many Jewish friends, and one good friend who was a Harley Street surgeon who told me that he had become a specialist in nose reconstruction, which is a type of plastic surgery, and he became a great expert and people came to him from all over Europe. He would ask them their reason for wanting to change their appearance, it was part of his job to know the person and his or her reason for taking this quite drastic action. Of course, at root the reason was fear, pure and simple. And these unfortunate people would sometimes break off all contact with their families, and try to blend into the countryside, and it became a sport among a certain type of gentile to see if one could sniff them out.

And so it was with me, I could see people sniffing me – not sniffing at me, that is quite a different sensation that I have also experienced – in order to see if I was one of them. I learnt what it is to be a Jew. The hostility to the Jew that some people nurse is not a thing that suffocates its object; on the contrary, it stimulates and energizes and we see that, but in learning to live with this sensation the Jew, of necessity, develops an invisible skin which deflects certain emanations from other people. When, at the end of a working day, the Jew returns to the bosom of his family, they gather around a table for the evening meal, and they tell each other jokes about how they cope with life outside, and draw strength from one another before they venture out into the world the next day. I remember a particular occasion, I stood at the counter of a shop in Aberdeen called Price and Sons, the wife of the owner was serving me, Mrs. Price I imagine, standing before me on the other side of the counter, and I said to her, 'would you be so kind as to quote me the price for a ton of such-and-such animal feed.' I went to this shop from time to time, it was a wholesale outlet for farmers only and a very good one, and because I ran a business I needed to know what I was paying for my feed and ensure that I was getting it as cheaply as possible. This harassed woman looked at me for a moment with a certain expression, and after a slight pause, quoted me a price. Now, perhaps this woman bought her feed from someone in Glasgow called Cohen, and this Cohen wouldn't extend her credit, or they had a disagreement, I'm quite sure he didn't cheat her because Jews are not cheats. And I'm sure Mrs. Price was a good Christian, and she would have heard things about the Jews as a child in her Sunday classes, and she thought to herself, 'this woman (my good self) is not from these parts, she calls herself Mrs. Smith but they say she has a past and that she is a Jewess, and now she has the effrontery to tell me that a ton of my grain is ten shillings more expensive than Jock McLeod's down the road, I can put two and two together, can I not. Let her buy her grain from her own people'. This woman became quite agitated and ordered me to leave her shop, and made hand gestures for me to be gone.

I was shocked and I was extremely angry. I turned to look at the faces of the other customers, and they avoided my eyes and were nodding their heads imperceptibly, which was disconcerting to say the least. Now what was I to do? Was I to say, 'Ah, but I'm not Jewish, if that's what you think! I'm a Macdonald of Glencoe on my father's side, and an Edinburgh Wigmore on my mother's side'? Or was I to leave without making a fuss, and go to McLeod's to buy my grain (on the assumption he will sell it to me), as I imagine a real Jew would have done? Or was I to stand in the middle of the shop and tell the people there, 'I'm a farmer like the rest of you. Your prejudice shames you, you're a disgrace to yourselves and a disgrace to Scotland, I shall not come here again!'? A Jewish farmer could return to his wife and his children, and perhaps even his old mother-in-law, and tell them what happened in Aberdeen that day, and they will laugh about it together, or shake their heads, and put it behind them. But I had no one at home to share that particular story with, so I just swallowed and got on with my life. I found it neither stimulating nor energizing because I wasn't a Jew and I wasn't married to one. But it deepened my appreciation of that race and what it had to contend with.

Soon after I was kicked out of the British Legion for being too pro-German (you see how very complicated my life was becoming), I was on a plane returning to Edinburgh from London, courtesy of the people at Keren Kayemet. I had just completed a series of appearances at fundraisers for Youth Aliyah, and I was longing to get home. This type of work is most rewarding but also exhausting. I was in my window seat in the rear of the fuselage, where I like to sit on a plane, tucked up with the book I was reading, when a man came to sit in the seat next to mine. Now I hate talking to strangers in any public conveyance – on ships I keep to my cabin as you know – because travel is a penance and I find that the time passes most quickly if I have a book in my hand. I have devised strategies for politely discouraging people from talking to me, and if I wished to be impolite I could have pointed out to this man that there were many perfectly good unoccupied seats elsewhere on the plane – it was less than half-full as I recall – but before I could collect my wits the man was sitting and talking, all in one motion. But instead of turning to me and asking me a foolish question, such as, 'are you traveling on business or pleasure?', he simply launched himself into a description of his private life in the most candid manner as if he was talking about a third party to an old friend, making no demands whatever on me as a listener, and what this man had to say was far more interesting than the book I was reading.

He was a good physical specimen, he spoke extremely well and he had red hair. Now I love men with red hair and I cannot explain why that is. Men with red hair, as you know, often have poor complexions and invariably have freckles which are not attractive in a man. Papa had black hair before it all fell out, to the last strand, Orde's hair was fair to mousy, Sutherland's was brown, my ambassador's hair was grey, but when it comes to hair, my preference is for red. He was also well-educated, amusing, and had perfect manners. I found that I had to interrupt him several times with precise questions which he answered without inhibition, and before long I turned my body in my seat to face him, the better to watch him as he spoke. Nineteen women out of twenty would not have been drawn in by this man, because his confession was too personal to be appropriate or credible, and the subject matter too strange, but I was amused and touched. He was entirely self-absorbed, and showed no interest in me, which I find appealing in a man, I never allow a man to pick me up, that is always the woman's job. It was not a long flight, and the plane had landed long before my curiosity had been remotely satisfied, so I invited him for lunch at our house, mother's and my house, in Murray Street. We arrived there, deposited our suitcases in the hallway, mother was away in London with Jonathan, so without further ado I took this unusual man to my bed.

His name was John Rowland Russell Smith, and he came from one of the best families in Scotland. The Russells go back hundreds of years and in their various piles hung family portraits by Gainsborough and Reynolds – those that hadn't migrated to museums to pay for the new inheritance taxes. The Russells had a lot of ground and they generally farmed it profitably, good yeoman stock from the Moncraig area, the backbone of Scotland; Roberton, one of the best-known farms in the country, was theirs. John's grandfather, Sam Smith became a cotton magnate and he moved his family to great houses in Cheshire and Dumfreeshire where John's father and uncles were born, and they all went to Trinity College at Oxford. One of the uncles was T.O. Smith, a fellow at All Souls, an astonishingly brilliant young man. Then one day he had a – I won't say he had a nervous breakdown or even a mental one – a sort of revulsion against humanity, and vanished into a house in the south of England where he was cared-for by a devoted couple, and occasionally saw members of his family for ten minutes, or fifteen. He opted out of life, but John's father did not, he became headmaster of Loreta, by Edinburgh, one of the great Catholic schools of Britain. So all in all, the Russells were a grander and more accomplished lot than my own people; and one mustn't forget the salacious Bertrand Russell who was, I think, a second cousin. Now

A Green Rose

John grew up on an estate on Loch Ard in the Trossocks, a place of surpassing beauty, and considerable acreage, 8000 acres of glorious country, shooting, fishing. He had many gifts and graces, he painted delightfully, and played the piano very well. Fished! My goodness, I was told by a man who was a very good fisherman that John was one of the four best trout fishermen in Scotland. He thought like a fish, I've seen him take a fish from waters where nobody believed any fish existed. And, above all, he was a farmer, and an acknowledged expert on the subject of sheep.

Of course, none of the above was revealed to me on the plane to Edinburgh. No, indeed, on the plane John told me of his enchanting wife, an Austrian woman who had been an enthusiastic member of the Nazi party before the war, and had only avoided internment during the war by dint of her now belonging to this great family. Since the war, this indomitable female had managed to spend all of John's inheritance, had recently walked out on him and their six year old son, and had moved in with a man in London who, I understood, was having no better luck with her. I asked him why he was still married to this woman, and he answered impatiently that he still loved her and didn't believe in divorce. Meanwhile his farming enterprise was failing and the bank was about to repossess the farm and its equipment. Through determined questioning I discovered that his father died when he was eleven, and his mother when he was sixteen, whereupon he took himself on a European tour on bicycle which terminated in Germany, and there he took a job in a shipping concern and met his future wife. Naturally I asked him if, at that time, he became a Nazi sympathizer and he confessed that he had. He described this humiliating state of affairs to me with perfect equanimity, and I was strangely charmed. His son was about to be expelled from his school, he had a mad, nymphomaniac sister-in-law who kept bursting out of her lunatic asylum and quartering herself on him, and he had just had his golf clubs stolen. When mother returned home a week later, John was still there, and it was left to her to uncover the more creditable aspects of his biography. I had already made up my mind to take him on. Mother expressed her gravest misgivings.

I don't think it was so very strange of me to have wanted to do so. I wanted Jonathan to have a father, and indeed John was very sweet with him. I wanted my son to have siblings, and we duly produced two delightful children. I wanted to try my hand at farming, in fact I had quite serious ambitions in this direction. I would be returning to my Scottish roots; if Lorna belonged anywhere, surely it was on a farm in Scotland. Finally I liked and trusted the Russells, and I think this was the decisive factor in my decision to marry John. They welcomed me into the fold with great warmth – they were more courteous to me than the dear Wingates – and I very much wanted to be associated with people of great culture and long lineage. And I liked him, I liked him very much and enjoyed looking at him and touching him, but I hadn't fallen in love with him – I was spared that particular torment – and I was never bound to him in the way I had been bound to Orde. So this was my first great mistake on my return from Abyssinia.

Our first years together were happy ones. John was a wonderful-looking man, not only did he have a fine figure, broad shoulders and deep chest, narrow hips, and well-shaped legs, his colouring was charming; his red hair and green eyes with a gleam in them, he looked like a Regency buck. When he was dressed to go to the Queen's garden party with a grey top hat set slightly over one eyebrow, I was very proud of him. The first time we set out to Buckingham Palace we didn't arrive at all because it was a lovely day and I thought it was too beautiful to go to a garden party, and so we went to the woods and made love to each other instead, much more fun. Those times we did arrive we did so in the strangest of equipage. At one time I remember we went in a Ford van which had no windows except in the front, and the assembled who were watching the arrivals were taken aback to see John in all his splendour get out of this. Another time we went in a filthy Land Rover. You see, John was a delightful creature, he was not only splendid to look at in his earlier years when I first married him, but he had gaiety and grace. One could put him in any room, and within a few minutes people would be standing with him, smiling and giggling as he talked with his easy and unusual manner, little Lucy said that her father reminded her of Eric Morecambe.

As I have already written, I had longed to be part of my father's administration of Tilliefoure. I wanted very much to learn how to administer land, I wanted to take on the responsibilities of growth, building, planning, a development of the countryside. When I married John, he was unable to purchase anything in his own right because his relations, finding that he was running through his fortune at a great rate when he was married to his first wife, made a marriage settlement which was an inflexible one. He was not allowed to take any capital out, all had to go to his children on his death, therefore he was not able to buy himself anything but a very small estate. So I invested all my capital in two excellent farms in East Lothian in the Lamma Muirs, and in these I was greatly interested. I knew nothing about farming because my father had never allowed me to take any part in the care of Tilliefoure, and I learned all I could from John, and although he was no great doer, he knew a lot about the theory of sheep farming. He was not interested in cattle, his love was black-faced sheep, and that delightful animal, so gallant and gay to look at with its great curling horns and its black velvet face and black velvet stockings and its golden eyes, a mountain sheep indeed, no wonder he was so fond of his black-faces.

He was very sensible about the theory of their management, the trouble was he would not do anything about the practical side, he would not keep his employees under control, he was frightened of his servants, he was concerned only with the lighter side of black-faced sheep care. He would spend hours considering how to mate this pup with those ewes in order to get the right shape, he was an artist, you see, and he wanted to see the perfect sheep emerge. But what of all the others that had to be sold simply for lamb, for wool? That had to make the money to keep the rest of us going, to butter our bread too. And this was something that he was not prepared to do very much about.

I found the whole theory of farming fascinating, and I used to sit up in bed reading all the books I could lay my hands on, including a quite unique publication – there can surely be nothing like it in the English language – called 'The Farmer and Stock Breeder', an immensely fat magazine coming out weekly costing in those days nine pence in old money, crammed with the most enthralling information, wonderful photographs giving you from week to week a conspectus of the whole range of British farming. The man who edited it was a genius, no doubt about it, they gave him a knighthood or something he was surely the best editor in the British Isles, and I used to take this paper into my hand, and I would sit reading and learning. Of course I dismissed those articles concerned with the disposal of slurry, the mechanics of pig farming, how you put them into this sort of a house or that sort of a house, what temperature, to what dreadful diseases those poor pigs are prone, dairy farming left me quite cold. But when it came to grass management, cattle breeding, the new varieties of sheep, there are men in the Scottish farming industry who are highly-gifted, they're doing great things, they're bringing in five different breeds of sheep in order to produce one, five different excellences; milk here, growth there, proliscacy somewhere else.

 I was excited and I wanted to try new ways of, not so much making money as of saving money because, as you know, much of farming doesn't depend on great new ideas – nature doesn't allow such new modes of thought - so much as cutting the corners. A great deal of subsistence farming comes from saving money rather than making it, and I had schemes for in-wintering our ewes because we in East Lothian had a hard and healthy climate, low rainfall, great difficulties in the winter. In the spring the cold wind came to cut the grass from under the feet of the grazing animals so that they were under-nourished. We were always having to spend vast sums on feeding the sheep on hay, and of course our cattle on cake, to keep their central heating apparatus going. We had 70 head of breeding cows, and a couple of bulls, and 1500 head of sheep, and these animals had to be kept in good heart, and the winters were very long and very hard; they got no diseases, I think it was too damned cold, it killed the germs. But the beasts themselves, if they were to be brought to anything, they had to be husbanded at the most expensive level. For example, I wanted to try out new systems for wintering the ewes, and putting up shelter belts for the cattle; shelter belts are best made up of trees; one plants and in ten or fifteen years you have your belts, but we were only in Elmscliff for twelve years, so I had all sorts of schemes for putting up shelters of a cheap and disposable kind.

 I was becoming more involved and more proficient with every passing season, and I developed a passion for the work. I would have expected John to be glad of a wife like me, a willing worker, a fellow-enthusiast! But he took it badly, which was most upsetting to me. He didn't want me to make any suggestions because he wanted his farm to be his own kingdom and his own domain, and I think that most of the time he resented my overpowering presence, he insisted that I keep out of the farming side. I would say to John, for example, 'couldn't we go up to see the Blue-Faced Leicesters in Kinross shire, the new breeds of sheep that they're producing up there? I'm sure they'd allow us to look over their enterprise if we rang up and tried to get in touch with them.' 'Not so', said John, 'I'm not interested in them' It was so damping, you see, because John's idea was to enjoy his sheep as a man might enjoy a piano sonata, he was not concerned to try new fields, to practice new tunes, he only wanted to do that which he knew and which was the easiest. So John was not ambitious, and the little sparking plug went to waste.

His head shepherd was an exceedingly idle man, Mc-Guffy. His son was splendid as was his nephew who were the second and third shepherd, they would have listened to me and we did occasionally have talks together about new ideas but I would never have suggested things to them behind John's back, that would have been improper, and McGuffy and John were resolved on one thing, they were not going to do any more work than they had to, so my schemes were all slaughtered at birth, and they told me to keep out of things. Well this made life even more difficult because I would have loved to take an interest in the farms and the absurd thing was I owned the damned things, but I was not allowed to be interested in them, and of course I knew nothing about sheep the difference between one sheep and another was a mystery to me.

John and McGuffy had an annual ceremony which was designed to cut me down to size. Every autumn when we took our pedigree tups to Lannock, our tup lambs which of course were the flower of the flock. No, they were not the flower, we kept the flower of the flock to become foundation fathers but we used to take the secondary and tertiary lambs so that other people might buy them to become the foundations of their flocks. John used to say to me, 'would you like to come up to look at the tups', and I always said, 'yes, I would', and I'd go up in the early October evening to the tup house where electric lights were on, and the shepherds were all ranged in a line along the hurdles, and inside the white stonewashed building under electric lights there would be six or seven beautiful young male creatures with white fleece and their black faces and their curling horns and their golden eyes, quietly milling about among the straw, and John and McGuffy would say to me – McGuffy never said a word, none of the shepherds spoke – John would say to me, 'well now, which one do you think is the best?' I was geared now, I said, 'well, that one over there looks rather a good-looking beast is he not, nice straight back, seems to have the right sort of conformation, I knew all the jargon. It's often easy to spot the best animal but the test comes when you're asked to spot the second best and the third best and the fourth best, so after having chosen the best, they'd say, 'yes, he's quite good', that would be an accolade, but then I was at sea, quite lost. Which was the second best, I had no idea they all looked exactly alike to me, and then I'd say 'well, that one, third from the left, seems to have a good kind of fleece on him', and there'd be a dead silence and I'd look round and see a slow smile of satisfaction that came across the faces of these two men, it was obvious I'd made a fool of myself, you see.

Oh dear, it happened every year, and I had to undergo it. By and by our financial straits became pressing and our conflicts more severe. It had fallen to me to put his house in order from the beginning, I got rid of his wife; his lawyer had been exhorting him to divorce her for years, but he, unable ever to make a decision, wouldn't do it. I got rid of his sister-in-law who was an international tart and had been wandering Europe since the age of 18, thrown like a football from the arms of one man to the other, I sold his farm which was failing, and bought him another which was a successful one, had he been prepared to work at it. What had I been thinking? Did I imagine that he would thank me for taking him by the scruff of the neck and shaking out his fleas? How naïve and insensitive was I? Of course John was as guilty as I in entering into a relationship which both of us must have realized was quite wrong from the start because, you know, he didn't even like me, poor man, and he made this quite plain a year or two after we were married, he told me, quite serenely, that he didn't like me. I liked him but I didn't want to marry him of course, I did it because I felt I had to put my hand to a practical plough.

After three or four years, an extraordinary thing happened to us, this is something that I think one would have to give to the bio-physicists, I don't know who else could come up with the answer. Supposing you have two creatures in their prime of life, both with its field of force surrounding it, because all creatures have a field of force surrounding it, and in most cases when one's field crosses that of another, you feel either a greater or less repulsion, and then you fly apart, or you feel a greater or less attraction, and then you come together. Sex has very little to do with it, it's a matter of personal magnetism, a fluid, but very occasionally, I've never known it happen before, you find that when your field of force touches another, you neutralize each other, and this is what John and I did to each other. It was really as much to do with physics as anything else, I feel, because neither of us was deficient in magnetic fluid, but when we came near each other, we were immobilized, we became static. Now the trouble was that not only did we find each other totally unattractive, without being repelled by each other, but as we lived with each other over the years, the springs of life dried up and we were not only unable to feel attraction to each other, we were unable to feel attracted to anybody else either.

And so one had this awful state of affairs that I – I can only speak for myself – who loved making love because it is one of the greatest joys of life, perhaps a very simple one but of all the simple joys it is the greatest, living constantly with a splendid physical creature of the opposite sex, sleeping beside him year after year, feeling no desire whatever to put out a finger and touch him, found that his presence had dried up all desire for others. I never wanted to look at another man, and never did, I was totally faithful to John in thought and word and deed for 17 years, and this not because of my high moral principles but simply because I'd lost all desire. And he, poor man, I do believe, he had one fling a couple of years after we were married, he had an affair with a local farmer's wife which lasted about a year, but after that, poor John, he no more cared for women than I cared for men. And both of us, of course, losing our magnetic field of force, had an effect on other people who came near us – although you don't expect people necessarily to want you to make love to them all the time, they do expect you to have the smell of humanity about you.

John and I no longer had the smell of humanity about us, we were not concerned with each other, we were not very concerned with anybody else, we were zombies in a way, and this had a very bad effect on all the people who came into contact with us; our neighbours, even the simple souls with whom John had to do business. It has a very far-reaching effect when you change your shape, your smell, your texture, you become a very different kind of human being. Poor John and I changed, and in some sort destroyed each other. Two completely incompatible human beings, condemned to live with one another for 17 years and traverse a wilderness with very few oases, we were both to blame, each of us guilty of a deadly sin. I, the greatest of them, pride, and its executive arm, presumption; first you are quite sure you're right, and then you think you can bring about the solution that your overweening pride proposes. Poor John was guilty of sloth, and together we brought about each other's purgatory, exquisitely adjusted, I may say, to the needs of our malfeasance

Let us say that there are two men: One is a misfit, maladroit, a man of violent passions, of average appearance, of average height, crooked teeth, often scowling, badly dressed, assertive, ill-mannered, thinks deeply and cannot lie, and from an undistinguished family. The other is tall, handsome and perfectly formed, he is gracious and diplomatic, amusing and engaging, has exquisite taste, plays the piano enchantingly, fishes like an angel, he has the nature of an artist, and he comes from a noble family. If they were two characters in a Jane Austen novel, which of them, by the end of the novel, do you think would become Lorna's true love?

By far the worst effect on my life of my marriage to John was my separation from my Jewish friends. When I married him at the age of 36, I'd been thinking about my friends' concerns and I'd been serving them as best I could for something like 17 years, half my life, and John, by the most unfortunate mischance, was an anti-Semite. There are all kinds of shades of anti-Semitism and John, being a gentle soul, was a gentle anti-Semite. He didn't advocate extermination or final solutions, all he did was to repeat the slanders which we all know so well. I thought when he said these things before our marriage that it was because his first wife had been a professed Nazi – she was of course an Austrian – and he had picked up the only knowledge he had of he Jewish race from one who was its enemy. But after we were married it was born in on me that he had his own dislike of Jews based upon nothing at all because he knew none.

A Green Rose

It was a problem for a man like this to be married to a woman like me. The trouble began at once, he uttered various myths, he repeated them to me, about the Jews, we all know what they are, and I refuted them indignantly, and he, seeing that this was my attitude, became silent. Then came the time when we had to accept or refuse the invitations, the official invitations that flooded in on us from all my Jewish organizations with which I was connected. Naturally the Jews were delighted that I'd married again, being on the side of life, they do not believe in perpetual widowhood; I remember one letter I had from some unknown admirer who said, 'I'm so glad that you married again, now you will have somebody to look after you' . But of course, we had to appear in public together, and although John's manners were so good that they remained intact, he was cold, and my Jewish friends were puzzled, it was inconceivable to them that I could have married somebody who did not support their cause or be friendly to their race. But John showed no sign of either, and after one or two entries into the kind of public life I'd been living, semi-public life, side by side, I came to the conclusion that I couldn't possibly take John with me again to any of the Jewish public functions to which I was invited because he was so obviously hostile, and the smoothness and coldness of his manners did not conceal his hostility

I had to make up my mind, was I to go on as I had for so many years, serving my friends' cause, being devoted to them, talking about them, thinking about them? I loved them as I'd always loved them, always would, the noblest people in the world I think, and I don't except my own race to which I'm devoted. I'm glad I'm a Scot, but I would like to serve the Jews. But unhappily I had to make a choice because I'd chosen to marry John, it was not a matter of love, it was not something natural and forceful, its own raison d'être, I'd decided to marry John as a matter of principle, of policy and so it was doubly incumbent upon me to make a success of this marriage. I had to make a choice between a sour and angry husband who would continually resent my service to my friends, who'd never accept them in his house with any grace or greeting, or else I must go the whole way and serve the marriage which I'd constructed, it was an artificial thing, perhaps, but I felt it was my responsibility.

It was a terrible decision, it took me some months to arrive at it, years in fact, but John was adamant that he didn't want to receive any of my Jewish friends, that he didn't want me to go anywhere among my Jewish interests. I had to make up my mind to choose, and so, having taken on the responsibility of this man I felt it was time to say goodbye to all that I loved best, and so I said goodbye to them. I don't know what they thought, they've been far too tactful and gentle to tell me how they took my total resignation...I simply opted out immediately.

Another interesting thing that happened was, after I married him, and it was born in on me that he didn't approve of my work for my friends, I lost the power of making speeches; very interesting, it must be something to do with self-confidence. Making public speeches is a curious thing, you have to establish a kind of rapprochement between you and your audience. Again, it's this magnetic fluid, it's almost a physical thing, there's a flow between you and them, they flow back to you, you flow out to them, it's very exhausting, it's not exactly an actor's role, one is truly engaged from one's deepest emotional feeling, one's heart, but all the same you have to project yourself, and I found that after I married John, perhaps because he was so obviously unenthusiastic about me and all my works and ways, after all those years I lost the power of making a good speech. It was quite sudden, and I realized it at once, I lost my self-confidence, it was like a tightrope walker, I looked down and saw the abyss and I decided to make for the platform as quickly as I could, and so I did. I think I only made two bad speeches, then I gave up. And a few years later when I had young Lucy, I gave as my excuse the fact that I had two young children to care for and I could no longer remain the chairman of my charity. This was the reason I gave, and it was quite an honest one, I mean in truth I had no nannies and I wanted to stay with these two young creatures. .

Then one day in 1964, John complained of pains in his chest and it was his first heart attack, and I realized that I might have pushed him too far, he certainly told me that it was because of me. This was the end of my career as a sheep farmer, so I sold the farms together with our very good herds, put the money back in the bank and I took the family to Dorset.

Chapter 18

Now, finally, I have come to the kernel of the matter, my reason for writing this memoir. The historians. Yes, those high-minded intellectuals entrusted with the job of making sense of the infernal muddle which man has wrought. What were they to make of Orde Wingate? Immediately after the war there were a slew of war journal-type of book, mostly written by Wingate's boys and written while memory was strong and many of them were delightful and highly respectful, but the first historian out of the starting gate – if indeed he was an historian – was a journalist called Leonard Mosley, a distant relative of the awful, embarrassing Oswald. Yes, a moment's silence for poor old Oswald. Leonard wrote a short, racy book about Orde called 'Gideon Goes to War' and it was clear from page one that he nursed a true affection and admiration for his subject, which made the book quite readable. This

I have adduced from others for I could not bring myself to read it, indeed I did not cooperate with Mosley, I wouldn't even talk to him on the phone, neither him nor a dozen other prospective biographers because I thought it was too soon for a biography of my late husband for reasons I shall presently give; I didn't want the first serious attempt at biography to go off halfcocked.

Mosley produced his book with or without me, and not unnaturally, he had ambitions that the book should be read, and he believed that he had the wherewithal to accomplish this, in the form of a sensational discovery. He had, intrepid reporter that he was, uncovered evidence that Wingate had proposed to lead the Jews in an attack on the Haifa Oil Terminal, in order to hold Britain to ransom. This story could only have come from Tony Simonds, indeed Mosley appears to have met Tony, so I shall assume that Tony was his source. I will also assume that Tony, dear man, not knowing the full story himself, at the same time trying to be discrete, only hinted darkly at his and Orde's transaction. Mosley, evidently in a hurry to get the book to press, fleshed out the hint the best he could, and created a dramatic scene with a novelist's flourish in which Orde is supposed to have said this, that and the other.

I am many things but I am not a hypocrite, and I did at no time climb on my high horse and denounce Mosley to the heavens. What he had written was quite inaccurate – blowing up the terminal would have been foolish beyond words, and would have gained nothing for the Jews, as I have said above – but apart from that one large detail, Mosley had been essentially correct, and had done well to discover it. This after all is the work of the newspaper reporter. So Mosley took the manuscript to the publishing house of Arthur Barker in London, and secured a contract of some kind; all well and good. He had met Orde in Cairo once or twice, and he was undoubtedly an admirer, so it is clear that he wished Orde no harm, in fact, to the contrary.

Mosley, sensing that the book lacked something (what the book lacked was about two years dedicated research, and the approval of the widow and the family), offered the manuscript to Lord Beaverbrook for serialization. I don't say that Mosley enjoyed doing this, but one has to pay the bills, does one not. Beaverbrook was not a Wingate fan. In 1938 while Orde was rushing about London like an angry bluebottle, trying to gain support for the Jews of Palestine he went to see the diminutive press baron, and urged him to go softly on the Jews. Beaverbrook was one of the four of five most powerful men in the land, a friend of Churchill and an enemy of the Jews, and he was not cooperative. Orde saw he was getting nowhere with him, so he started haranguing him. Coolly taking stock of this impetuous advocate, Beaverbrook interrupted Orde's discourse and said, 'I have decided…' and was undoubtedly about to deliver himself of a crushing riposte which would send the young captain out of the office and out of the building with his tail between his legs, when Wingate, like Zeus hurling a thunderbolt, rose to his full height, and cried at the man behind the large desk, 'it is not you but God who decides' (and Beaverbrook was not just a believer but a non-conformist believer, and he knew that Wingate spoke the truth), and stormed out of the room. He returned to me in Welbeck street, he came in the door humming a tune, and told me what he had been up to that morning. A few days later Beaverbrook wrote in his editorial,

> 'Here is a piece of advice from a newspaper which has always been sympathetic to the Jews and is anxious for their safety now. Beware Zionism'

Indeed, they are always sympathetic. So Mosley took his book to Beaverbrook and said, (I shall borrow Mosley's literary style here), 'I say, your lordship, I have proof that Wingate betrayed his country, how about serializing my book in your excellent newspaper so the world can see who he truly was', whereupon Beaverbrook answered, 'by gad, Mosley, I will run it in six weekly issues, to whom am I to make out the cheque?' So the people of Britain, at least those who subscribed to the Sunday Express, woke up one Sunday morning in the summer of 1955 to read that General Orde Wingate had been a traitor.

I was by now living in East Lothian with John, and as we were not Express readers ourselves I had to be told of this by mother, and she was quite hysterical. The reaction in other newspapers to this revelation was muted but shocked, and of course I refused to speak to anybody in the press about it, I wouldn't answer the phone for about two months. I would have called Tony, not to berate him but to commiserate, but I thought better of it, and in fact we have never spoken about it. When I went in to Aberdeen to do the weekly shopping, one or two people may have stared at me, I kept my chin up and pretended not to notice, smiling sweetly and nodding hello to everyone who looked in my direction.

Emmanuel called from Haifa in Israel and of course I came to the phone, and he told me that he had had all the newspapers calling him day and night for him to confirm or deny Mosley's story – he was named co-conspirator in this plot – and he told me that everyone in Israel was as one voice in calling the story a complete fabrication, and Mosley had been denounced in the Israeli press. Emmanuel was willing to come to London to take Mosley to court, but I think I managed to calm him down by telling him that the British press wasn't like the Israeli press, and this sort of libel appears every day, no one is safe, and the best thing was to let the brouhaha die a natural death and people will forget it and move on to the next thing. I believe that Emmanuel knew nothing of Orde's activities in April 1939. But the poor Wingates! Not even bothering to call me first, Sybil took the night train and came straight to me. It wasn't clear to her or to me why she had come. To hear a denial direct from the horse's mouth? To give me a shoulder to cry on? Naturally I kept nothing from her, and told her the truth of the thing, which surprised her greatly, but didn't in the least disappoint her. In fact she thought that on balance Orde's plan had been perfectly sound, and he was clearly right about future events, and Chaim entirely wrong. At no time did she suggest even by the smallest word or gesture my culpability in this affair; Sybil, bless her, the most loyal of beings. In retrospect, I think I might have spared the Wingates a lot of heartache, and served my late husband better if I had agreed to speak to Mosley when he was writing the book. I would have found a way to redirect his enthusiasm, and this unpleasantness could have been avoided. The serialization of the book generated a number of articles and radio interviews with various soldiers and verbalizers, and then, as I had told Emmanuel, it all died down. But it had not been good; a certain amount of doubt about Orde had been sown in the mind of the British public, which of course had been Beaverbrook's intention, and none of us were very pleased with Leonard Mosley.

Next up was General William Slim. He was one of Orde's superior officers in Operation Thursday, a well-liked man with an easy manner which helped his advancement in the army, and he duly went all the way to the top. In 1956, Slim's military memoirs were published, Defeat into Victory, I would say a very good title for a book of that type. What endeared Slim to soldiers, and to readers of his excellent book, was his innate modesty, his willingness to carry blame for mistakes made, and the fact that he didn't denigrate his colleagues. If you are a reader of military memoirs as I am, you will appreciate what a rare bird Slim was. I'm not going to get bogged down with a lot of unnecessary detail; Peter Meade, Robert Thompson, Derek Tulloch and others have all written about this if you wish to know more. Briefly then, when, twelve years after the fact Slim recalled the Chindit campaign, he made a number of errors and, more importantly, he contradicted contemporary statements, orders and letters of his own. The effect of these errors and misrepresentations was to show Orde in a poor light. The book arrived about a year after the Mosley debacle, and the Wingates read it and were astounded, having never expected an attack on their brother from that quarter; The Chindits, who had always loved their 'Uncle Bill', were baffled and deeply hurt. Slim had been such a strong admirer of Orde, supporter too, what had happened to make him revise his original evaluation? Anyway, it was after the publication of Defeat into Victory that we decided that it was time for the authorized biography of Orde to be written, only thus would we be able, once and for all, to set the record straight. Who would be its author?

I had been approached by a number of historians over the years who put themselves forward to write such a biography, but had prevaricated because Derek was planning a book (it was taking him an age), and also because I was afraid of certain things coming to light (as was the case). I was of course not in the least ashamed of what Orde and I had done while in Palestine, but one wasn't sure how Orde's commitment to the Jewish cause would be received by the British public. They had not forgotten the ugly events of 1946-7 when Jews had killed British servicemen, wounds were still fresh, and since I now felt Orde's reputation as a British soldier to be my primary duty and responsibility in life bar none, I had to think carefully how to approach an official biography of my late husband.

This type of political calculation has never been my forte. Now, about six or seven years previously, there had been a telephone call from Robert Graves – I was living with mother in Edinburgh and she took the call – and he told her that he would like to write about Orde. I discussed this with mother and she prevailed upon me to at least hear the man out, so it was arranged that I would meet him when I was next up in London, whereupon I sat down and read practically everything the man had ever written and it was an impressive body of work. We met at the house of Tosco and Mary Fyvel whom I knew from Palestine, and Graves told me that we had met once during the war – I had no recollection – and he had spoken to Orde all evening, and was a great admirer, and he wished to write an historical novel in the style of 'I, Claudius', that is to say, a historical reconstruction using all known facts in order to create a dramatic portrait. He told me that he could only undertake such a task if I would agree to tell him everything there was to know about my late husband. 'Well', thought I, 'Graves is not a military historian and yet if anyone could establish Orde in the imagination of future generations, it was Robert Graves'. So I called Granville in order to sound out the family on Graves' proposition, and I arranged to go to him at his club.

Here I must tell you something of my relationship with Granville, I'm not sure it is relevant to the subject at hand, but it is a part of my story. Granville was, at one time, in love with me. We were closer in age than Orde and I because Orde was one of the older siblings, and Granville the youngest. He declared himself about two years after Orde's death. He had taken me out to dinner at a very good restaurant in Edinburgh, and we were conversing in a perfectly normal manner, and suddenly he said, 'Lorna, I don't know if you are aware of this, but in some parts of the world, when a man dies, his brother is obliged to take on his widow'. 'Yes',

A Green Rose

I thought, 'Granville is proposing marriage, I should have known he had come to Edinburgh for a reason'. I could see that the man was in difficulty, Englishmen are not very good at this sort of thing, clearly Granville was afflicted, I had probably suspected it for some time, so I gently put his hand in mine, looking into his sad eyes, and said, 'Granville, I cannot return to the Wingate family '. He accepted my decision as final and I took the dear man back to his hotel. Now Granville and I remained on good terms until he decided that I was delinquent, but his wife Judy suspected that he carried a torch for me and, quite sensibly, refused to have anything to do with me, scarlet woman that I am.

A number of years having elapsed, I was meeting Granville at his club somewhere in London, he was well on his way to becoming a judge, and a very good one, and I told him of my meeting with Robert Graves. Granville, it has to be said, was not a great reader of books, and when I tried to describe to him what Graves had in mind, he shook his head and wrinkled his forehead, I thought he was going to take out his gavel, and he said that it wouldn't do, Orde required a serious historian, a military historian, not a writer of novels. I went away and thought about what he had said, and I decided that I would take Granville's advice but not for Granville's reasons. Graves had been clear, and emphatically so, that he would have to know everything. He would want to delve deeply into Orde's Zionism, and selectively lying to a man of that intelligence would be an exercise in futility, I don't think I would have dared. So the following day I wrote to Mr. Graves, thanking him for his offer, but regretfully declining.

The Wingates were a marvelous family, my admiration for them knew no bounds but they were not Zionists, and they only half understood their brother's great passion for the Jewish cause. They were an English family with a proud military tradition, and they wanted Orde to be remembered as a great English soldier, which he most certainly was. Evidently one could be a great English soldier while ser-ving the Arab cause, one could be a great English poet while serving the Greek cause, but the Englishman who serves the Jewish cause is a traitor. This placed me in an inescapable dichotomy. In seeking to protect the Wingates from hurt and embarrassment, I played myself false. I should have stuck with the truth. Many years later I ran into Robert Graves in Guernsey, he had a brother living not far from La Monnaie, and by now he was a very old man indeed, and I told him that my not allowing him to write Orde's life had been the worst single decision I had ever made, possibly the worst in the history of English letters.

Granville and I now produced a shortlist of the top military historians of the day, and one after the other they turned us down. Various reasons were given but it was only Basil Liddell Hart who told us that he found himself out of sympathy with Orde's Zionism; I wondered to what extent Mosley had frightened these august scholars off. I mention in passing that Robert Henriques had put his name forward in about 1950, and Malcolm Hay about a year after; more of Malcolm Hay in a later chapter.

I happened to tell one of my Marist monks that I was on the look-out for a biographer for my late husband, and he pointed me in the direction of Christopher Sykes, who was also a Catholic. Now Sykes was a good candidate, his name forever associated with the Near East through his father, so I wrote him a letter, and he replied in a positive manner, a meeting was arranged. We met, we talked, more consultations with the Wingate plenipotentiary – Granville was adamant that the story about the Haifa oil terminal must be scotched – and the job was Sykes', and this of course was my second great mistake arising from my debacle in Addis Ababa.

He had taken a rather plush solicitor's office in Sackville Street, Piccadilly for the numerous interviews he intended to hold, and when it was my turn I sat down with Sykes for a number of days and talked about Orde. It just poured out of me, this was a cathartic experience for me, and he took notes – he was thoroughly professional – but I had my doubts from the first hour I was closeted with this man. He was giving away clues about the inner workings of his brain, and I could see that he was uncomfortable with his subject, which of course is the kiss of death for any biographer, and when we came to the matter that concerned Granville so deeply, Sykes said, 'Of course, Mosley made that oil refinery story up, didn't he?', and I replied, casually, 'oh completely, he conjured it out of thin air' but as I said that, I was actually thinking, 'if Sykes hasn't understood by now, after listening to me talk for two days, or however long it had been, that this is precisely the kind of thing that Orde would have done for the Jews – and more – then the man is a heartless fool with no imagination'. Poor Sykes; not willing to let sleeping dogs lie, he devoted two pages and an appendix in his book to reassure the reader that no such idea could possibly have been mooted by Wingate. The lady doth protest.

By about the half-way mark in the interviews with Sykes, I knew we were in trouble. I called Granville and asked for a council of war. He, Rachel, Monica, Sybil (I can't remember if Nigel was present or not) and I all met at Granville's house the following day, and I told them that Sykes had been a big mistake, we had to find a way of stopping him from proceeding with the book. 'He doesn't understand Orde at all, and he doesn't like him, he is full of bad ideas and is not to be trusted.' So Rachel said to me, 'Lorna, surely you are over-reacting', knowing well how I had over-reacted in the past, and the discussion went on for a good while and finally we all agreed that Lorna was over-reacting, and I duly returned to my work with Sykes, with a heavy heart but feeling at least that the responsibility for what would follow was now shared by one and all of Orde's custodians. By the time we'd reached Quebec in the chronology of Orde's life, I had faced and accepted the fact that Sykes was not going to listen.

Sykes' manuscript was submitted to me and to the family for corrections and we now saw clearly the scale of the disaster. He had inserted many dreadful things about Orde, some, and I say this quite advisedly, were downright lies that he'd picked up in his research and others were misinterpretations or falsifications. He claimed that Orde was drawn at one time to the British Israelites. Where on earth did Sykes get such a notion? Sybil was horrified, and the bugger slipped it in after we had read the manuscript, it was pure malice on his part. His text was full of little ironic asides, and he cheerfully expressed himself baffled by one or other of Orde's actions, supposing that his bafflement only added to the Lawrencian mystique of Wingate. Confused himself, he confused the reader, and since his writing was turgid and incoherent, the text neither enlightened nor pleased; the portrait was one of a colourful military Dervish, it might have been made into a West End musical.

Sykes had just not been up to the job, he had failed to understand his subject, and in not understanding he had got himself into a terrible muddle. That is the charitable version. The less charitable version is that Sykes was guilty of sharp practice, he wanted to obtain not only the money connected with such a biography but also the acclaim that would come to a man who'd written other books of various kinds, and was now the serious biographer of a public figure. He didn't like Orde, he had no use for him, and he should have refused to accept the assignment as Liddell Hart had done. But the fault lay not with him – he was a flawed creature anyway – but with me, I should never have chosen him.

I had passed an enormous body of information to him which he very cleverly and cruelly edited so that all the hard stuff was edited out and only the flashes of trivial gossip, some of it mildly malicious, remained, always of course scrupulously attributed to me in a footnote. He quoted me as follows: 'So I went down to the cabin where my mother was sitting and I said to her, 'I've seen the man whom I should like to marry'. I told old Sykes this along with all the stuff that really mattered and he put it in because it had a schoolgirly, gossipy feel to it, made it all sound rather silly, but I was utterly stricken, for I had been in the grip of a huge passion; I emerged from the text as an insipid china doll. On the subject of Orde's Zionism he was worse. I remember how his lip curled – that's one of the clichés that writers use; my flesh crept, I was rooted to the spot. I wondered if these things can really happen. Can your heart stand still? Well it can, one's flesh can creep, and I saw Christopher Sykes' lip curl – when I was telling him the story of how Orde took out his first group of Jewish settlers on a foray into Syria, his band of brothers. I suppose I was rather emotional because it was a turning point in his life. Christopher Sykes was a man of very limited sensations, to him such moments meant nothing.

What was unforgivable, however, were his observations about the Chindit campaigns. Here he was on solid ground, no Jews, no wives, just armies and battles, and yet again he willfully misunderstood the progression of events, finally slipping into Slim's canards with regards the final days of Orde's generalship. Well, the Wingates, poor loves, were distracted with worry, and so was I, I sat weeping over the manuscript, I don't think one cries if one's heart is broken, one certainly cries if one can't get on with the defense of the people one loves, and one cries with rage and frustration.

I was now in my sixth year of being Mrs. Smith, living on a remote farm with three young children and battles enough of my own to fight. I might have made a stab at writing a biography, but who'd believe the widow? This is one of the reasons I haven't run to Orde's defense during the years he's been betrayed by so many people. Nobody would give a widow credence, particularly when she is known to be a verbalizer like myself. I would have to wait for a champion, a proper champion to come forward.

Granville bore the burden and heat of this debacle, he called it his 'little salvage operation'. He said that we have got to have things taken out, and Sykes is a very vain man, and he will only take out so much, so anything he says about the Jews or about you will have to stand because we can't ask for more than quite a small quota of deletions, and I thought this was perfectly proper and right, and so I agreed; *I* had chosen Sykes, so *I* would throw myself on my general's sword. The book would have the imprimatur of 'authorized biography', Orde's reputation would suffer, it would take a deal of undoing to put right the harm that Sykes had done. But more trouble was on its way.

In 1962 the Official Histories of WW2 were published. This is something that is done after every war, however small, and it is done, as much as anything else, for the benefit of the simple soldier who can open it, and find an account of the meanest engagement in which he was involved, in which perhaps his friends may have died, and can say to himself, 'we did our bit and it hasn't been forgotten'. It also can be used as a reference work for other historians, and for military planners, and of course the whole shebang is paid for by the Ministry of Defense. In a conflict of this scale, it necessarily took a while to assemble the vast amount of information, and in this case it took them seventeen years. I don't know how many pages the complete set comprises, but it is not the sort of thing one goes out and buys at a bookshop, it sits in the main libraries of Britain and the Commonwealth.

Volume III of these Official Histories dealt with the Burma campaign and when it was published, as I say, in 1962 it caused a storm of protest from the Chindits themselves, they went quite spare with fury. Soldiers and officers who had served under Wingate read the accounts of battles, orders, who-did-what-and-when, and it was just a travesty of the truth and these ordinary soldiers, unlike the authors, had been there, in the heat of battle, and knew of what they spoke. The Official Histories demeaned Wingate personally, downgraded the value of his work, and consequently denigrated the achievements of Wingate's officers and men. The Chindits Old Comrades Association, with which I was still proudly associated, put together about 50 testimonials to Orde in a direct challenge to the assessment of the Official Histories, and some more senior people lodged an official protest.

As with Slim's volume, this small episode in a vast literary undertaking was a complete aberration. Nowhere else in the entire Official Histories of WW2 has an account generated controversy on this kind and on this scale. So now we must ask ourselves, 'who were these historians?' There were two men primarily involved in writing-up the Burma campaign, General Woodburn Kirby and Brigadier Michael Roberts. Both served in the Indian Army, both hated Wingate. Kirby (see p.220) actually ran foul of Wingate in 1943, so this was a visceral matter for him, perhaps also a sort of inter-regimental jealousy of a type common in any army. Their role in this unhappy episode has been completely uncovered by the excellent detective work of Thompson and Meade, and several others, and I can only feel sorry for Roberts' wife and Kirby's widow, who had to live with the disgrace.

But there is more. You will recall that on a previous page I wrote, 'Slim had been such a strong admirer of Orde, and supporter too, what had happened to make him revise his original evaluation?' Slim was in Australia when he wrote the book, and he had asked a friend of his in England, a fellow Gurkha, to read his draft chapter by chapter. This friend, a military historian living in England, with access to the documents and files that Slim needed to complete his work, was none other than Brigadier Roberts. Thanks again to the work of honest historians who examined the correspondence between the Slim and Roberts it can be seen clearly that Roberts traduced Slim into taking a negative line with Wingate and the Chindits. He basically said, 'look, general, we all know that you spoke well of Wingate at the time, generous to a fault as always, blaming yourself and giving credit to others as per usual but, my dear general, Kirby and I are literally knee-deep in documents and testimonies, and I can assure you that a picture is emerging here of a martinet, ego-maniac, imposter and a danger to the fabric of the army and if you will allow me, sir, I should like to suggest one or two corrections to your draft…' Slim, doubting his own better judgment, and afraid to make a public fool of himself – undoubtedly mindful of Mosley's assertion – gratefully allowed Roberts to rewrite the section dealing with Wingate. Poor Slim let himself down badly, and the Chindits never forgave him. Roberts and Kirby left no stone unturned. If Kirby and his ilk had deployed as much single-mindedness, cunning and energy against the Japanese in 1942, there would have been no need for the Chindits.

But there was always Derek. I think it is fair to say that I ruined Derek Tulloch. I enticed him and goaded him into taking a job he didn't feel he could do, and when he failed in the decisive test, I raged at him to his face and later here, in these pages, where he cannot answer. Derek took his moment of disobedience very much to heart, and never forgave himself. His career had been ruined by association with Orde, and he now dedicated his life to restoring the good name of his dead commander. He remained in close contact with the Wingates and even with me although our relationship remained fraught. He encouraged the writings of Calvert, Fergusson, Meade, Thompson and many others, all the while accumulating documents and testimonies for the book he planned, one day, to write.

In 1964 when he let it be known that he was gathering material to write a book about Wingate, he was taken aside by an officer junior in rank to himself, and told that if he attempted to 're-write Wingate', he would be court-martialed and would lose his pension. Knowing the lengths to which the army had already gone to consign Wingate to oblivion, he didn't take this threat lightly. For the next eight years he struggled to find the words to tell the truth about Wingate without letting his fury and bitterness show through. It destroyed his health, and when the book was finished he suffered a nervous breakdown, and died two years later. I never had the chance to tell him how much I admired his writing, for it is an excellent book, deeply researched, unsparing in detail, exuding Derek's integrity and modesty. I should like to have begged his forgiveness for the harm I caused him. The book sold, I was told, 2200 copies, which is a creditable number for a book of this kind, but it was bought and read by believers, the naysayers still held the field.

Chapter 19

When I was fourteen grandpa Paterson died, and papa decided to renounce his title because he said it would put 10% on his bills. He was a very good businessman and went into this type of thing in great detail, I'm sure he didn't do it to spite mother, but she was infuriated. I think he just couldn't be bothered with having a title, there are such people. Their marriage was a battle from the outset, and she, being the stronger of the two, prevailed and finally crushed him. She received his hard-earned fortune for her pains, and survived him by twenty seven years. She had selected his successor several years before he died; Malcolm Hay had been a friend of papa and a frequent guest at Tilliefoure, and he fell in love with his friend's wife. My heart went out to papa of course, but I must be fair to Malcolm. He was besotted with Ivy, this was the great love of his life. He had a title, one that he could bestow upon his spouse, which made her Ivy Hay of Seaton, it meant the world to her. And he was one of that rare breed of Christians who loved the Jewish people and fought for them all his life. He sat in the House of Lords and there was a force for good. It was a match made in heaven, so am I the one to criticize Hay for stealing another's love?

The Scots have a tendency to internal feuds within the family and our family was no exception. Papa's father was a delightful man with blue eyes and fair complexion. I knew him because mother took me to see him in his house in London. His manners were more beautiful than any other person's I ever met, completely natural and quite unfailing, his courtesy to everybody sprang from a gentle heart. Because grandpa Paterson had denied his son Walter permission to join the navy at the age of eighteen, Walter never forgave him, and cut him out of his life completely, and would not attend his funeral, so mother and I went in his place. 'Aye the Scots, aye fucking and feuding'. Papa was an extremely solitary animal, he had few friends, and introduced me to no relatives, he only met Orde about four times in eleven years, twice before the wedding, and only once after. He disliked Orde and detested Rachel and Sybil Wingate. When they came to visit me in Scotland, he considered their manners to be beyond description bad. I'm afraid papa turned into a royal misanthrope, but I never stopped loving him, and wishing to be loved by him. The end came in 1956, it came suddenly and I didn't say farewell, he'd literally drunk himself to death. I wouldn't have got a penny from his estate but for the statutory minimum that Scottish law decrees for surviving offspring, mother got the lot.

As a girl I loved my mother deeply, I did everything she asked, I agreed with everything she said, she was brave and clever, with excellent judgment in all things, she kept nothing from me, drew me into her most intimate confidences, we were best friends, indeed she was the best and most beautiful mother a girl could have! I see her in my mind's eye, almost sixty years ago, on a bright, sunny day, she is about 50 yards away from me, across a large expanse of manicured gravel, stepping down from father's brown-maroon Bentley, beautifully dressed with an enormous hat, my heart was racing with pure joy. She had come to collect me from St Leonard's at the end of my first term there, there are many expensive cars about, and no shortage of well-dressed mothers, but none to compare with my own dazzling mother, she seemed to have such flair!

I did not fall in love with Orde in order to defy mother, for I was not a rebel. I was and always have been conservative in outlook, in that I wanted things to remain the same, I never wanted to stop looking up to mother, I never wanted to leave Tilliefoure. If I had not been so very much in love with Orde, I'm sure I would have keenly felt the loss of mother's approval and the withdrawal of her affections. I thought that I had come to a crossroads in my life, and having made my painful choice I would learn to live without mother at my side. So when, in response to my letters dutifully written to her from Palestine, she announced that she would come out to visit me, I was not only thrilled, but I was also honoured that she would make such an important trip to see her ungrateful offspring. Happy as I was to be reunited with her, my greatest joy was to witness her full reconciliation to Orde. She arrived with two trunks of clothing and hats and parasols, she had bought an entire trousseau for the tropics – she arrived at the end of May and would remain until the end of July – and installed herself in an apartment adjacent to ours which we had rented for the purpose.

My view of her had altered after two years of marriage. I have already described the effect on me of Mrs. Wingate, in fact the entire Wingate effect, so I knew that there was something off-key about mother, however my affection for her was undiminished. She showed a keen interest in what we were doing. After studying a copy of the letter Orde had written to cousin Rex, she threw it on the table and declared, 'this is the Magna Carta of the Jewish race!', and from that moment forward she became not only a convinced believer in the cause of Zionism, but a devoted follower of my husband. I was a little taken aback by this extraordinary about-face, it seemed to me that there were now three where there ought to have been two. For the two months she was in Palestine she exhibited no wish for independence, she attached herself to us in a positively zoological manner, held at arm's length, however, by the field of force put out by a newly-married man and wife. And she showed such deference to me! The Arabs, who make a study of power and understand its uses better than any other race, have a saying; 'the sheikh's dog is a sheikh'. She told me, immediately after what she called her epiphany, 'how right you were to want to marry that man! Will you ever forgive me for the unkind things I said to you about him?' 'But mother', I said, 'that was such a long time ago.' I knew then that there was a subtext to this exchange, but it would take me many years to decipher it.

Mother's Zionism was a very real thing. Like me, she warmed to the Jews and she became extremely sensitive to anti-Jewish prejudice wherever she found it. This gave her Zionism an anti-church aspect, she saw herself as 'Defender of the Jews' and she could become most indignant. I remember when Jonathan was born, Chaim Weizmann very kindly agreed to be Godfather to my baby, and he and Vera, who happened to be in London, attended the baptism, a small affair consisting of just them and the family. The following day we saw a very brief mention of the ceremony in one of the newspapers, which elicited, a week later, a long letter to the editor from a minor public figure protesting the selection of Chaim Weizmann as Godfather, I recall this line, '...that the son of one of our most famous generals should have as a Godfather a non-communicant...' Mother went bezerk. She wrote letters to the newspaper, to the vicar who officiated, to Lambeth Palace, to the Archbishop of Canterbury and about a dozen other notables demanding a condemnation of the comments (with copies to me and to Chaim, and they were all very long letters), the woman had prodigious energy.

Mary Fyvel told me the following story about mother: She and Ivy met up in Jerusalem, and decided to go to a fashionable café in the center of town on Ben Yehuda Street, and there was a table outside with four British officers having tea and éclairs, which was the specialty of this establishment. It was the occasion of Ernest Bevin's visit to Palestine, and there was a good deal of tension because, apparently, the revisionists were going to try to kill him, and a number of arrests had been made. The coffee house was filled with Jews, mainly ladies of a certain age, and these four British officers, sitting in the sunshine and minding their own business. Mary and Ivy walked into the café, Ivy paused as she passed the table with the soldiers, and said in a loud voice, 'I would rather be the poorest Jew in the poorest slum, than be a British Officer!' Mary said that the ladies tittered behind their hands, I think they were embarrassed for the officers who politely got up and left. Mother's heart was entirely in the right place, I feel that such sentiments did her great credit, but as I said, she was sometimes a little off-key.

When Orde was killed, mother stepped back into my life, she took matters in hand and was invaluable. She organized and fussed, but it was not easy for me, at the age of twenty seven, to return to a relationship that I had left when I was fifteen. We were two such different women and she was not by nature a tolerant individual, and soon we were at loggerheads. She was enraged that I turned down the opportunity to become an MP. She was bitterly disappointed that I wouldn't take her to meet Lady Anderson. If I told her how much money I'd raised for the Jews she would have been furious because she worked harder and longer to raise less than half that sum for her own worthy causes in Aberdeen. If I told her that I'd turned down a marriage dowry of a destroyer, a castle, a penthouse in New York, not forgetting the Rembrandt, from one of the richest men in America, she would have instantly split my skull. She thought my conversion to Catholicism unseemly and theatrical, and she loathed John Smith and considered me a fool to marry him. I have given my reasons for marrying John, I think getting away from mother should be added to the list. He wasn't my only recourse, but he was probably the only one at hand when she had become particularly unbearable; is not timing everything? The fact that she was opposed to the union may also be added to the list. She took my persistent rejection of her advice as a personal affront and, looking back, I believe she was correct. She had become such an aggravating presence in my life that whatever she suggested to me, or I imagined she would suggest to me if I gave her the opportunity, I did the opposite. I came to the realization very late in life that mother was by far the stronger of the two of us, she was my inspiration when I was a girl and my nemesis in my middle age. Only for the eleven years in which I belonged to Orde was I free of her overbearing influence.

 Mother's tactlessness sometimes bordered on the farcical. She had a habit of writing on the back of every book or picture or photograph that she owned, some opinion of her own. Malcolm Hay's younger son, Brian, came to stay with her in Aberdeen, bringing his wife, and Ivy had prepared a room for them thoughtfully, and had laid out on their dressing table a photograph of Brian's late mother. Rather a pretty photograph I would say, taken in 1915 or 1918, and on the back, in my mother's bold, round hand was written, 'Florence Hay, first wife of Malcolm Hay of Seaton', and then underneath the words, '...a French woman'. I remember how angry mother was with Brian, 'Why did he not take this photograph away with him', she said, 'when I was kind enough to put it out for him?' Well, I couldn't convey to her the feeling one gets when one turns over the photograph of one's mother and finds written on the back in the hand of one's stepmother some sort of information such as 'a French woman'. You either feel these things or you don't.

As the years rolled by I became wearier and wearier of mother and I began to avoid her. Her greatest reproach, and surely the most justified, was my failure to protect Orde's reputation and in 1963, long past the point of endurance she published her own biography of Orde in the form of letters addressed to her grandson, Jonathan. Titled 'There was a Man of Genius' she gave free rein to her admiration for her son-in-law. I forced myself to read it, and I think the tone of the thing was positive, I agreed with much of what she wrote, however, without wishing to carp, she displaced me and replaced me in the book. I had over the years told mother stories about things Orde had said and done in my presence, and she put them in the book, as if they had happened in her presence, I was edited out, as in a Soviet photograph.

When mother arrived in Palestine, she became an ardent follower of Orde, and I wrote of how graciously she apologized to me for having so badly misjudged him. Well now the hidden subtext to that apology was revealed with garish clarity. Mother considered me entirely unworthy of Orde, and probably felt that she would have made him a far better wife, and certainly a better widow. I should like to have discussed this proposition with dear Peggy.

A Green Rose

Some time in 1962, I received a telephone call from a man called John Heyman, who introduced himself as David Lean's producer. I had never heard of John Heyman, I'm not one of those people who remain in the cinema when the film is over to see who wrote the score for the film, or who the best boy was, or what he was, but Mr. Heyman sounded quite authentic, and he asked if he might come to East Lothian, and talk to me about a project concerning my late husband. Well, Lean was the man who made the best war film I had ever seen – if you can properly call it a war film, it was certainly a film about soldiers – which was Bridge over the River Kwai; who better to tell the story of the Chindits? I wanted this man to myself, so I told John that I was expecting a visitor on the following weekend, a Hollywood film producer called Mr. Heyman. I might have said 'Hyman', because I didn't want John to imagine that he was a Hayman who dabbled in stock-breeding in his spare time, with whom he might wish to compare notes, and sure enough, after a reasonable gap in time, John announced that he would be going off fishing for the weekend. Come the Sunday I was in a fever of anticipation, I had been to the hairdresser and had a facial, and I was wearing a very acceptable outfit, dressed as 'the widow'. He arrived exactly on time, he came in a large black car with a uniformed driver, and I was standing in the doorway as he walked towards me. I don't know what I was expecting, a smaller, older man like Lew Grade perhaps, but this man was really wonderful-looking. He was tall and debonair, with an intelligent expression, and dressed like a banker, not much older than me, and, as you may imagine, my attention was starting to drift, and I was glad that I had taken the trouble to look reasonable for this meeting.

Mr. Heyman clearly had no plans for a long, relaxing day in the Scottish countryside, he was very business-like, and was in and out in less than an hour. He told me that

David had just finished making a film about TE Lawrence – it hadn't come out, and I certainly knew nothing about it – and that Mr. Lean and Mr. Bolt wanted to 'do Wingate next', I think that is how he put it, and that he had come to secure the film rights to Orde's life story from me! 'And you shall have them, dear boy,' thought I. We talked for about an hour in which time I told him a little about the Sykes saga – the Official History wasn't in place by this time – and he allowed me to waffle on, then he suddenly looked at his watch, apologized delightfully, and sped off back to London. He'd obviously come just to get a look at me, to see if I was a steady proposition. A contract arrived in the post within three days which took me a day to read, in which I agreed to give Lean's people access to all my papers and cooperate in every way, and I had to undertake to be loyal to Mr. Lean for at least three years, and not to go to another film-maker, and for just this, I would be paid 10,000 pounds. That was the price of a very large house with a garden in Edinburgh. I signed the contract and sent it back, and within days I received the check; my bank manager was so pleased he took me out for lunch at the bank's expense to celebrate. 'Why do they say that show business people are undependable', I remember thinking.

It was very astute of Mr. Lean to send his producer to me before I had a chance to see Lawrence of Arabia, because if he had come to me after I had seen it, I might have asked for two houses, or even three. It was not only a very good yarn, Bolt was obviously a gifted writer, but such a very pretty Lawrence they found! One would imagine that they held a beauty contest to find the right actor for the part, because Lawrence in the flesh was narrow-shouldered and knock-kneed, and looked like an unhappy English schoolboy. If this was what Mr. Lean could do for Lawrence, imagine what he could do for Wingate! In due course I met Mr. Bolt in London, and one immediately had the sense that one was dealing with a top team of people in which everyone knew exactly what they had to do, what their role was, in order to accomplish their mission. Mr. Bolt was the screenwriter, and he wanted to find out if there was 'an angle' for the telling of the story, and he wondered aloud whether I should not be a part of the story because, of course, there were no women in 'Lawrence'. I asked him, in passing, who they had in mind to play Orde, and without a moment's hesitation, he said, 'oh, there is only one actor who can play your late husband and that is Richard Burton'. Well, I was an experienced woman approaching middle age, but I think I might have blushed when he mentioned that man's name. Mr. Bolt then flattered me with one or two little remarks such as 'Jack Hawkins told me that you were a great beauty, and that is clear to me – and most filmic'; I was learning a new language. If he was complimenting me, it wasn't for his own immediate advantage, because he was gone within an hour, but he told me that they were working on another project, following Lawrence, and that they only ever worked on one project at a time, so I wouldn't be hearing from them for at least one year. 'A well-oiled machine', I remember thinking, as I saw him into his taxi. Well, by the time this dear man had finished with me, I needed a double whisky, which was not at the time at all my drink but nothing else would have sufficed, and a long hot bath. I returned directly to my hotel room and proceeded to give my imagination full rein. 'If Burton is to play the brilliant young general, who better to play his tempestuous young wife than Elizabeth Taylor? Had I not read somewhere that she had embraced Judaism? What feeling she would bring to the role! But how would I appear in the film, I wondered. Would I come across as a latter-day Lady Macbeth? I didn't at all mind being played by a cinema goddess with pouting lips and a large bust, and I didn't much care if they portrayed me as a loose woman if it would help pay everyone's salary – I believe the salaries are generous in the film business – but I wanted to know what words they were going to put onto my pouting lips; I would have to see the screenplay in advance! And would they be very dismissive of Peggy? I should have opposed that!' In this manner I set new terms and conditions for participation in Mr. Lean's next-but-one film.

I never heard from David Lean or his writer again. If I had been told that as I was lying in the bath I think I might have slipped quietly under the soapsuds, but the truth dawned slowly over the years that Orde was never going to get the Lawrence treatment. When 'Lawrence' came out, it gave every producer in England and America the idea that the public was clamouring for films about eccentric British soldiers, and sooner or later they all came knocking at my door. 'Lawrence' inspired a number of thespians to wish to try their hand at portraying Orde Wingate. This was a sad commentary on the alteration of Britain's place in the world. Lawrence's books inspired a generation of soldiers and orientalists, and Lawrence the film, a generation of actors and screenwriters. No one in post-war Britain wanted to actually be an Orde Wingate – the Army Council's fears were wildly optimistic – but everyone wanted to act Orde Wingate in a film. What would Orde have done in a world like this? To what could he have turned his hand, at the age of 44? It would have been frightful. I think I was glad that he had been spared the ordeal of living in modern Britain

> *My name is Ozymandias, King of Kings,*
> *Look on my Works ye Mighty, and despair!*
> *Nothing beside remains. Round the decay*
> *Of that colossal Wreck, boundless and bare*
> *The lone and level sands stretch far away.*

Anyway, this was the eighth plague, the plague of locusts, they all found me, appeared on my lawn some of them, and I became exceedingly weary with this business.

One locust I shall not forget, and I mean this in a positive way, was Peter Sellers. Four years after John Heyman, that is to say, after my contract with him had expired, I was approached by a well thought-of Jewish screenwriter called Wolf Mankowitz who came to stay with us in Dorset. Mr. Mankowitz just moved in hoping, I suppose, to find inspiration in the widow, and after the fifth or sixth meal I asked him if he had any financial backing lined-up – I was becoming something of an expert – and he told me that Peter Sellers was committed to the project. 'Is Mr. Sellers a producer now?' I asked with genuine curiosity. 'No, actually Peter wishes to play your late husband'. I asked Mr. Mankowitz to leave the house immediately. A few days later Mr. Sellers called me himself to apologize for not having come in person as he had been away filming but he had something very important to tell me, could he please drive down to see me now? The prospect of having this very amusing man under my roof was irresistible, and he arrived at about 11pm in his Rolls Royce in an exhausted state, he mumbled something and went straight to bed. I tapped lightly on his door at about 11 o'clock the following morning with a cup of tea, whereupon he became abusive and I hastily withdrew, the poor man didn't seem to know where he was.

Well, he rose in his own good time and presented himself downstairs for a meal, I'm not quite sure what meal he expected at that hour, and proceeded to tell me about his experiences in the armed services. Adam and Lucy came home from school in a high state of excitement expecting to find Inspector Clouseau in their house, and by this time Mr. Sellers who was disheveled and unshaved and not fresh-smelling, was sitting on the sofa in floods of tears and not entertaining me at all. I was not a cinema-goer but I would take the children to see the latest offering at the local flea pit, and this is where I was introduced to the work of Peter Sellers, obviously a gifted comedian, and this man was now telling me that it was his life's ambition to portray Orde Wingate in a film.

I have already mentioned the interest Orde aroused in London among writers and verbalizers during his lifetime, and indeed after his death, a number of film people attached themselves to me because of the name – my charms notwithstanding. Jack Hawkins became a friend, as did Trevor Howard (a fierce Scottish patriot), Kenneth Moore, all top British actors of film, not so much of stage. What attracted these men to Orde so strongly was their own wistful longing to have been heroic soldiers, which many of them claimed to have been, in their circle, but in fact seldom were; they were all Walter Mitty types, and all confessed to me freely, when sufficiently drunk, what a terrifying experience the army had been, and of course none of them had fired a shot in anger. To be a brave soldier in a modern war, and survive the encounter in which one's bravery has been noted was a rare enough thing. They had also come through the war with an intense dislike of generals and other officers, which is not surprising if one is of a sensitive disposition, and therefore they looked up all the more to Wingate who had a reputation for disobedience and telling his superior officers where to get off.

In the case of Mr. Sellers it was also the fact that Orde 'spoke up for the Jews'. He was trying to persuade me that he 'read' Wingate, and could bring him to life on film, when suddenly he became very animated and asked me to imagine that we were in a military barracks and were standing outside a building looking through a window into a room, there were two men in the room, one was the commanding officer seated behind his desk, and the other was Captain

Wingate, standing before him. Mr. Sellers was rushing about moving furniture, and creating a 'set', and talking about camera angles. He then proceeded to extemporize a conversation between Orde and his superior officer – he dashed back and forth playing both roles. I'm quite sure Mr. Sellers hadn't prepared this little pantomime for me, in fact, when he started to extemporize he seemed to have no idea at all as to why the two men were in the office, but as the debate between these two characters developed, it emerged that they were discussing what to do about an imaginary soldier who had abandoned his position during a battle. This was done, as I said, on the spur of the moment and entirely from his own imagination. I was as fascinated by Mr. Sellers' performance, in my mid-forties, as I had been by the Indian rope trick at the age of five. Well, I think my jaw must have dropped, and my goose pimples stood up, and any other cliché you may care to mention because by the time this strange man had finished I was emotionally undone, tears everywhere. This man was indeed born to portray Orde in a film, I was suddenly glad not to have heard from Mr. Lean with his Burtons and O'Tooles. While he was performing his riveting little make-believe for my private benefit, all his bedraggled sadness and vulnerability fell away and he shone like – what else? – a star. Mr. Sellers did not offer me a check, and of course I never heard from him again. This is why they call Hollywood 'the dream factory'.

I must mention in passing James Robertson Justice a most charming and gallant friend who was an actor, and there was nothing Walter Mittyish about him at all. He was a devoted admirer of Orde, he was in the RMGR, curiously enough the man was a marine engineer as well as being an excellent ornithologist, and he used to appear from patrolling the Channel. He wanted to organize a Jewish navy, dear fellow, warm-hearted creature, whenever he came to see us, he would bellow, 'where is the *Sar Ha'zava*, which is the name given to the commander of the Israelite army in the Book of Samuel; in those days one still knew one's Bible.

My final encounter with the world of films was with Alan Moorhead, dreadful little man, who had been commissioned to write a script for a film, and the Wingates were so pleased to have captured such a name, and I was pleased to meet him, I'd read his book...books, Gallipoli and others, you know, very well written, exciting, and he turned out to be such a disappointment. After a number of days of conversation about Orde in which he, strangely, did most of the talking, he had persuaded himself that Orde had a Napoleon complex and suffered from sexual repression on account of his upbringing. I told him that he was a bloody sensationalist little journalist, and a shit, and I threw him out of the house. What a furor! Telephone calls from the producer, and Granville wrote me a most unpleasant, rebuking letter which ended with a suggestion that I drink less. He seemed to be saying, 'here is a first class writer, come to make a film about our brother, and his drunken widow is preventing him from getting on with his work'.

This was more than unfair, it was nonsense. Moorehead had the support of the Wingates, full access to the papers, the documents, if he wanted to make a film, let him get on with it, what did he need me for? No, the problem was not with me, in fact I could almost lay it at Granville's door. The difficulties in writing a screenplay about Wingate were one and the same as the difficulties in writing a book, I would have thought that was fairly obvious. The problem lay in the sanitizing of Orde's biography, Granville's primary concern – supposedly in the name of the family – which robbed it of any coherence. Granville understood perfectly well why Orde's good name was being besmirched in Britain, it was his identification with Zionism, and Granville's response was not to proclaim and justify his brother's belief, but to play it down, as a means of disarming Orde's critics. This was a very foolish policy, and one that was bound to fail. Granville should have stood up and said, 'if my brother is guilty of betraying his country to an enemy, show me that enemy! The loyal Palestinian Jew? And who decides who is and is not an enemy of Great Britain? The Colonial Office? The House of Lords? Beaverbrook? And if the Jew is our enemy, does that make the Mufti our friend? And Hitler? Britain was given a mandate by the League of Nations to create a Jewish homeland in Palestine, let her honour her pledge! My brother had the right of it!'

But poor Granville was not of the same mettle as his brother. I don't think for a moment that he was against Zionism, but he had no stomach for the fight, and nor, I suppose, had I. This letter from Granville was, I think, the last straw. I decided that I had had enough. Not right away, but in the course of the following weeks.

I did not come into this world with illusions, I think I have always been a realist, but I had found it to be a very cruel and unforgiving place indeed. If Granville was right and I had become a disgrace and an embarrassment to the family and to Orde's legacy, I would retire from the field and quietly disappear. If Granville was wrong, all the more reason for me to up sticks and leave, for I should only continue being hurt to no purpose.

I was preparing the family for another big move, and so it was back to the packing crates. The wife of a soldier gets used to this kind of thing, but I was getting on in years, I should have been settled for life by now. I thought Dorset would be a haven for John and me, we were renting an old Mill at Fivehead Neville – they have such wonderful names in Dorset – it was incidentally the part of England Orde had loved the best, and where he wanted to retire. But I soon regretted leaving the fastness of our Scottish property, I was worn out by the film people, by the Wingates, by mother, I was too close to the center of things I didn't at all want, I needed to put myself beyond these people's reach, I had been thinking about an island somewhere. Anyway, when one packs, one has the opportunity to get rid of unwanted possessions and have a general clean-up. One has a pile for giving away, and a pile for throwing away. I think I might have been depressed and generally under the weather.

    I set light to the pyre in the garden, and when it was burning nicely, quite deliberately and methodically I emptied out all my drawers, all my boxes, all the contents of the muniment room. It started to drizzle with rain, I didn't want a scorched mulch so I went to the garage to get some paraffin and poured that on, because I wanted a real fire now. I went into the house and tore the Fildes portrait of me as a seventeen year old bride off the wall, and threw it on the pyre. It was very large and I had to burn it in stages. Letters from Orde, letters from Clementine Churchill when Orde was in hospital with typhoid, the letter from Hennessy, newspaper clippings about 'Loincloth', letters from Sykes, birthday cards from the Wilenskis, photographs of Hannibal, the letters from Derek, the letter in green ink from Chaim, a photo of me with two Bedouin sergeants in Transjordania in 1937, I smashed the glass on the framed testimonials from Youth Aliya and cut my finger, a signed photograph of Madame Chiang Kai shek, Orde's passport, his driving license, letters from Chindits, the letter from Granville, an entire box of condolence letters, a photograph of Jeffrey Locket coming out of the jungle, my ration book, a box of maps of Palestine, letters from Haile Selassie, photographs of my mother, snapshots from Ceylon, a love poem written in pencil by an admirer on the back of a menu, my school reports. I remembered a box of my earliest family photographs I'd placed in the spare room, there were daguerreotypes, a photo of mad Aunty Ivy as a girl, photographs of Tilliefoure, Lorna on horseback, I rushed back to the house and brought the box out, it thought it could escape my impulsive wrath but it went to the flames. I ran to the kitchen and grabbed a carving knife, and carefully cut my image out of a portrait painting of John and me, and threw me on the fire. I scoured the house for every last vestige of my past and when I was certain that it was all gone, I felt a lightness, the lifting of a burden, I took deep breaths. The heat had dried off the mulch, and the pyre burnt down to black ashes, it was done, I was free.

The Wingates had been helping themselves to my papers for many years. Monica would come to stay with me in Scotland, and in Dorset, and I could always tell when she had been in the muniment room. Jonathan had left home, and on the rare occasion he came to see me he would help himself to any knickknack or letter that took his fancy, I resented this and resisted it. Perhaps my family knew me better than I knew myself, because these letters and keepsakes had been precious to me, and some of them probably had value, historical or commercial value, and I didn't think myself capable of such determined madness as I showed on that day; they evidently did think me capable.

I was now in my fifty-third year, and drinking steadily, in that detail Granville had been perfectly correct. I was not yet addled but I was a long way from resembling Vivienne Leigh, I seem to have deteriorated rather rapidly, my teeth were coming loose in my mouth, my tummy was slightly bloated, and my hair was quite grey. I couldn't get out of bed before I had drunk half a bottle of wine, and I couldn't fall asleep without taking a bottle to bed with me, and between that bottle and a half were several other bottles to keep me afloat during the day.

Chapter 20

I kept returning to the idea of an island. A Greek Island might be fun, one could almost buy an entire island in those days, but the children had to be educated, and John for his part refused to consider it. I needed to get away, I would sit down at the kitchen table with the children with the AA Greater Road Map of the British Isles open in front of us, and together we would compete to identify the remotest and most inaccessible islands – I had no idea there were so many – and then Adam's finger went off the map and landed at the Isle of Guernsey and he said, 'mummy, what is that?' 'That doesn't count, it's not in England!' protested Lucy. 'Ah, but it is!' said I. Indeed it is so close to France one wonders why the French allowed the English to have it. Why hadn't I thought of it before? The Channel Islands were once considered a suitable place for lighthouse keepers and sea birds, and whatever allure it had would have been soiled by the Nazi occupation. But it was probably full of old houses, and I remembered the old town of Quebec City with its old-world French charm. Did they speak English there? Were there suitable schools?

Lying to my husband and children that I needed to take care of business in Scotland, I set out on a reconnaissance, travelling by train to Plymouth and then by packet boat to Guernsey, a sea journey of four hours. As I was sailing, it was a glorious sunny day with a stiff westerly and a lot of movement on the water, I reflected that mother would never make this journey. I commandeered a very old taxi and a still older driver, and with the aid of a map we crisscrossed the island so that I could see for myself which part I liked the best, I felt like a little boy in a toy shop. I knocked on doors and spoke to many people whose average age was probably seventy five, and on the second day I found exactly what I was looking for. It was slap in the middle of the Island, a very old farmhouse, stood at the top of a beautiful valley, and its acres were in the valley so you could see them laid out in front of you from the house. One approached the house through an arch giving onto a courtyard with ancient paving stones and, heaven help me, wisteria growing all over the house, and if it wasn't wisteria it was an enormous white rose bush that reached up to the roof. It was called 'La Monnaie'. The old couple was not ready to sell, it would take me another year and an inflated offer to get them to part with their farm, but my heart was set on Guernsey. I returned to Fivehead Neville laden with gifts for the children and an expensive electric razor for John, and then I sat them all down.

The house was riddled with dry rot, if I had bothered to have it surveyed like any normal person I would have been warned, but it wouldn't have stopped me from having it. We had builders living with us for two years, the house had to be gutted and new beams installed to hold up the roof, and when that was done, then all the woodwork in the roof was replaced. There were five bedrooms, John's was on the ground floor because of his heart, Jonathan had his own room, one each for Adam and Lucy. There was a library on the first floor, it was a long room which was also the living room with a lovely fireplace at one end and a piano at the other, a spiral staircase that went up to the next floor. John was a good sport about it, he started playing the piano again after many years, and he did play beautifully. And then, peacefully, his heart gave up on him, and he died almost exactly a year after our arrival on the island.

The renovations cost me more than the house itself, and I found myself deeply in debt. If I had sold La Monnaie there and then, I should have made a profit, but I could not bring myself to take this road. Renovating this ancient farmhouse represented, I think, my only tangible achievement since I don't want to say when. A forced sale might have brought a smile to my bank manager's face, but it should have demoralized me and it would not have gone well with the children who were weary of moving.

Having not spoken to mother for about a year, I called her up and asked her for 50,000 pounds. It was twice what I needed to pay off my overdraft, but since I knew that this was an action I could never repeat, I thought I should have a small cushion in place. I had never asked my parents for a penny all my life, and the sum I now requested represented less than one fiftieth of papa's estate, I knew she would not cavil. She of course made me jump through one or two minor hoops, and then she sent me a check. I was grateful, it relieved me of an enormous amount of pressure, and I stopped drinking for a year.

I think Guernsey was rescued from obscurity by an unsung accountant. When Harold Wilson raised taxes in Britain, this anonymous individual noticed that Guernsey and its adjacent dots were beyond Mr. Wilson's grasp, and he passed on this arcane fact to one of his wealthy pop-star clients. A stampede of young, rich, fashionable tax exiles migrated to this charming backwater and this was happening at exactly the time we arrived, but had nothing to do with my decision to move there. I was an exile from my past, but the island attracted many categories of British exile. The most interesting was Una Moyne Brown, she had been sent to Guernsey by her own family which was Guiness, as a form of quarantine. She spent too much money and was too eccentric to be let loose in London. Oliver Reed, the actor, was a tax exile in Guernsey, an unpredictable drunk but a very attractive man. These people discovered me as a curiosity, and initiated me into a very colourful world, for a while I became quite 'with it' and adolescent, smoking cannabis and reading books by Aleister Crowley and Gurdjieff, but I soon returned to my faithful alcohol and the English classics.

It was at about this time that Derek's book finally came out, he kindly sent me a copy in the post with an apologetic inscription, and I sat down and read it. It was exactly the book I would have expected from Derek, and on the whole I was pleased that he'd written it, because no one was in a better position to know what went on during Operation Thursday than Derek, and this was really what the book was about, all Orde's previous experiences were merely an introduction. But he wrote about his early days with Orde, and here my name did crop up, as did Peggy's. Derek was kind to me, he could never be cruel, he didn't have it in him, but old wounds were opened. He included a long and very good letter from Peggy to the author concerning Orde's character, and the break-up of their engagement. Her love for, and praise of, Orde was undiminished through 40 years, one word she used which I think is key, and describes him entirely was 'incorruptible'. That is a marvelous word, it means 'pure of heart', and indeed he was. Derek did not attempt to describe me as a person or speculate about Orde's relationship with me and since he had known me personally over many years this was a conspicuous omission in a biography; it made me feel little and unwanted and it suggested to the reader that there was something to hide. I started feeling sorry for myself, and it made me want to have a glass of something. Seeing his mother unusually down in the mouth, in a moment of pure inspiration, Adam who was I think eighteen, produced an old Grundig tape recorder that I had quite forgotten about in the back of a cupboard, dusted if off, and sent off for the old fashioned tapes that go on it. He told me not to be so wet and to record my own bloody recollections of Wingate. So I put myself to bed for a month, and started to record the bones of this present work. Extemporary verbalizing was awfully hard, it needed a great deal of concentration, no notes of any kind, I didn't want to waffle beyond a point. It was exhausting and gave me no comfort whatever, in fact it had the opposite effect, for I saw that it could never become a book of any kind because it would hurt and upset too many people, a few who deserved to be upset, and many who did not. When I came to the end, I didn't set fire to the tapes, I put them in the draw of my bedside table, and locked it with a key.

My life now consisted of my house, my dear and plucky little Lucy, and my most resourceful Adam. I had made a beautiful room for Jonathan but he came to see me only once a year, sometimes less. He was in the Artillery like his father before him, and he was doing reasonably well, quite enjoying the profession, but always under a shadow, he felt. The name Wingate was charged, it meant something very positive or very negative to his superiors, and Jonathan couldn't just be himself, so in some ways the army was the worst place for him so he decided to try something else.

When Jonathan did come over to Guernsey, it was a great event for us, he was loved by all his family in his own right, but he never knew it. We were very much bound together, two shipwreck survivors on a raft, terribly intimate and, when together with a bottle between us, there was no thought of eating or sleeping, we had too much to talk and laugh about. I fear that Adam and Lucy may have felt on the outside on such occasions, but they were few and far between. As time went on, as I deteriorated, he relished seeing me less and less, one cannot blame him. I think, of course, how it would have been for him if he had known his father; if it would have made the burden of being Orde's son heavier or lighter. He had a great deal of his father in him, not just characteristics, but qualities, but he didn't believe in himself; he felt like an imposter whereas his father believed in himself absolutely. I look at Granville's children, who have come out so very well, and regret the absence of Wingates in Jonathan's upbringing.

In 1976, Jonathan brought a very pretty girl to Guernsey and introduced her to me as his fiancé, she was a Sloane like Diana Spencer, a little hoydenish for my taste, but perfectly suitable. They married and had two little girls, he went off to work in the City and I felt sure that all would now be well for Jonathan, and my mind was put at rest. I received no visitors from the mainland, it was a rule. Monica came one last time to see the renovation, and when she learnt of the fate of my muniment room, she was distraught and never returned. I continued to receive letters from writers and researchers but I threw them away, they were of as much interest to me as the electricity bill. I mentioned in an earlier chapter the excellent detective work of Meade and Thompson. There were many others who worked to reinstate the reputation of Wingate, the center of such activity was Manchester University and I was happy and grateful for their efforts, but I wanted nothing to do with them. For some reason these people had the idea that I had information that I had not yet divulged to the world, but of course would want to divulge to them. A man called Elliot-Bateman was particularly insistent, and I was forced to tell him that if he set foot on my property, I would have to shoot him with a shotgun that I keep loaded in the hallway cabinet, and he took my warning to heart. Unfortunately there was no cabinet and no shotgun.

When mother gave me the money, I entered into a compact that I would call her once a week without fail. I did this for a while, two or three years perhaps; I would fortify myself with a few drinks, prepare notes, deep breath, and dial her number in Scotland. She had become a worthy woman in Edinburgh, she poured herself into charitable work and, as I mentioned, she raised a lot of money for her various causes, and I don't feel that she got the recognition she deserved, she should have been an OBE. She was only married to Hay for six years before he died, but she retained the title. She had all her life been slavishly English, she was a very great snob and a social climber, and her accent was pure Noel Coward, too posh to be real. When she raged at me on the phone, I could discern the odd Australian vowel coming through. I put up with this weekly verbal beating for as long as I could, and then finally I could do it no more.

It was a Sunday morning, our day for talking, and it started off lightly enough with my recounting to her my empty threat to shoot dear Mr. Eliott Bateman, to amuse her, I suppose, and to signal to her that her daughter retained some of her vim and vigour. Mother was in the process of severing the family connection with the Aberdeen firm of solicitors who'd handled our business for 55 years, and we both agreed that it was rather a sad parting, and the Sunday preceding she had mentioned that she'd sold papa's fishing tackle to a senior partner of this firm, a rather nasty man called Brown. This came to mind as I was delivering my empty threat to dear Mr. Elliot Bateman[5], so now I asked her what had become of papa's Purdy guns. Now Purdy guns are a family heirloom, you sell off your jewels, your cars, your house, your wife, but never your Purdy guns. Sensing some mild form of possible criticism in the question, she flew off into a rage and said she knew nothing about guns of any kind, then she mentioned that there was a gun in the house in Edinburgh, well, my heart rose because the loss of a Purdy gun is a sad thing for a family, but she told me she thought it was a pistol.

'Well', said I, 'if you did sell the Purdy guns, it would be a great pity, mother, because with two grandsons to follow after him these boys would have prized such guns above anything, they'll never be able to afford to buy them for themselves'.

Now I spoke in ordinary terms such as I'm using at this moment, but my mother took this as a serious insult that I was offering to her, she said she knew nothing about guns, the guns had been sold by the executors'.

'Who were the executors?' said I.

'They were Mr. Brown and myself.' she said,

'Hold on to your hat mother, how much do you think Purdy guns are worth nowadays?'

'I don't know and I don't care', she responded.

'Well, a second hand pair of Purdy guns now makes 5000 guineas'. There was a pause while this information was sinking in, and she screamed back at me, tearfully,

'If you had been kinder to me, Jonathan would have had the guns', and then she slammed down the receiver and that was the end of the conversation.

The following Sunday it was my 57th birthday, or just after, and when I rang her I found her at the end of a seven day brood, and in a state of hysteria. I've never forgotten that wonderful bit in Baden-Powell's 'Scouting for Boys', where he gave some simple remedies for common ailments, and one of them was the remedy for hysteria. 'Threaten the patient with a pair of scissors'. My mother enjoyed scenes and she'd used her hysteria as a weapon all her life. Our conversation lasted nearly forty minutes, I remember, and although I was brought up to this kind of thing, I confess that I was very tired at the end of it all. It was like standing beside a drain that has been choked with filth, and suddenly it floods open, and down the gutter comes a roaring torrent of decay. I suppose she's been storing up in her mind over the past twenty five years, even more of the envy and the hatred and the malice which she began to feel for me so many years ago, and which it took me half a lifetime to recognize, and another half a lifetime to accept, but it was a horrible experience.

I won't weary you with what she said, because it was scarcely sane, but it was not manic, it was hysteric, and she was not mad, she was bad. I could never get mother out of my system. Never. I loved her very much, that's one reason. Another is the tie between a mother and a child is a real tie, and it may even be that it's an umbilical tie, it can't be changed or removed simply by wishing. Sybil told me, and I believe she was correct, that every fault I had was from my mother's upbringing. I don't hate my mother, for many years I feared her, but now I felt sickened as I heard her raving on with such desire to wound in her clawing way, with such hope that things go wrong with me. With such a fastening on any difficulty or disadvantage, or enmity that I may encounter in other people, such joy in my difficulties, such resentment if I seem to be happy.

She told me at great length that I had achieved nothing in life, and that I was a wretched failure compared to her, that the only thing I'd succeeded in doing was in having three fine children and that she supposed she'd better apologize on her knees to me for only having one...she was infinitely ahead of me in all attainments, she'd written splendid books, she had hosts of friends, I had none of these things to my credit. To which I replied, 'indeed mother, yes, how right you are', which is a phrase one finds oneself using with people of this kind in an endeavour to calm them, but it doesn't, it maddens them, because what they want is a reaction, you see. Which is why she became so furious with my father because he would not react to the storms and the scenes which all blew up out of nothing, as this one did. But I look back on my life and I must say I don't think I've done very much. I was an unsuccessful daughter, only a partially successful wife, and a less than perfect mother. I've been a loyal but detached friend, to the causes I've espoused I have probably been an embarrassment. I may have been an inspiration to a few people.

John used to tell me that on the night before each of his birthdays, he used to dream, not anything so impressive as a foretaste of the year to come, but a general feeling of happiness or unhappiness which invariably proved to be true to coming form. Well, on the night before my 57th birthday, I dreamt that a great black woolly spider was scuttling about on the floor, and mother reached down and picked it up, and pulled its legs off one by one. I never spoke to mother again.

I had a beautiful garden at La Monnaie, I did a bit of weeding on and off and I'd pay companies do the serious work of gardening, I wanted the exterior of the house to be of the highest quality. It wasn't to impress visitors, because I had none, I think I wanted to recreate the Tilliefoure of my childhood, and when I picture my old home, I picture only the exterior. I barely remember the interior other than that it was all polished wooden floors, and it contained thirty stone fireplaces. But I remember every detail of every façade, even now I could sit down and draw that large and rambling structure from memory, chimney pots and all. I wanted to see things grow beautifully, I had a real eye for a beautiful flower, I wanted the old roses, the French roses, I wanted beautiful things in the corners, if it wasn't clematis it was apples, I didn't mind if it got a bit tatty out there, it shouldn't be spic and span, but the windows were always properly maintained, painted, I wouldn't let things fall into disrepair. Inside the house I wouldn't say my standards were incredibly high. I had cleaners occasionally but they were short-lived, they didn't work, discipline wasn't maintained very well, and I wasn't a great cleaner myself, terrible cook.

I would make a very good blancmange and I made porridge and I enjoyed making leak and potato soup, that was the only thing I really liked out of all the things I cooked. The children were lucky if it was on the list, and if it wasn't on the list it was basics, and the children had to muck in, fish fingers was a staple. I don't know how they got by but they did, not much frozen food, a lot of baked potatoes. I tended to let things go to seed in the fridge, and they sat there for a lot longer than they should. I liked to watch the children eating but I couldn't bestir myself to cook for them, I was a shambles.

I loved cookery books, they were my and Lucy's particular weakness, I kept buying them. Elizabeth David was a wonderful writer, beautiful recipes, and we had all her books grandly sent to us in a parcel from the bookshop, ordered in – I'd read about them in the national newspapers. Lucy loved them and would look at them and say, 'we'll try that, but nothing was baked out of it, nothing was cooked out of it. How did they get by? Children are very resilient, I suppose. The kitchen had been rebuilt from scratch, it was designed as a French kitchen, a large open space with the dining table in the middle, full of equipment, and it was where we always sat at all hours of the day or night, but it was like a film set, no real cooking took place there.

Adam was a tear-away, handsome and wild, he had wonderful hands, he could make things, but he wouldn't get out of bed. I asked Michael Calvert for help, and he was instrumental in getting Adam into the army, it was what he needed at the time. While he was away, I was alone with Lucy, and she would come home with her school friends, I'm sure I was a great embarrassment to her, and I often kept to my room, but other times I would entertain them with my phenomenal memory. One of the girls was doing Shakespeare's Coriolanus for her 'A' levels, and I found that I was able to recite entire passages of it from memory, and then parse them, all while I was under the influence. I had no idea how good my education had been until it showed itself to my daughter and her friends, Miss McCutchin would have been proud of me.

After my final, irrevocable break with mother, I allowed myself to drift, I had become a certified, chronic alcoholic. Occasionally, usually after I hurt myself, the children would send me off for a cure – they called it detox – and I would be on the wagon for six months or a year, then I would lapse. I played cat and mouse with the children, I kept finding new hiding places for my booze, and one day they were quite defeated until Lucy noticed black marks around my mouth and realized it was coal dust. It was very funny in its way, funny in the re-telling. I don't know how or why Lucy and Adam stood by me so staunchly, why they felt so very protective of me. I was a sick and thoroughly disgusting woman, I deserved a bullet in the head, I took up space. I had two dogs who left their hair on every piece of furniture and fabric in the house. They jumped on me one day and caused me to fall down the stairs, and I broke my hip. What caused me to fall was my drunken state, but I blamed the dogs. I would lie in bed at night, sipping my gin, eating chocolate mints, reading a book and listening to the radio. One night I felt I was falling asleep, I removed my teeth and put them on the bedside table, unwashed, with chocolate still on them. The dogs found them and chewed them, upper and lower, thinking they were a chocolate flavoured bone, and in the morning my four-poster was littered with individual teeth licked clean, but with dog hairs sticking to them. Why am I telling you this?

Mother died in 1983. Her funeral was low-key, all her old biddies from Aberdeen turned up, she had been living in a home that she'd raised money for, she was a Dame of the Star of St. John, a few friends from along the way, a few family members, and my children. I didn't go, I didn't want to be there, I didn't want to be seen. She left some of her money to her three grandchildren, and quite a lot of furniture. With mother's passing something switched in my head and I stopped drinking. It was a gradual change but accumulating. Lucy and Adam wanted to leave the island and I encouraged them to do so, but they wouldn't leave without me. I sold La Monnaie for a great deal of money, we pooled my money with their inheritance, and we set up shop on the mainland so that they could be productive and make lives for themselves, yet never far from my side, I was never alone.

One day Adam pulled the tapes out of the bedside table, and placed them on my kitchen table with the Grundig, and plugged it in. Lucy had an Amstrad word processor and taught me to use it and they strapped me to a chair and commanded me to write about my life, which is what you are now holding in your hand. If you have read it to the end, it makes of my life a satisfactory ending.

CPSIA information can be obtained
at www.ICGtesting.com
Printed in the USA
LVHW081703281019
635578LV00037B/1615/P